W9-CMR-766

Creativity in American Philosophy

Creativity
in American Philosophy

CHARLES HARTSHORNE

State University of New York Press
ALBANY

$\mathcal{B}$
$85{-}1$
$\cdot H37$
1984

$10/85$

Published by
State University of New York Press, Albany
© 1984 State University of New York
All rights reserved
Printed in the United States of America
No part of this book may be used or reproduced
in any manner whatsoever without written permission,
except in the case of brief quotations embodied in
critical articles and reviews.
For information, address State University of New York
Press, State University Plaza, Albany, N.Y., 12246

Library of Congress Cataloging in Publication Data
Hartshorne, Charles, 1897–
  Creativity in American Philosophy.

  1. Philosophy, American—History. I. Title.
B851.H37 1984   191   83–15562
ISBN 0–87395–816–0
ISBN 0–87395–817–9 (pbk.)
10 9 8 7 6 5 4 3 2 1

96924

To D. C. H.

Contents

CONTENTS

Acknowledgments

For permission to republish or quote from—in parts of this book as specified in brackets—the following essays the author thanks the respective journals or publishers:

The Monist [chs. 1 and 7], "From Colonial Beginnings to Philosophical Greatness," in vol. 48, no. 1 (1964), 317–331; "A Revision of Peirce's Categories," in vol. 63, no. 3 (1980), 277–289.

The Journal of Philosophy [chs. 6 and 10], "Royce's Mistake—and Achievement," in vol. 53 (Feb. 2, 1956), 123–130; "Santayana's Defiant Eclecticism," in vol. 61, no. 1 (1964), 35–44.

Journal of Theology and Philosophy [ch. 5], "James's Empirical Pragmatism," in vol. 1, no. 1 (1980).

International Philosophical Quarterly [ch. 9], "Whitehead's Revolutionary Concept of Prehension," in vol. 19, no. 3 (1979), 253–263.

Philosophical Review [ch. 15], Sheldon, *God and Polarity*, in vol. 64, no. 2 (1955), 312–316.

Review of Metaphysics [ch. 18], "Weiss's *The God We Seek*," in vol. 25, Supplement (1972).

The American Scholar [ch. 19], "Mortimer Adler As Philosopher: A Criticism and Appreciation," vol. 41, no. 2 (spring), 269–274.

The Philosophical Forum [ch. 16], "The Structure of Givenness," vol. 18 (1960–61), 97–111.

ACKNOWLEDGMENTS

Martinus Nijhoff (The Hague, Netherlands, 1966) [ch. 12], "Idealism and Our Experience of Nature," in *Philosophy, Religion, and the Coming World Civilization: Essays in Honor of William Ernest Hocking,* ed. Leroy S. Rouner, 70–80.

The Library of Living Philosophers (Open Court Publishing Co.) [ch. 13], "Lewis's Treatment of Memory," in *The Philosophy of C. I. Lewis,* ed. P. A. Schilpp, 395–414.

Preface

This is the second of two volumes dealing with the history of philosophy, especially of metaphysics. The first, *Insights and Oversights of Great Thinkers*, discusses some thirty European philosophers, from Democritus to Wittgenstein and Merleau-Ponty. In both volumes I try to learn and teach truth about reality by arguing, in a fashion, with those who in the past have sought such truth. Admittedly, the other party to the argument is in most cases not there to reply; but scholarly care and imagination can to some extent give him a voice. I try to avoid the straw-man fallacy. My models here are Peirce and Whitehead. They did not, as some do, waste their own and their readers' time by attacking never existent (often rather stupid) opponents. They objected to views that had really been held by intelligent people. I try to do likewise, without, however, always documenting my sources. These books are written to show not my learning but my understanding, the understanding of a reflective student for more than sixty years of speculative philosophy through its twenty-five centuries in the West (and to some extent in Asia also). I believe one cannot do justice to metaphysical issues by considering only one's contemporaries. There are gains in the history of philosophy, but also losses. Changes in intellectual fashions have their capricious aspects. Intellectual history serves as storehouse of old ideas and laboratory for testing what seem to us new ones, as we try to imagine what earlier thinkers might have said about them.

This book can be read independently but will gain in significance if read in connection with its more comprehensive predecessor, which gives a background for it. Neither book is merely historical or merely systematic. My effort throughout my career has been to think about philosophical, that is, essentially a priori or metaphysical, issues, using the history of ideas as a primary resource.

"Creativity" in the book's title is intentionally ambiguous. The word refers, first, to the originality of philosophers in the United States of America and even in the British colonies that preceded them. The implication is that these philosophers were better than mere disciples or imitators of Old World philosophers. The word refers, second, to a major theme in our philosophical tradition, creativity itself as a philosophical category of cosmic significance. True enough, Bergson, Cournot, and Berdyaev in France, Varisco in Italy, and Fechner in Germany have had versions of the idea; but nowhere has the topic been more persistently and searchingly investigated than in this country (Peirce, James, W. P. Montague, Dewey, Whitehead). I am convinced that this concept is an unsurpassed, though long neglected, key to many philosophical problems and their history.

In the first nine chapters I consider those of our philosophers who have contributed most directly and powerfully to the development of a philosophy of creativity—sometimes, as in the case of Edwards, partly by arguing with unusual vigor against one or more of its presuppositions. In the remaining chapters I consider writers who seem interesting and relevant, though in less central ways, to the theme. Ten of the thirty-two writers mentioned in the table of contents are still living, but all were born either before the twentieth century or in one of its first four decades. I have omitted some important philosophers whose work has been primarily in ethics (for example, Charles Stevenson, John Rawls) or in aesthetics (DeWitt Parker, Monroe Beardsley). Also some philosophers whose training was in other countries (Rudolf Carnap, John Findlay—a superb writer and thinker), with the exceptions, justified by the unique extent to which they learned from and became influential in American philosophy, of Whitehead and Tillich. Perhaps another exception should have been Gustav Bergmann. The writers dealt with in chapters 1–9 include all but one (Santayana) of Max Fisch's "six classical American philosophers." Santayana (Chapter 16) I consider somewhat marginal to the main line of development of metaphysics in this country.

With Max Fisch I treat Whitehead as American, although Anglo-American is more accurate. But it was an American university, Harvard, that gave this mathematician, physicist, and logician the opportunity he needed to devote himself full time to reading, teaching, and writing philosophy. England, like Europe generally, has been too much given to exclusive specialization to afford Whitehead this opportunity. Whitehead gladly accepted his new role as philosopher among our philosophers. He stopped reading physicists and gave all his attention to philosophers. He related himself to our traditions, and in fact they were more congenial to his speculative imagination than the British tradition, Ockham to Moore and Russell, could reasonably be said to be. The British neglect of Whitehead's philosophical work confirms this judgment.

Chapters 2, 4, 7 are slightly revised versions of Lowell Lectures given in Emerson Hall, Harvard University, in October, 1979. Sixteen and one-half chapters (2–4, 8, 11, 14A, 15, 17, 18, 20–27) and parts of most of the others are here published for the first time.

The reader will find that I combine hearty enthusiasm for the philosophical traditions of my country with sharp partial disagreement with nearly all their representatives. A youthful admiration for Emerson, Thoreau, Royce, and James partly explains the enthusiasm; the discipline of my Harvard training (1919–1923), study abroad (1923–1925), exposure (as editor) to the writings of Peirce (1925–1933), association as an instructor and research fellow at Harvard with Whitehead (1925–1928) and with critical colleagues in philosophy, theology, and science at the University of Chicago (1928–1955) partly explain the form taken by the disagreements. My thinking is somewhat akin to that of Peirce and Whitehead; but I have learned much also from Emerson, Royce, James, Lewis, Dewey, Carnap, and many others, including the very intelligent Episcopal clergyman who was my father. Finally, my thinking is my own. Metaphysics (and it is metaphysics—*pace* Heidegger—with which this book chiefly deals) cannot be divested entirely of a personal element, though metaphysicians should, and I do, strive valiantly to transcend the merely personal. Always the degree of success or failure in this is for others to judge.

I feel gratitude to the writers-editors of certain books of readings in "American Philosophy," meaning philosophy as represented by citizens of the United States of (North) America or their colonial predecessors. These writers-editors include W. G. Muelder, Laurence Sears, and A. V. Schlabach (*The Development of American Philosophy*, Houghton Mifflin, 1940, 1960); P. R. Anderson and M. H. Fisch (*Philosophy in America*, D. Appleton-Century, 1939). Fisch's *Classic American Philosophers* (New York: Appleton-Century-Crofts, 1951) was also very helpful. These three books, and several departments of philosophy that asked me to teach courses on American philosophy greatly helped me to appreciate our national heritage in this branch of inquiry. In general I am inclined to regard books of readings as the most valuable introductions to a subject. Every time I think of Benjamin Rand, philosophical librarian at Harvard for many years,

I feel gratitude for his selections from the history of philosophy. It is fine to go back to complete works by the great ones; but life is short, considering what a vast mass of such works there are in which we might find stimulating ideas. When I was suddenly asked to teach aesthetics for the first time, having never before thought of doing so, it was the books of readings that made a quick initiation into the heart of the subject possible.

Although the order of topics is largely chronological, I do not call this book a history. For a history in the standard sense consult *A History of Philosophy in America*, Vols. 1, 2, by Elizabeth Flower and Murray G. Murphey (New York: Capricorn Books, G. P. Putnam's Sons, 1977). It gives massive information about sources, in the Old World and the New, of the philosophical ideas dealt with. Consulting this book will have the advantage for a reader of my works that its authors' biases or blind spots, which all of us inevitably have, will be very different from mine. Thus in dealing with Emerson, Flower and Murphey manage to miss entirely the idea of "compensation," of which he was so fond (at least the word does not appear in their index), and they do not mention his theological determinism, which I show to be central (and unfortunate) in his thinking. Their readers will learn a great deal about the contexts and influences under which our philosophers have developed their thoughts. But when it comes to the question of truth (in a more than historical sense) of these thoughts, their readers will be largely on their own. Evaluations bearing on this are few. They interpret philosophies sympathetically and largely as their representatives saw them. I emphasize the distinction between what we *now* have reason to see as ill judged or badly mistaken in their writings and what we *now* have reason to see as well judged and a likely approximation to the truth about God or nature. I try to present the story of philosophy as a gradual sifting of possible views, a process that tends to eliminate cruder errors and thus constitutes a sort of testing laboratory for those ideas that empirical science logically could not falsify and therefore cannot in the proper sense verify. These are the metaphysical ideas, whose truth consists in making sense and whose falsity consists in not doing so.

The philosophers dealt with in chapters 1–7 did their work before I came to exist (at least as a philosopher); but those discussed in the remaining chapters were all, except for Santayana and Nozick, personal acquaintances, and with all I have been to some extent in intellectual dialogue. They form a somewhat arbitrary selection from the large number of American colleagues whose work has given me food for thought during the six decades that I have been a conscious member of the community of philosophers.

As usual my readers and I benefit from the superior editing of Dorothy C. Hartshorne, who in the last hundred days has found it possible to make perhaps five hundred (or is it a thousand?) valuable suggestions for turning mediocre into good, good into excellent, unclear into clear, or clear into very clear writing, and in this way to enable me to achieve in two books a higher level of communication than I could possibly do otherwise.

I also wish to express appreciation of the encouragement of Mr. William Eastman, one of many who have been students of mine and who later proved important for the world and, incidentally, for me.

CHAPTER 1

From Colonial Beginnings
to Philosophical Greatness

When the American settlers crossed the Atlantic and later the mountains and prairies on their way westward, they tended to leave certain things behind, the fine arts most obviously, but also theoretical science. Three things, however, were not left behind, at least not for long: the arts and concerns of government, religion, and philosophy. The first could not be dispensed with, nor the second; and indeed, the very reasons for leaving the Old World were often intensely religious. Also philosophizing, like religion, is almost native to our species. Moreover, the diversity of religions among the colonists favored philosophical reflection, and it led to the early establishment of freedom of thought to a degree that had been uncommon in Western civilization generally. So we need not be surprised that Jonathan Edwards was a far better theologian and philosopher than any of the colonists were scientists (with Benjamin Franklin perhaps an exception). Down to the end of the nineteenth century the country produced only one natural scientist of superb quality, Willard Gibbs; and it is typical of the situation that few United States citizens have even heard of him. Pure scientific theory was not greatly encouraged in a land where the need was for applications of existing knowledge to transform a wilderness into farms, habitations, roads, railroads, and other means of communication. The inventor, not the scientist, was most honored. Practicality was in order. But the political and religious questions were not to be evaded, and reflection upon them could be accepted as practical enough. Such reflections easily led into the depths of philosophy. Thus it was perhaps almost predictable that Gibbs should have been followed by a half-dozen philosophers of great distinction, and many others of only lesser merit.

1

It is supposed by many Europeans that most philosophical ideas originated in Europe and then, in a delayed and usually inferior form, found their way across the Atlantic. Of course this has happened. But it has also happened that the first formulation of an idea appeared in this country; and in some cases Europe still has not caught up! And even when a European did say it first, the American version may have been independent—or, sometimes, an improvement, not a diminution. Thus Royce's version of the argument for metaphysical idealism has some elements which in clarity and cogency surpass anything in Berkeley or Hegel. And finally, in the "six classical American philosophers," so designated by Max Fisch, we have had a group not surpassed in any country during the past one hundred years. I doubt if it would be too much to say, not surpassed in all continental Europe.

I have been speaking of superiority in philosophy. Science is another matter. In it provincialism tends everywhere to be transcended. However, conditions in this country have until recently been less favorable for scientific than for philosophical creativity. Energy and talent that in Europe went into basic scientific reflection tended here to go into secondary experimentation and applications. But, on the other hand, what in Europe went into the cultivation of each country's own philosophical heritage, or of its borrowings from Germany, here went into a courageous and informed confronting of the international philosophical scene. Since there were in philosophy no tempting physical applications or ingenious experimental tests whose devising could distract from theoretical inquiry, and since the ferment of religions, with none established or clearly dominant, kept pointing to theoretical issues, American philosophers were relatively free to be as theoretical as they wished.

In the classical period (c. 1870–1950), for special circumstantial reasons, six men, five of them associated with Harvard University, and four of them for many years on its faculty, achieved great distinction in philosophy. These are Charles Sanders Peirce (1839–1914), William James (1842–1910), Josiah Royce (1855–1916), John Dewey (1859–1952), Alfred North Whitehead (1861–1947), and George Santayana (1863–1952). Each of these impressed many scholars by his genius, and five of them, Santayana being the exception, were also competent and creative in one or more branches of science: Peirce in astronomy, physics, mathematics, symbolic logic, and experimental psychology ("the first in this country"); James and Dewey in psychology; Royce in symbolic logic; Whitehead in mathematics, symbolic logic, and physics. True, Whitehead's training was entirely

British; but it was Harvard University and a great chairman of its philosophy department, James Haughton Woods, who changed intellectual history by inviting Whitehead, aged sixty-three, to teach philosophy, something he immediately said he had "always wanted to do."

Peirce, James, Royce, and Whitehead combined a positive but critical interest in religion with knowledge of exact science and the history of philosophy. Dewey and Santayana were deeply skeptical of religious traditions. Peirce, James, and Royce influenced one another considerably; Peirce and James influenced Dewey; James and Dewey influenced Whitehead, who also read Santayana with care. Whitehead, as he told me, found Royce too loose a thinker for his taste; he learned about Peirce (apart from his symbolic logic) too late to be influenced by him.

Peirce was called, by a distinguished British mathematician (Sylvester), a "great" mathematician. He had few rivals in the world in symbolic logic, and it would be hard to find a philosopher since Leibniz who commanded as many branches of knowledge as he did. James uniquely combined technical psychology and technical philosophy; Dewey was a leader in educational theory. Whitehead was right that Royce could not be counted upon for close reasoning; yet he was one of the most profound students of German philosophy who ever lived, in Germany or out of it, and there was in him—as Santayana, a sharp critic, said, "something simple and sublime." His analysis (in *The Problem of Christianity*) of the idea of community, what makes a group of people a nation or other cooperative society, is profound. It is probably partly his early influence that makes me so unusually immune to the alleged truism that altruism is merely an aspect of enlightened self-interest. I see more truth in "self-interest is a corollary of enlightened altruism." True, my reasons for this attitude are in part quite different from Royce's.

It may be difficult to judge, but I take the six men who are listed above to have possessed an awareness of the intellectual landscape of their time unsurpassed by any contemporary group. Their training and equipment to deal with the totality of the knowledge of their day was at least as good, even considering how much more there was to know, as had been the equipment of Hegel, Fichte, Schelling, and Schopenhauer in Germany. For the American group was, for the most part, in the middle of the problems produced by scientific advances, not on the periphery of them. But they were also richly sensitive to the religious and humanistic heritage from ancient Palestine and Greece. It was a golden opportunity, and it elicited some

3

golden results. I for one am not convinced that we have any less to give than to gain from interchanges with Europe or Britain, though I should be less sure of this had not one very great Englishman—so typically non-English in some ways—thrown in his lot with us for a dozen grandly productive years.

To make possible the upsurge of American philosophy in the period mentioned, it was necessary that the base of philosophizing be broadened to include more than politics, religion, and somewhat stale echoes of European science. Gibbs may have been the only great natural scientist of his day and country, but the northeastern universities began about that time to be alive with scientific activity. And it so happened that two young men with philosophical inclinations, Charles Peirce and William James, were exposed early and intensively to this ferment. They were also brought up to have religious interests, treated in a highly intellectual way, and were possessed of a noble trust in reason. A third young philosopher, Royce, came under their influence, and also under some of the influences which had molded them. All three men were well aware of German—and James, at least, of French—thought. The German influence also came to America through philosophically gifted immigrants and in many other ways. This influence did not make the philosophy of this country a mere weakened echo of German idealism. For our principal philosophers were exposed, in a way no German is likely to be, to the entire force of the English and Scottish tradition, with its ideals of clarity and sobriety. Thus, while Peirce apparently did his first careful philosophical reading in Kant, he also discussed the reasoning with his mathematician-father, who showed him many logical flaws, and with Chauncey Wright, a scientist and vigorous disciple of John Stuart Mill, with whom he had "daily" argument for years. Peirce, James, and Royce gave the philosophy of this country a foundation broad and deep.

I also find that almost the entire gamut of philosophical problems confronting Western man has been centrally dealt with during the two and one-half centuries of philosophizing in this country and that nearly all the important points of view have been represented, and well represented, by one or another of its philosophers. To survey the resources of philosophy generally, one scarcely needs, any longer, to look across the Atlantic. There is somewhat more need to look across the Pacific; but there are competent Buddhist scholars among us also.

The most famous recent philosophical movements in Europe—Bergsonianism, existentialism, phenomenology, analysis—are not, one may suggest, so superior to the American classical philosophers as has been widely assumed. A great deal of Bergson, without his neglect of intellectual devices, is in Whitehead; Peirce might be called the first phenomenologist of all, and in some ways (in my opinion) he remains still the best; James and especially Whitehead are rich in subtle phenomenological accounts (when Whitehead called metaphysics "a descriptive science," he meant that concepts are to be derived from concrete experience). As for sensitivity to the central role of language in philosophy, Peirce in his theory of signs was in some ways at least the equal of Wittgenstein. For instance, he said, long before the latter, that the certainty of mathematics is a matter of our own sign-using conventions.

But even if my own efforts (including months of study with Husserl and Heidegger) to appreciate the continental and British achievements have been somewhat unsucccessful, so that my remarks in the previous paragraph should be largely discounted, it still would not follow that the American movement deserved to be neglected. The claim to have rendered obsolete all philosophical speculation, all metaphysics in the grand manner, may plausibly be made. But, I submit, it ought in honesty to test its case against the strongest, not the weakest, of recent representatives, those who combine the old imaginativeness and courage with adequate knowledge of modern logical techniques. These representatives have worked largely in this country, rather than in Europe. It is quite obvious to me (and I have made it my business, as no one else, I think, has, to know the facts) that the most penetrating, imaginative, and yet careful, speculations of the last one hundred years have occurred here, not elsewhere. Wittgenstein may be subtler than anyone else as an *un*speculative philosopher, though it might be hard to say what he sees that neither Peirce nor Dewey was aware of. G. E. Moore may have been a better man to scare a young student out of daring to speculate than we have had, though A. O. Lovejoy was searching, without wishing to scare anyone. But unless positivism, or positivism plus a poetic existentialist anthropology, or plus a subtle theory of language in its more banal or harmless aspects—unless these are the precious gifts of philosophy to culture, Europe has had little to offer of late. And in any case these things are now capably represented among us.

Has there been progress, in the sense of solutions to problems, in the course of our philosophical history? To answer this question is to declare one's own philosophy. I think that there are five major problems that have been pervasive from Edwards and Theodore Parker to Peirce and Whitehead and that the treatment of these problems by the last two is incomparably more illuminating than that by the earlier thinkers. This treatment is speculative, not positivistic or (as the British sometimes now say) merely "therapeutic." The problems are solved, not dismissed or dissolved. (It was Dewey who first said that philosophical problems are abandoned, not solved. But the Peirce-Whitehead theory of creative relativity tries to solve problems.) Many of the writers who today deny the solubility of speculative puzzles, or who answer speculative questions by arguing that they need not arise if we are careful, do not know or understand this particular form of solution. And if I am wrong, if the thing to do is to dismiss or avoid the questions, then there have been, or are, those among us who are capable of defending that position, in one or another of its several forms. It is, however, amusing that British writers today seem almost unable to see that anything philosophical is going on here unless it be of the positivistic or therapeutic sort. It is true that we have fallen into a bit of a trough from the wonderful heights of the recent wave. But another wave may be forming.

The five speculative problems are: God and cosmos, mind and matter, freedom and causality, substance and event, and, finally, a priori and empirical knowledge (or reason and experience). One may add to these a sixth problem, which is rather practical than speculative, (political) equality and sovereignty. Most of the colonial philosophers had much to say about God. Edwards and Johnson had radically idealistic theories of matter; Edwards anticipated much that has been current lately concerning the alleged compatibility of moral freedom with strict causal determinism and argued this question at length and with great sharpness; he almost anticipated Whitehead's analysis of substance into a special kind of event-sequence (perhaps following some hints of Descartes). The fifth speculative problem, that of reason and experience, was sharply formulated by Parker.

My view—naive enough, some will think—is that none of the five problems was satisfactorily illuminated anywhere in the world in the seventeenth, eighteenth, or early nineteenth centuries, but that several of them at least can now be given a reasonable solution, thanks chiefly to the work of our "six classical philosophers," especially Peirce and Whitehead—work chiefly written, though not always immediately published, between the years 1866 and 1933; that is, during the last third of the nineteenth and the first third of the twentieth centuries.

In the more than fifty years since 1933 much good detailed work has been done, but in general not quite of a fundamental nature.

We have been going through one of those skeptical eras, like that of the Second Academy, which may seem to themselves almost definitive, but which so far have always been followed by new outbursts of speculation. And there are signs that antispeculation will not be the last word this time either. Meanwhile, it may not be amiss to take a good look at the over-all adventure of American thought from Edwards to Dewey and Quine, so that we shall not perchance exchange our best inheritance for an inferior European product or a superficial contemporary fashion.

Whether Europeans can profit by the study of our tradition is for them to consider. We learned from them for centuries; if they are too preoccupied, or for some other reason unable, to learn from us now, it is possibly their loss. It must be admitted that multitudes of young philosophers in this country today seem determined to Europeanize themselves as much as possible. The glamor of the Old World, with its incomparable artistic riches, and its one-time speculative grandeur, still fascinates. Perhaps it is for the best that it be so. We do not want to fall into mere provincialism ourselves. But our own tradition is at least worth a closer look than some of us appear to suspect.

That the foregoing talk of 'solving' speculative problems will sound quaint to many, I well know. And doubtless it is wise to take all such talk with considerable reserve. But the fashionable clichés about the essentially illusory nature of metaphysical ideas are, I am very sure, not nearer to literal correctness. We must, with Hume and even more than Hume, be skeptical of our skepticisms, or we shall only be duped in a different way from the overconfident metaphysicians. Let it be not forgotten that Kant thought he knew exactly the limits of human knowledge or of humanly significant questioning. His work produced one of the maddest speculative outbursts of all. The wise balance here is not necessarily attained by giving free rein either to suspicion of, or to confidence in, the human power to find rational over-all meaning in life and the cosmos. Moore, Wittgenstein, Sartre, Heidegger (like Richard Rorty in this country—see his *Philosophy and the Mirror of Nature*), ably represent one extreme, but where in England, Germany, or France today are the able representatives of the balancing contrary attitude of speculative confidence? Heidegger never gets free of anthropomorphism, and even in his anthropology he eschews what most of us mean by rationality.

Whitehead's statement of more than forty years ago is still plausible: that while Europe has lost her speculative freedom and courage, this country has not. The chief qualification to be added is that, if the present trend away from our heritage were to go far enough, the Western world as a whole would be in the plight Whitehead saw Europe to be in. Let it not be so. For the Western world needs all its heritage to survive. Marxism has an alleged solution to all our six problems, and this claim is one of its assets. If we have no better solution, or no solution, this is scarcely a source of strength.

It is rather alarming that the Marxist solutions are, to so large an extent, merely duplicated by many of our living Free World philosophers. Of course a Marxist can be right and indeed must be right in some of his beliefs. No one can be uniformly wrong, and certainly not so successful a type of person (by some criteria) as the Marxist, in many countries, is proving to be. But consider: the Marxist says the solution to the God problem is that 'God' stands for a superstition encouraged by certain vested interests. Just so do many of us think. The Marxist says that mind is an emergent quality of certain material systems and that matter can exist in total independence of mind. Just so say many of us. The Marxist thinks (or at least does not clearly deny) that human liberty and strict causal regularity are compatible and that moral freedom is the "acceptance of necessity," or, at least, of the laws of nature. This is today a fashionable philosophical position everywhere. The Marxist view concerning events and substances is perhaps less definite, but similarly nebulous and not significantly different is the view held by many of us. The Marxist thinks that all knowledge is empirical, with an element of rational interpretation that is ultimately pragmatic, and this, too, is a favorite doctrine among us. So here are five speculative problems concerning which we apparently are scarcely wiser than the Marxist world. The chief difference is that the latter has more confidence in its answers than most of us have, a difference perhaps not wholly in our favor.

I believe that the Marxist is in serious error on all five topics, although least so in respect to the fourth (substances and events). I admit that he does have some true insights; for instance, "the transformation of quantity into quality" has a certain validity. But we have a heritage superior to any he is utilizing, and why should we not cultivate that heritage? The point is not that unless we know Marxism to be philosophically mistaken we shall lack grounds for opposing totalitarianism. On the practical points of freedom and sovereignty we know well, nearly all of us, that present-day communism ought to be opposed.

The value of reminding ourselves of our superior speculative insight is rather in the positive inspiration that it might furnish us and our friends. It is the confidence, boldness, and energy of Marxists, and our own lack of these qualities, that is perhaps our chief danger. The Marxist has a system, and this heartens him and helps to keep up his fervor. We cannot respond with a uniform generally accepted system of our own. Our method of freedom rules that out. But it might be well if many of us freely came to accept a system that carries thought to the highest level open to us. For we believe that we have something precious to maintain that Marxists would destroy, and yet mere political freedom seems not enough if all we do with our freedom is to gravitate toward the very tenets which Marxism makes authoritative. Should not the difference appear also in the content? I believe that the Marxist content is basically wrong at some points. But so may ours be if we do not take care.

Is there really no connection between our faith in the rights of persons not to be tyrannized over for the alleged benefit of future generations (as this benefit is defined by a ruling clique) and the belief that only one, namely God, has an unconditioned right to prefer His wisdom to that of the rest of us? Has the definition of a liberal, one "who knows that he is not God," really been superseded? Or does it now mean "one who knows that there is or may be no God"? Is there not some loss of cutting edge with this shift? But if there is a connection between human equality and the common immeasurable inferiority of all of us to deity, then it might help our political idealism to arrive at the most enlightened view of deity that our history makes available.

Can faith in the value of freedom have simply no connection with superior insight into its universal metaphysical principle? If that principle is merely causality, then we have nothing to offer that has not been common property for more than two thousand years and certainly nothing hidden from Marxists. But suppose the principle is the secularization of the theological idea of creativity, of action that no causal explanation can ever derive from antecedent conditions, or of decision whose possibility can indeed be causally explained but not the realization of precisely this possibility rather than others that would have been equally explicable from the same conditions.

Can our greater faith in the value of consciousness and ideas be simply unrelated to any superior insight into the cosmic role of mind? If that role is to emerge from mere matter, that is, if mind is not of cosmic dimensions at all, then we can be no wiser than the communists on the basic point. But suppose mind really is the explanation of matter, as many great intellects, from Leibniz and Berkeley to Peirce and Whitehead, have held? Then it is we and not the Marxists who are free to understand this.

Is it really likely that we shall make the most of our principle of the preciousness of individuality if we have no carefully conceived doctrine of the nature of enduring individuality in the stream of events connected together in space-time? The communists mock at our notion of soul or self, claiming that the social group is the enduring identity, not the person. If in reply we merely assert the individual against the group, then we are likely to fall into an anarchism no better than the collectivism we oppose, and rather less realizable in practice. The Buddhists long ago rejected the 'soul', but they did not fall into either anarchism or collectivism. Their wisdom at this point is essentially duplicated, more or less independently, by the 'Buddhisto-Christian' view of Peirce, and still more completely, and with improvements, by Whitehead's 'philosophy of organism.' Incidentally, it is worth noting that Emerson, Peirce, and Whitehead had affinities—of which they were to some extent conscious—with Far Eastern thought.

Can mere empiricism give us a standard for judging the forces of history, and for distinguishing, however cautiously, tentatively, or roughly, between the ethical and the triumphant, as the Marxists, with some inconsistency, refuse to do? More than a century ago Theodore Parker argued vigorously that religious and ethical first principles, like scientific ones, cannot be empirical. Royce continued the argument, and James unwittingly provided a brilliant example of the hopeless inconclusiveness of empiricism when applied to trans-empirical problems. Peirce, Whitehead, and some more recent writers have carried the analysis further.

The value which I have been imputing to recent speculative philosophy, chiefly American, though with partial analogues in Italy (Varisco), France (Lequier, Boutroux, Bergson, R. Ruyer), Germany (Fechner, Wenzl), and England (Ward, Alexander), and elsewhere, does not, of course, imply its acceptability as it stands. There are at least four respects in which I personally find it unsatisfactory. First, concerning the method and logical status of speculative philosophy: Are its statements analytic, synthetic a priori, consequences-of-meaning postulates, phenomenological insights, or what? I find neither Peirce nor Whitehead sufficiently clear at this point, though not so unclear as many of their critics suppose. Second, though Whitehead seems to me to have come closer by far than any other metaphysician in the grand manner to ridding theistic philosophy of its well-known antinomies, nevertheless, his exposition on this topic is marred by ambiguities and apparent or real inconsistencies, suggesting that he was groping toward a theory he did not quite reach. And in the last conversation I had with him he indicated just that. If his view can be freed of these weaknesses, we may well put Whitehead above most great theistic philosophers, who have not even been in the neighborhood of a tenable theory of deity. The rest are all impaled upon the horns of ancient dilemmas that arise from their very principles. Whitehead's difficulty here arose, on the contrary, chiefly from his not quite adhering to his general principles when he came to the religious problem. He did not wander far from them, but far enough to get into trouble. Yet the remedy was in his own hands. This, though to a lesser extent, is also true of Peirce. It is not true of Augustine, Thomas, Spinoza, Leibniz, Kant, or Hegel.

Third, Whitehead's rather platonic theory of 'eternal objects' seems to do insufficient justice to the case for a more nominalistic view and is doubtfully consistent with the ultimacy assigned to process or 'creativity.' Peirce suggests a conception of the "evolution of the Platonic forms themselves" that may provide a clue.

Fourth, since Whitehead, new interests and new criteria have emerged in philosophy, for instance, a new attention to the centrality of language in human thought. Everything has to be reconsidered in the light of these new concerns.

But no work of high genius, such as many careful students have found Whitehead's to be, can be evaluated by a raising of the eyebrows, whatever our remarkable contemporaries at Cambridge or Oxford may think. It needs to be reconsidered, yes, but re-considering is still considering. The cultures of England and this country have by their confluence produced no greater joint product than Whitehead's vision of cosmic creativity. Even it, of course, is but a stepping-stone. However, the claim of many to need no such stone will be more impressive when we see them reaching more exalted philosophical objectives without its aid than they are now contenting themselves with. I dare to say that one might about as easily reach great heights in philosophy without benefit of the work done in modern America as to reach them in physics without using the work of modern Germans. Is this statement extreme? If so, it can cause little harm. The most one can do with European provincialism, in which some citizens of the United States choose to participate, is to mitigate it ever so slightly. The economic bases of that provincialism alone seem to guarantee its persistence far into the future. How many foreign scholars or students can afford our books and journals, not to mention adequate travel and study in this country? This is one of the nonrational factors whose power in philosophy is, sadly enough, much greater than in natural science. In the latter, the financial sacrifices are recognized as imperative; in philosophy they are appreciated at best as luxuries.

The vigor of the American philosophical development would not have been possible without careful consideration of the work of German, French, and British writers. Our scholars have often been in a position to travel and to import foreign publications and foreign scholars, and we have not made it a point of honor to refuse to learn from them. This good fortune and this modesty are sources of strength. However, our danger has become an inverted snobbery, turned against our own past.

My proposal is, then, that philosophy in this country, not of course only here but particularly here, has arrived at a metaphysics in which human freedom and human consciousness are given a congenial setting, unfavorable both to collectivism and to anarchic individualism, but favorable to reason in religion and religion in reason, and furnishing an ethical principle (not, of course, an ethical code) that is valid for all rational beings, independently of factual circumstances. Those of us who can accept this doctrine are in no danger of wondering what it is that our political freedom enables us to enjoy. For communist orthodoxy would sweep every item of this faith away or reduce it to silence and inability to communicate itself.

Having, in effect, brought the cold war into the discussion (and it may bring itself into every discussion, if we do not do what we can to see that it is more successfully conducted or favorably ended than hitherto), I must take some further steps. A philosophy of cosmic freedom and creativity can consistently exercise tolerance toward other philosophies, even those seeming to deny freedom. It can and should go further and admit that in some ways communists show themselves to be more creative and, in that and other respects, more in harmony with the theory of universal creativity, than our own views have usually been. For instance, the communists have a more realistic sense of the tragic side of life than have most of us. Yet tragedy is logically inherent in a philosophy of freedom such as Whitehead's. There can be no absolute harmonization of multiple freedom, even by divine 'persuasion'; not because God is weak but because it is meaningless to speak of absolute control over free beings. And for a metaphysics of freedom, a simply 'unfree' being is also an incoherent notion; hence, the notion of absolute control or absolute providential guarantees is logically, not just factually, vacuous. And the higher the level of freedom, the greater the inherent risks of conflict as well as opportunities of valuable harmony. Thus human life is bound to have aspects of great danger.

12

How shall the miserably poor who now inhabit much of the world acquire some share in the wealth they see around them, and not someday but soon? For they refuse to wait. The Marxists answer this question; their answer is open to grave objections; but, alas, we have scarcely offered an alternative. (We have made a beginning, but a small one.) Our native optimism, not our best speculative philosophy, is at fault here. We did not believe that the dilemma of the all-too-even race between population and resources could be so desperate as the facts show it to be. Indeed, we all along refused to read Malthus intelligently and thereby lost a great opportunity to prepare ourselves for what is now upon us. Dewey, so far as I know, ignored the Malthusian problem, and Peirce and Whitehead take it too lightly. Royce, the careful student of Hegel, ignored Marx, though surely Hegel's greatest contribution, for good or ill, was precisely his unintended part in the production of Marxism.

It is not that Whitehead, for instance, was committed to a socio-political or ethical code that is held to be uniquely fitting for all situations. Quite the contrary, he denies this. But he did not focus, as we now need to, on certain tragic aspects of things: race prejudice, stubbornly persisting in all our cities in spite of rapidly rising consciousness of rights on the part of the victims; population increase beyond any comfortable possibility of production increase; and finally the grim dilemma: Risk nuclear destruction or lose the chance effectively to defend freedom anywhere. The communists at least have a sense of permanent emergency. We still (and this is perhaps as true of West Europeans) want to get "back to normalcy," that is, to a tragedy-free, comfortable domestic existence. It cannot be.

The communists also have a sense of the subordination of the individual to the general welfare, which, as they formulate it, is again open to grave objection; but to which, again, we tend to offer no real alternative. Individual self-interest is not an ultimate idea; for ultimately every individual perishes—and indeed everything we know will presumably perish except God. Here is the genuine alternative to mere individualism. But we have given it lip service, have not quite believed it. The "glory of God" is more literally the aim of existence in Whitehead's or Peirce's philosophy than in conventional Christianity.

The "times that try men's souls" also sift their philosophies. If I am right, suitable working ideas are in principle derivable from neoclassical metaphysics, as I call it; but they need focusing on the actual needs and dangers.

CHAPTER 2

Jonathan Edwards
on God and Causality

Edwards (1703–1758) was a giant intellect, but an intellect in prison. The confining bars are apparent in the very doctrine for which he has been primarily admired by some: his contention that moral freedom is compatible with strict causal determinism. In this position our first great American philosophical writer was following a false trail, blazed, nearly two thousand years before by the Stoics and not effectively corrected by Augustine, Luther, or Calvin. Though the doctrine was not new, it was defended by Edwards in extreme form with great candor, energy, and cleverness. This defense forced attention to the issue, and—as I shall suggest in dealing with Royce— that is one service a thinker can render his branch of knowledge.

All Edwards's energy and skill, however, could not conceal the fact that the doctrine was not the result of his inquiry, but its presupposition. The logical acumen was employed, not in a genuine examination of the credentials of determinism, but rather, as with many writers of today, merely in the effort to rebut some—by no means all or the best—arguments against it. It has indeed been characteristic of determinists (though less so in recent decades) that they have generally been incapable of treating this question as an open one. Genuine reasoning must at some point so treat a question or it will almost surely go astray, take some short-cut to its goal.

As it is easier to see now than it was then, Edwards inherited a theological tradition that was bound to fail the man who attempted to think rationally about his faith, and this not necessarily because that tradition concerned itself with the mysteries of God, but rather because it confused these mysteries with certain all-too-human interpretations. Only after the prestige of the tradition had been severely damaged was it possible to institute a genuine inquiry, whether from a religious or a philosophical standpoint (Barth or Whitehead), into the credentials of the old way of doing things in religious metaphysics. Edwards was an exceedingly brilliant and honest man, but he simply could not have imagined the extent of the revisions required if his efforts were to achieve lasting validity.

Let us look at some basic contentions of Calvinism—in substantial part shared by European theology in general for more than a thousand years.

God has created or creates the world. And what is it to create? If this word is a humanly intelligible one, some human experience must provide its meaning. What is that experience? Is it observation of the "potter with his clay"? But the potter acts on clay only by using his hands to turn a wheel. And the potter can do nothing without clay already there. God has no hands and is said to create matter itself. So the meaning of 'create' can hardly come from this example. Is it the observation of the sun causing its rays to go forth? But this, too, is one physical thing from which other physical things proceed; moreover, it is a wholly unconscious and involuntary operation (to all appearances). We also hear of overflowing fountains, and God has been said to be so rich in reality that he naturally overflows into creatures. This clearly adds nothing to the sun analogy.

There is, of course, the analogy from reproduction. We are children of God. But in the divine case, as usually conceived, the purely immaterial generates the material. The word 'generates' cannot here say what it literally seems to say. What then? Are we reduced to the bare word 'causes?' But this word must acquire meaning somehow, and the history of philosophy shows how difficult a problem the word names.

In modern scientific use, causes are antecedent conditions, certain types of events, from which the characters of subsequent events are (more or less) predictable. Is the divine cause an event or feature of events? We are told that nothing divine is an event, that God's thoughts are not in time. But this is not all. The world is said, by most theologians, to have been created freely. God might have 'made' a different world, or even none at all. But a cause at liberty to produce not only all sorts of effects, but also no effect, is a very strange cause indeed!

There is another difficulty. Not only do most of the examples concern physical causes of physical effects, whereas we are seeking to conceive an 'immaterial' cause of physical effects, but we have to conceive also the creation of minds, or at least, of thoughts and feelings as well as of bodies.

Let us now consider what Edwards did with this problem.[1] He held that, in the world, causal order is absolute, all events following upon their conditions according to strict laws, without the least chance or randomness. Human choices are not excluded in any degree from the strict orderliness. Yet the choices (in favorable circumstances) issue in free acts, because we *do what we choose* or wish to do, and that (it is contended) is freedom in the good sense. We do not choose as we choose to choose, for that would mean a vicious infinite regress of choosing to choose to choose . . . (I have heard Einstein argue in this way). Freedom is in the ability to execute choice, not in the choice itself. But the choices are completely caused, and in any given case one chooses in the sole way then possible for one to choose. Our decisions are always inevitable, in the sense of the only then-and-there causally possible ones.

In favor of this doctrine Edwards urges that otherwise, or if we allow any weakening of or deviation from the strict principle of causality, we shall have cut off the possibility of knowing the existence of God. For God is knowable as Universal Cause, and hence to claim to know God is to accept the causal principle.

Let us look at this argument with (if possible) the same sort of pitiless logic that our heroic ancestor applied to the Arminian view of human freedom (held by James Arminius, Dutch theologian) which Edwards combated. Let us not spare him, as he did not spare an intellectual foe.

We must, he seems to be saying, admit that from causal conditions subsequent events are strictly derivable; for otherwise how can we derive the divine Condition from the (logically though not temporally) subsequent world, its effect? Now here Edwards commits a non sequitur. To infer God is to infer divine Cause from worldly effect, Condition from conditioned; to refute "free will" one must (in principle) make precisely the opposite inference, from worldly (or divine) cause or condition to effect or conditioned. Since when in logic is "*P* does not entail *Q*" inferrible from "*Q* does not entail *P*"? For example, "this is an animal" does not entail "this is a fox;" yet the reverse inference is valid. Edwards has merely assumed, not shown, that causality cannot have the one-way character that entailment certainly does have. It may well be that in each case the condition is the only one which the conditioned could have had (and hence the former is inferrible from the latter), while yet the condition could have issued in a different conditioned result, so that the latter was not inferrible. Indeed, most theologians have held that the divine Condition could have issued in a very different total result, or perhaps in none at all!

It is true that we need also to make causal inferences (predictions) from condition to result; but this does not refute Arminian freedom (that an actual choice is not the only one then and there causally possible), unless not only do we need to make causal predictions, but also there is a necessity for an in principle *unlimited* possibility of inferring the future. How is such a necessity established? Physics today explicitly limits prediction; if psychology does not yet do so, the suspicion is in order that this study is still so far from precision that it does not yet see what the issues really are.

I think the reader of Edwards will not find any valid argument for assuming the symmetrical absoluteness of causal order, backward and forward. A relative order will suffice for all manifest human needs.

So far I have merely been saying that Edwards has not made out his case. But we should go further. There is a very strong case against him, which he never sees clearly. The divine Condition (1) was or (2) was not free to produce another world instead of this one. Either God acts by causal necessity or not by necessity. Either way, the extreme Calvinist is in trouble. (Some interpret Calvin's determinism as not unqualified.)

(1) If God acts by necessity (as Edwards seems to suggest, "determined by the good"), this is the paradox of Spinoza and Leibniz that this world is the only possible one. (True, Leibniz says it is merely the "best possible;" but then he also says that God is "morally necessitated" by his goodness to create the best possible world, from which it follows that, since the goodness of God exists by eternal necessity, the best possible creation is really the only possible creation.) Thus the distinction between "necessary" and "contingent" collapses, and we no longer know what we mean by either term. "Everything whatever is necessary" says nothing distinctive about anything. And how, pray, can "the good," an abstract general term, entail the concrete detail of the cosmos? God is "determined by the good." Very well, if the world is the uniquely possible result, then "the good" must be as definite and detailed as the world and, indeed, indistinguishable from it. So you are really saying that God in creating the world is determined by the world, which is hardly illuminating.

An ideal for action that entails a concrete act is not an ideal, but merely the act over again. Ideals never imply any precise mode for their execution, and as ideals they cannot do so. Edwards is merely misusing "the good" so that it loses all meaning. And if we follow what he says in justification of the divine predestination of sinners to damnation, we shall find, not without shock to our moral sensibilities, that God's being determined by the good merely means doing whatever it happens to please God to do, which by definition is called "good." No requirement of kindness or sympathy for the creatures is called into play. If people dishonor God (as many do), they deserve nothing from God except punishment.

(2) Suppose, as Douglas Elwood holds, the Edwardsian position is "God could have created a different world." Then in the divine case, at least, choice is free in the very sense Edwards denies absolutely in the human case. Is there then an infinite regress of divine choosings to choose? If this does not follow, the Edwardsian argument from regress must be invalid. And if we have no freedom in the Arminian sense (anticipated by Philo, the Jewish theologian of the first century A.D. and Faustus Socinus, the seventeenth-century Antitrinitarian) what can we mean in attributing such freedom to deity? (Human words either have human meaning or they do not; if not, human beings ought not to employ them.) An Arminian does not face this difficulty; for he can say that, as we have a feeble spark of freedom of choice, so we can suppose God to have the infinite or perfect form of such freedom. We can analogically extend our inferior liberty into a concept of divine liberty. But Edwards has nothing to extend. He starts with zero, and with this nothing, nothing can be done. True, he recognizes "voluntary," doing what you wish to do; but we have seen that, at least in application to deity, this is not enough. Our freedom may be hemmed about by divinely instituted laws, as Edwards says; but the divine instituting of the laws cannot be according to a prior law, unless we have again the endless regress. And if this freedom is not according to any law, then law-transcending freedom is admitted. Yet how could such freedom even be conceived by a creature that has no experience of it?

My conclusion is: Edwards's show of rigorous logic is a sham. He is indeed capable of sharp reasoning, but he uses logic not to get at the truth but to discredit opponents. The moment the application of exacting criteria would make trouble for his theological commitments, there is an end to his inquiry. After some early sallies into partially free speculation, he asks only the questions that will serve his apologetic purposes. This is a brilliant instance of the theological "sham reasoning" of which Peirce rightly complains.

What were the sources of the impasse, the blind alley down which this wonderful mind strayed?

The basic source was a confusion between piety and intellectual commitments, or between religion and philosophy—in particular, a form of philosophy, unluckily, which did not lend itself to the undistorted expression of piety. This philosophy was Neoplatonism. In this doctrine one tended to identify God with an eternal form, immutable, ever-complete, of which all becoming is an inferior "shadow," contributing nothing to the Form. Causal order was the analogue, in becoming, of the perfect Unity which is immune to becoming. Derogated, with becoming, were materiality (extendedness in space), receptivity to influences, and (though this was stubbornly denied by many) genuine creativity or freedom.

It is a dazzling paradox, indeed, that in a tradition in which "creator" and "creature" were supposedly the key concepts, creativity, the presupposed principle of both, was left in Cimmerian darkness, or was implicitly denied. For what is it to create? (We return to our initial question.) Man was said to create by molding matter, God, by molding nothing, as it were. But the concept of matter, after two thousand years, remains a masterpiece of obscurity, and hence so does the notion of man molding it. And when God creates (with or without matter) voluntarily and freely (we have seen the absurdities of trying to conceive a necessary creation), must this not mean that there is a divine decision, such as might not have been taken, to do this. "Let there be light." This divine fiat *must itself be a creature* (if it is not eternally necessary), and the resulting universe is thus a creature of the second order. Of course this is hinted at in the doctrine of creation through the Son, but nothing is gained by this complication unless in the Son or in the Father there is a created or contingent decision.

What the foregoing analysis seems, to me at least, to show is that free creation is first of all self-creation, free self-determining, and its first product is the thought or volition of the creator. The volition is free, not in the sense that another volition is back of it, but in the sense that another volition was possible in its stead, for that very individual. This is precisely the Arminian principle. Without it there can be no intellectually viable theory.

Edwards says that reason alone cannot deal with the theological question; in particular, it cannot solve the problem of evil. Of course it cannot, assuming the Calvinistic blind alley of no creaturely creativity. But if the first creation is always in the thinking or deciding of the creator, then, since we also make decisions and think, we

19

must have a humble version of genuine creativity. And then the world is not simply "made" by God, but rather is the result of the creatures' creativity, as inspired, ordered, guided, by divine Creativity, yet by no means wholly determined by it. The Supreme Creator produces lesser creators. And what else could supreme creativity produce but inferior "images" of itself, humbler forms of the same principle? How from infinite or perfect decision-making could one get to zero decision-making in the product?

Admit, then, creativity in the creatures. Evil becomes intelligible as the chance interplay of creaturely acts. There must be an aspect of chance in this interplay. For if X's decision is A and Y's is B, then the conjunction AB, which was not the decision of either, will begin to influence the world. Will AB have been divinely decided? If the creatures really, in a humble way, "make" (note the word) their own decisions, then it cannot also be true that God has made these decisions for them. There can be only one decider for a given concrete decision, or the concept of the decider loses its meaning. Back of God's decision there is no causal necessity; if then back of mine there is God's, covering mine in all details, only the word "decision" is common to both. And then we do not know what the whole argument is about and theology as such is impossible.

In supposing that one can really conceive "volition" as the sole possible outcome of antecedent conditions, the entire question is begged. That a concrete deciding experience, or any experience in its fullness, could follow uniquely from a complex of conditions according to laws is something we can verbally enunciate, but any clear meaning for the words is necessarily lacking. Edwards's contention, the "strongest motive" must determine the volition (since by definition its being the strongest means just that), is the merest word-juggling. The size or weight of motives is not a determinable magnitude apart from behavior.

Actually, the "strongest motive" could not wholly determine the deciding experience; for the weaker motives, equally by definition, must also have some influence, or they would not be motives at all, however weak. So the upshot must be at least a synthesis of all the motives. And how can many motives uniquely determine a single experiential state? We now need an additional motive to assign each of the competing motives its exact place. Here, too, a regress yawns. It will not do to say that the magnitude of the motives relative to each other assigns the places. For either this is merely the empty formula, "Each motive has the place it has, and this *defines* its strength," or there is some other meaning to strength, and then the problem remains. A synthesis of motives can only be a creative one, an emergent whole of factors that never uniquely imply this whole.

Before Edwards, the Colonial theologian Urian Oakes (1631–1681) had stated a similarly uncompromising position.

> The Lord . . ., doth not only stir up Second Causes to act at large, and set them agoing, and leave it to their own inclination what they shall do; but he leads them forth, and determines them to this or that object . . .
>
> Otherwise, the Lord might possibly suffer real Disappointment, and be defeated of his Ends in some Instances. . . . He might be so far unhappy, as to his *voluntary Happiness*, which results from his having his Pleasure done in the world. . . . if He had not the absolute and infallible Determination of all Events in his own Hand. But His Counsel shall stand, and He will do all his Pleasure: Isaiah 46.10.[2]

Let us analyze this argument. To be disappointed (in the special sense Oakes has in mind) is an evil; God (to be worthy of worship) must be conceived to be exalted above all evil; hence he cannot be disappointed; therefore he must be in absolute control of events. The argument seems cogent. But there is a flaw. To be God, to be worthy of worship, is not necessarily to be "above all evil." No doubt moral evil must be impossible for God, but not necessarily evil in the form of suffering. The rejection of every idea of a "suffering deity" subtly begs the question that is here at issue. For suppose it is impossible to be immune to suffering except by being immune to joy also. If that be correct, then to insist that God must be above all evil is either to imply God's impossibility, or (which comes to the same) to imply that God is utterly lacking in good as well as in evil. And surely it is worse to be incapable of joy than to be capable of suffering! (Buddhists perhaps dispute this, but on what ground?) Moreover, the supposition that immunity to suffering entails incapacity for rejoicing or bliss is not merely arbitrary; rather it is what life teaches us in innumerable ways. Life *is* sensitivity; openness to joy and sorrow, pain and pleasure, harmony and discord. God is said to be "living." What this means if a total divine immunity to sorrow or grief is assumed no one has told us.

Let us, from this standpoint, reconsider Oakes's reasoning. To be disappointed is an evil, granted. Therefore, when God suffers disappointment he suffers evil. Quite so. Does it follow, however, that the *capacity* for this evil is itself an evil? This I deny. Evil is significant

21

only where something might conceivably be avoided. A totally un-avoidable evil would be something that ought to be, but could not possibly be, avoided, and this is contradictory. We have argued that capacity for evil (suffering) is unavoidable in life. Ergo, this capacity is not itself an evil. I am serious in this counterargument; I submit that it constitutes a refutation. And note that the refutation does not depend on my proving the inseparability of the capacity for sorrow and that for joy. It is enough that Oakes cannot prove their separability. For his argument requires that they be separable. Conclusion: he has begged the question.

Arguments of this type are only too common in the theological tradition. God "must" be free from this or that "defect," where it has not been and cannot be shown that such freedom is compatible with the possession of any good or excellence. The arguer simply assumes that a certain verbal definition of "perfection" involves no inner absurdity. But in metaphysics the question of such absurdity is precisely *the* question at issue. So nothing can be proved by verbal definitions, without reason being furnished for trusting their self-consistency. Carneades long ago pointed to this defect in much theistic reasoning. What happened? For two thousand years his criticisms were ignored, until Hume reiterated them (with variations). So careless (or ignorant) has philosophy often been of its own past achievements.

Oakes and Edwards are concerned to impress upon people the absolute power of God, and they think to do this by making them aware of their own absolute powerlessness in God's hands. But, in truth, the absolutely powerless cannot know power at all. Zero infinitely magnified is still but zero. Thus the claims to exalt deity in this crude fashion cannot be made good. What really happens is that both the divine and the human are conceived in unworthy fashion. "If ever a man worshiped a false God," said Thomas Jefferson, "it was Calvin." The saying is harsh; but for this writer it is tragically true, granted that it is less than the whole truth. The denial of human initiative is not absolute in Augustine, Luther, and Calvin, but almost so. Edwards accepted the denial in extreme form.

The divine power can be absolute only in whatever sense its being so is compatible with a genuine power of self-determination (anything less being but a semblance of power, relative to some deluded observer) in the creatures. No theism will stand analysis if it attempts to evade this requirement. It is idle to *define* a "power" as "absolute" without attempting to show that the definition makes sense. The prior question is, does the logic of the idea of power permit such

22

absolutization, and if so in just what sense? The mere words guarantee nothing. Only our age, with its new sensitivity to the problem of meaning, can do justice to this matter. The age of Edwards could not do so, even though Hume (whose *Dialogues* came too late to influence Edwards) saw some aspects of the problem rather clearly.

I have understated the argument against Oakes because I have not appealed to the idea stressed in the Scriptures that God is a loving as well as purposive being. Love that does not rejoice in the joy and sorrow in the suffering of the one loved is less than love in the normal sense. A loving God cannot be equally "pleased" by creaturely happiness and creaturely misery. Something like sympathy is a minimal requirement of love, and for this very reason many have denied that God can love. But a religion must decide. Is there or is there not truth in "God is love"? I take Oakes not to have decided this. In his day people would tolerate such confusion or evasion. But in the long run such things are noticed and taken into account. And our age is less lenient in such matters than the eighteenth century was. Less and less evasion is tolerated.

Edwards showed his intellectual power in many ways. Thus (in his essay on the insufficiency of reason as a substitute for revelation) he anticipates Kant's antinomy about past time and, in a number of ways interestingly parallel to Kant's four antinomies, argues that reason cannot comprehend reality. He did not anticipate Kant's "religion within the bounds of pure reason"; but then, how many have been able to agree with Kant that reason can reach God via ethics, though in no other way?

The early writings of Edwards (especially his *Notes on the Mind*) show a sparkling genius. Circumstances were unfavorable to the development of his capacities. An example of his power to think sharply when he wanted to is his analysis of substance, of what it is to be an individual thing. Following a hint of Descartes, Edwards argues that a "thing" is actualized only as an ordered series of events (or, for Edwards's idealism, ideas in our minds), each of which is logically a contingent addition to the series as already actual. To say that the series continues in an orderly fashion because each event is a state of "the same thing" is, Edwards saw, a purely verbal explanation. Only because of the order is there the same thing. Thinghood and order are but one fact regarded in two ways, not one fact explanatory of another fact. As for the explanation of the thing-order fact, Edwards, like most theists, attributes it to divine will, as Descartes had done.

Edwards is close to the great Buddhist insight that the substance problem is only a special case of the causal order problem. The latter is the more general case, since a state of a substance is influenced not only by "its own" past states in the same ordered series, but by the past generally. Alas, the Colonial environment of a pastor of a Congregational church was not helpful in the pursuit of this line of inquiry. Nor was the time yet ripe for it. A similar backing away from the implications of an analysis can be seen in Berkeley's refusal to deal with mental substance as he hints at doing in his *Commonplace Book*. Only in Hume (later, William James and Whitehead) did the idea of substance, supposedly quite different from and equally fundamental with causality, begin to lose its tyrannous grip on Western minds.

In some ways Edwards was a tragic figure. His farewell sermon to the congregation that voted him out of his job was dignified and not self-serving. It showed a noble restraint and love of his fellows. This man with better luck might have come far closer than he did to the wisdom that philosophers and theologians have long been seeking. He did see that the beauty of the world is its final justification. He aesthetic theory, however, was typically Greek or traditional. Beauty is order, unity, avoidance of randomness and mere diversity. In truth, beauty is as much the avoidance of mere order or unity as it is of mere randomness or diversity. It is a middle way between two extremes, of which traditional aesthetics (from Plato to Edwards) saw clearly but one. Yet Edwards did throw some new light on the subject, though always hampered by his Neoplatonic-Calvinistic bias.

If the sermon "Sinners at the Hands of an Angry God" was Edwards in his least attractive vein, the two essays written considerably later and published posthumously present him in his best and most appealing mood. "The Nature of True Virtue" is a charming and insightful discussion of virtue as "the beauty of those qualities of the mind that are . . . attended with desert or worthiness of praise or blame." Beauty in this sense is compared to the "secondary and inferior Kind of Beauty" depending on "mutual agreement" or "mutual consent" of the parts of objects or of things with other things, or in general of uniformity in variety. He agrees with John Hutchinson (fundamentalist English lay theologian) that the greater the variety in equal uniformity the greater the beauty, explaining that "it is more considerable to have many things consent to one another, than a few only." (What counts, I remark, is not the mere number of contrasting things but the depth and diversity of the contrasts.) In this inferior beauty the will, disposition, or affection of the heart has no concern, hence its inferiority. Yet there is an analogy between it and the "true, spiritual, original beauty . . . consisting in being's consent to being in the union of spiritual beings in a mutual propensity and affection of heart." Those who know the chapters on "Peace" and on "Beauty" in Whitehead's *Adventures of Ideas* will see interesting similarities and differences.

There is much about love in this essay, including that which God "exercises to the creature," which love is "derived from, and subordinate to, his love for himself." "Though we are not able to give any thing to God which we have of our own independently, yet we may be the instruments of promoting his glory, in which he takes a true and proper delight." Edwards mentions the objection to our feeling benevolence toward God that we "cannot profit him," or to gratitude for his benefits since "we cannot requite him." He comes close indeed to seeing the paradox of a merely self-sufficient deity, wholly beyond influence by his creatures and with all possible good fully actualized no matter what creatures there are or are not, although in creatures promoting his glory "he takes a true and proper delight," and their true virtue is "especially agreeable" to him. He comes close to seeing but does not really see that he is talking nonsense. Our virtuous acts or decisions are divine decisions; so God is admiring his own actions, playing a game with himself. And he thereby acquires no value he would lack were there no creatures. God "has respect to the creature's happiness" but does not really participate in it. His love is totally without sympathy, and of course he does not sorrow in our misery. Edwards is making the absolute best rhetorically of a cruel doctrine. He is one of many, but who has done it better? Well does W. K. Frankena call him "perhaps the best philosopher Calvinism has produced."

If there is a more beautiful expression of the Neoplatonic form of worship than "Concerning the End for Which God Created the World" I do not know who has written it.[3]

Notes

1. *Enquiry into the Freedom of the Will* was published in 1754. See *Jonathan Edwards: Representative Selections*, ed. Faust and Johnson (New York: American Book Co., 1935) or vol. 1 of a six-volume edition of the works issued by Yale University Press, 1957–1980.

2. This quotation from Urian Oakes's *Sovereign Efficacy of Divine Providence* (1677) is taken from Anderson and Fisch, *Philosophy in America*, pp. 30–33. Or see Oakes's essay in the Augustin Reprint Society Publication No. 53 (Los Angeles: University of California, 1955), 15–20.

3. For an excellent treatment of Edwards, somewhat contrasting to mine, see *A Return to Moral and Religious Philosophy in Early America* by Rem B. Edwards (Washington: University Press of America, 1982). For an enthusiastic view see D. J. Elwood, *The Philosophical Theology of Jonathan Edwards.* (New York: Columbia University Press, 1960). Elwood accepts Edwards's compatibilist view of freedom.

CHAPTER 3

Some Early American
Critics of Determinism

A. Samuel Johnson (1696–1772).

This younger contemporary of the English lexicographer, author, and formidable conversationalist Dr. Samuel Johnson was in some degree the mentor of the seven years younger Jonathan Edwards and "directed" his reading of Locke's famous *Essay Concerning Human Understanding*. Johnson was an idealist in the sense of Bishop Berkeley, with whom he corresponded, and of Edwards. As Johnson put it, "an idea can resemble [or enable us to know] nothing but an idea," and an idea is essentially dependent upon mind. But he disagreed, apparently sharply, with Edwards's predestinationism or theological determinism, as one sees from paragraphs 22 and 23 of the eleventh chapter of his *Moral Philosophy*.

And as to my being so sinful a creature as I must confess that I am, this I cannot ascribe to God; for since the formal notion of sin consists in the voluntary opposition of our wills to the known will of God, or the constitution which He hath made, it must be the fault of my will, and not of His; and accordingly my own conscience tells me, whenever I do amiss, that I myself (and not He) am the cause, and true author of all the wickedness I commit . . .

If now I should ask, why hath God made me . . . capable of sin? This would be the same as to ask, why hath He made me a free agent? . . . Without liberty, I should be destitute of one of the chief excellencies of my rational nature . . . As sin

27

consists in a free or voluntary disobedience, so duty consists in a free and voluntary obedience to the known Will of God.[1]

Alas, Johnson had no clear grasp of the implications of freedom as meaning more than mere voluntariness. Predestinationists all grant freedom in *that* sense! In three passages in the same chapter Johnson shows that he has found no consistent alternative to the Calvinist position in its extreme Edwardsian form. In section 2 he tells us, "Chance is nothing but an empty name . . . a cover to our ignorance or inadvertence." And in section 12 we learn that all things are "contrived in the best manner to render them subservient to all the purposes of my subsistence and well-being, and that of the whole rational and moral system." In section 24 we encounter the response to the problem of evil which a deterministic theology can be expected to make, not the response suitable to a believer in creaturely freedom.

> As to the many pains, calamities, and dissolution to which I am liable . . . as I am a sinner, I need a course of discipline: it is fit natural evil should attend moral evil, as the best means for the cure of it: therefore God, having it in view that we would abuse our liberty, not only justly, but wisely and kindly ordered these calamities . . . to bring us to repentance and reformation . . . by mortifying our lusts and disengaging us from those objects that are most apt to ensnare and mislead us; and, at the same time, . . . since we cannot be completely happy here, they lead us to the hopes of a better state hereafter. (Ibid.)

Like so many other theologians, Johnson seems to have failed to read the Book of Job with much attention. His type of theory is repudiated in that document by the divine "voice from the whirlwind." Before process theology, beginning with Fechner in Germany and Peirce in the U.S.A. the problem of evil was scarcely open to reasonable philosophical treatment.

B. Ethan Allen (1737–1789)

"The knowledge of nature is the revelation of God." With these words, Allen, the revolutionary general and philosopher, affirmed his ground for belief. He continues (in section II of chapter I of *Reason the Only Oracle of Man*):

If we form in our imagination a compendious idea of the harmony of the universe, it is the same as calling God by the name of harmony, for there could be no harmony without regulation and no regulation without a regulator, which is expressive of the idea of God. Nor could it be possible, that there could be order *or disorder* [italics mine], except we admit of such a thing as creation, and creation contains in it the idea of a creator, which is an appellation for the Divine Being.[2]

It is notable that Allen implies that God's creative activity does not exclude all worldly "disorder" or guarantee absolute worldly harmony. The point rather is that without God there could be nothing, or only meaningless confusion, indistinguishable from nothing. The same notion is hinted at by that other deist Thomas Jefferson, who wrote that without God's control of the world there would be "unmitigated chaos." The implication is not that the world is absolutely ordered, but that whatever aspect of chaos there may be is mitigated, limited, so that significant goods are made possible and in the main, or on the average, certain.

Allen meant by freedom more than mere voluntariness. His account (section IV of chapter II) deserves extensive quotation.

The doctrine of fate has been made use of in armies as a policy to induce soldiers to face danger. Mahomet taught his army that the "term of every man's life was fixed by God, and that none could shorten it, by any hazard that he might seem to be exposed to in battle or otherwise." But that it should be introduced into peaceable and civil life, and be patronized by any teachers of religion, is quite strange, as it subverts religion in general, and renders the teaching of it unnecessary: except among other necessary events it be premised, that it is necessary that they teach that doctrine, and that I oppose it from the influence of the same law of fate upon which thesis we are all disputing and acting in certain necessary circles, and if so, I make another necessary movement, which is, to discharge the public teachers of this doctrine, and expend their salaries in an economical manner, which might better answer the purposes of our happiness, or lay it out in good wine or old spirits to make the heart glad, and laugh at the stupidity or cunning of those who would have made us mere machines.

Some advocates for the doctrine of fate will also maintain that we are free agents, notwithstanding they tell us there has been a concatenation of causes and events, which has reached from God down to this time, and which will eternally be continued; that has and will control and bring about every action of our lives, though there is not any thing in nature more certain than that we cannot act necessarily, and freely in the same action, and at the same time, yet it is hard for such persons, who have verily believed that they are elected (and thus by a predetermination of God become his special favorites) to give up their notion of a predetermination of all events, upon which system their election and everlasting happiness is nonsensically founded; and on the other hand, it is also hard for them to go so evidently against the law of nature (or dictates of conscience) which intuitively evinces the certainty of human liberty, as to reject such evidence; and therefore hold to both parts of the contradiction, to wit, that they act necessarily, and freely, upon which contradictory principle, they endeavored to maintain the dictates of natural conscience, and also, their daring folly of being electedly and exclusively favorites of God.[3]

It must be admitted, however, that Allen, like Johnson, fails to achieve a coherent philosophy of freedom. According to him, "creation, with all its productions, operates according to the laws of nature . . . in perfect order and decorum, agreeable to the . . . impartial justice, and immense goodness of the divine nature." That this passage [from section III, chapter II] is in conflict with the denial of causal necessity for human decisions seems not to occur to Allen. The more one reads in the history of ideas, the more revolutionary do Peirce's Tychism (the doctrine that chance is real and pervasive) or Whitehead's "disorder is as real as order" appear, although Antoine Cournot, another mathematician, did precede them in his form of theism.

Like the classical theists who were conventionally Christian, the deists could not arrive at an explanation of what the creation contributes to the creator, supposed to be simply, absolutely, and eternally perfect. Paine (in *The Age of Reason*) comes to the very edge of the problem and stops there. "The practice of moral truth, or . . . a practical imitation of the moral goodness of God, is no other than our acting toward each other as he acts benignly toward all. We *cannot* serve God in the manner we serve those who cannot do without such service; and therefore the only idea we can have of serving God is that of contributing to the happiness of the creation that God has made." [4]

The simple question arises: How does it serve God to have happy creatures? Is there a divine happiness that creaturely happiness can somehow enrich? If so, in what sense is God eternally and absolutely perfect? If not, can we serve God in any intelligible sense? Classical theists never quite see this elementary dilemma as neoclassicists see it. If they did, they would not be classical theists.

C. A Noble Unitarian

Perhaps it was the great Unitarian preacher William Ellery Channing (1780–1840) who, in the early days of our republic, came the closest of all to seeing the central importance of freedom in philosophy of religion. In his remarkable introduction to his collected *Works* (1841) he makes it clear that his objection to traditional theology was not merely, if even primarily, to its trinitarianism and deification of Jesus. Rather it was the idolatry (my word; not his) of identifying God with mere "infinity" (his word) and in not seeing that the implied denial of human freedom degraded human nature without truly exalting God. The monopolistic conception of divine power was the enemy, in his view. God's glory is in creating "beings like himself, free beings, (with) the reality, not the show, of power." Perhaps more remarkable still, Channing realized and fully acknowledged the greatness and nobility of the many writers who have accepted the error that he regarded as so calamitous. As Karl Popper later put it, "great men make great mistakes."

Channing was less clear, I find, than the Socinians (of whom he seems to know nothing) that the false conception of mere infinity as the essence of deity was associated with the false conception of mere eternity or immutability as equally divine. He was less penetrating about the relation of God to time and change than about the relation of God to finitude and the sharing of power. In both cases the logical mistake was the same. 'Only God is infinite,' or 'only God is eternal,' was converted illicitly into, God is only infinite, or only eternal. 'Infinity and eternity are uniquely divine' is correct, but no less unique to God is the (by others) unsurpassable form of finitude and temporality. The Socinian Catechism saw both aspects, as no one before Socinus and many after him have not seen them.

In another respect Channing, like the deists and Theodore Parker, failed to carry through his criticism of the tradition. None of them saw the subtle idolatry of talk about the "immortal souls" of us human animals. Not merely is eternity uniquely divine, even unlimited future endurance as changing individual—what is commonly

31

meant by immortality—on the neoclassical view is likewise restricted to God, who is neither born nor can die, but can and does, in uniquely excellent fashion, change. The creatures are born and die, and only their finite careers between birth and death are imperishable, everlastingly real—in God. But this final clarification of the divine uniqueness was reserved for the twentieth century.

Channing's reply to Jonathan Edwards's or Calvin's theological determinism was to the point. "We do not honor God by breaking down the human soul, connecting it with him only by a slavish dependence." [5] God may be the infinity of excellences, such as creativity or originativeness; but we are not the zero of these excellences. If we were we could know nothing of God, or of anything else. Thinking is always in some degree, however slight or humble, creative. Even mere feeling is that, as Peirce was perhaps the first to recognize in his concept of "spontaneity." Whitehead's theory of "concrescence" or "prehending" as "emergent synthesis" makes this explicit. Whitehead, though probably not Peirce, may have derived this insight partly from Bergson. The idea that only "reason" or "ratiocination" makes the future unpredictable, so that animal instinct and physico-chemical laws can be strictly determinative or nonstatistical is an error. Probably Channing did not see this; indeed, who at the time did see it?

Neither Channing nor the much younger, partly contemporary preacher Theodore Parker contributed much to the understanding of suffering and wickedness in a divinely created and ordered cosmos. The time for that had not come. As we are about to see, even the great and noble Emerson was helpless before this problem.

One of the many interesting facts about that most interesting man, Benjamin Franklin, is that one of his first intellectual experiments was to develop some logical consequences of strict theological determinism. Later he gave up the doctrine as having no practical meaning. Thus he was a pragmatist more than a century before the movement bearing that name.[6]

Notes

1. For this and the next quotation see Muelder, Sears, and Schlabach's *Development of American Philosophy* (Hereafter MSS), p. 50. Or, in *Elementa Philosophica*, Chapter 2 of *Ethica* (New York: Kraus Reprint Co., 1969), pp. 37–39. (First published by B. Franklin, Philadelphia, 1752.)

2. MSS, p. 85. From *Reason the Only Oracle of Man*, Philadelphia: 1836. (First ed., 1784, Bennington, Vt. New York: Scholars' Facsimiles and Reprints, 1940), p. 30.

3. MSS, p. 87. *Reason the Only Oracle of Man*, p. 96.

4. MSS, p. 101; *The Age of Reason*, chapter 17. *The Theological Works of Thomas Paine* (Boston: J. P. Mendum, The Investigator Office, 1859).

5. *The Works of William E. Channing* (Boston: American Unitarian Association, 1903), p. 5. See also Flower and Murphey's *History of Philosophy in America* (New York: Capricorn Books and G. P. Putnam's Sons, 1977), vol. 1, 407–408.

6. See Anderson and Fisch, Philosophy in America, pp. 131–143, for Franklin's *"Dissertation on Liberty and Necessity, Pleasure and Pain."* An edition of 100 copies was printed in 1725. It is omitted as "worthless" from the *Writings of Benjamin Franklin* (New York and London: Macmillan, 1905). For Franklin's somewhat more mature theological beliefs see his remarkably original and imaginative "Articles of Belief and Acts of Religion," in MSS, pp. 67–68; or *The Writings of Benjamin Franklin*, vol. 1, pp. 91–100. It was written when Franklin was twenty-two years old and is one of countless indications of the versatility of his genius. It seems hard to say what this man could not do, given time and occasion. Well did Thomas Jefferson say, when someone credited him with being about to replace Franklin as ambassador to France, "I shall succeed him sir; no man can replace him."

CHAPTER 4

Emerson's Secularized Calvinism and Thoreau's Approach to Anarchism

The Transcendentalists, of whom R. Waldo [the name he preferred] Emerson (1803–1882) was the most creative and Theodore Parker the most learned, are in some respects continuers of the Deistic tradition. But they also share some of Edwards's Calvinistic beliefs. Like the Deists they are (at least mildly) anticlerical, and like them, but also like Edwards, they find God in nature. However, unlike Edwards and the Deists, Emerson and Thoreau appeal neither to traditional faith nor to impersonal reason or formal argument, but rather to more or less individual insights or intuitions. Emerson and Henry David Thoreau (1817–1862) represent, indeed, in some respects a climax of intellectual individualism—almost anarchism. As Emerson put it in his essay on self-reliance, "Trust thyself, every heart vibrates to that iron string." But apparently the individual is to be trusted because he or she is an embodiment of the Over-Soul, the Universal Spirit, whose flawless harmony determines all things. Are we then back at the poet Pope's cosmic perfectionism ("whatever is is right") ?

That individuals collide and fall into discord with one another puzzled Emerson; that life involves such seemingly meaningless tragedies as the death of his own promising son deeply disturbed him. And there is indeed nothing much his philosophy could say about such things. For he held that the universal order was absolute and beyond criticism. He, too, was a theological determinist. "There is no chance and no anarchy in the universe. All is system and gradation. Every god is there sitting in his sphere." [1] (Shade of Jonathan Edwards!) Also, for every evil there is exact "compensa-

34

tion." "Justice is done here and now," he declared, not in heaven. The "law of compensation" is perfect. Why then his own small child's death—"a boy of early wisdom . . . of a perfect gentleness?" The theorist is frankly and entirely at a loss:

> Sorrow makes us all children again—destroys all differences of intellect. The wisest knows nothing. (1842)

And again, seven weeks later:

> I comprehend nothing of this fact but its bitterness. Explanation I have none, consolation none that rises out of the fact itself; only oblivion of this and pursuit of new objects.

And two years later:

> I wrote to Mr. F. that I had no experiences nor progress to reconcile me to the calamity . . . the senses have a right to their method as well as the mind; there should be harmony in facts as well as in truths. Yet these ugly breaks happen there, which the continuity of theory does not contemplate. The amends are of a different kind from the mischief.[2]

It does not seem to occur to Emerson that his denial of an element of chance and anarchy may have been simply wrong! Is it not strange that this man, who sometimes speaks rather loftily about the antiquated beliefs of the orthodox, should have entertained a view which implied that every event must have some ideal explanation, whether or not we can find it? For what belief could more extravagantly outrun all evidence and all justification than this one? After all, the Book of Job put the case once for all. There is nothing like perfect justice or exact compensation in the world we know. (It was Job's comforters who put forward such views; the fact that at the end of the story they are condemned from on high seems to escape many readers.) Why must Emerson, who surely(?) had read Job, wait until, at the age of thirty-eight, his own misfortunes bring home to him what all but small children have had opportunity enough to learn from the misfortunes of others?

So far I have been criticizing Emerson. But I regard him as a truly great man (he was an immense influence in my early teens), and his life and work is a valuable cultural inheritance which we ought not to overlook. Let us now try to explain why.

Emerson's faith in the essential goodness of the cosmos was connected with a certain rare nobility in himself. The universe, he thought, must be believed to have some spiritual architecture, some eternal and ideal tendency toward order, beauty, and love. Otherwise our own devotion to these things would be a meaningless impertinence. It was, however, Emerson's bad luck to have inherited a philosophical tradition that was so blinded by the vision of ultimate stability, control, and power that it often forgot that these things, to be significant, must (as Dewey so well says) contrast with real instability, anarchic freedom, and independence. There is no reason why the determination of things by providence should not be regarded as entirely right or good, provided it is borne in mind that the perfect mode of providential determination need not, and indeed cannot, lie in *complete* determination, in a monopoly of divine choice, leaving nothing open for the choices of others. To repeat what I have often written, such a monopoly is a nightmare, not an ideal. Substitute the true ideal, and Emerson's faith is no longer open to fatal objections.

I should like to give some illustrations (again from the *Journals*) of the ethical grandeur, mixed with a one-sided or ambiguous metaphysics, that was in this man.

God manifest in the flesh of every man is a perfect rule of social life. Justify yourself to an infinite Being in the ostler and dandy and stranger, and you shall never repent. (1836)

Happy is he who looks only into his own work to know if it will succeed, never into the times or the public opinion; and who writes from the love of imparting certain thoughts and not from the necessity of sale—who writes always to *the unknown friend*. (1848)

Love is necessary to the righting the estate of woman in this world. Otherwise nature itself seems to be in conspiracy against her dignity and welfare; for the cultivated, high-thoughted, beauty-loving saintly woman finds herself unconsciously desired for her sex, and even enhancing the appetite of her savage pursuers by these fine ornaments she has piously laid on herself. She finds with indignation that she is herself a snare, and was made such; I do not wonder at her occasional protest, violent protest against nature, in fleeing to nunneries, and taking black veils. Love rights all this deep wrong. (1848)

36

I think that as long as they (women) have not equal rights of property and right of voting they are not on the right footing. (1848)

If the women demand votes, offices, and political equality, as an Elder and Elderess are of equal power in the Shaker Families, refuse it not. 'Tis very cheap wit that finds it so funny. (1855)

(To say these things today would require no moral grandeur; to say them then did require it.)

I hope New England will come to boast itself in being a nation of servants, and leave to the planters the misery of being a nation of served. (1837)

In the morning watch on my berth I thought that morals is the science of the laws of human action as respects right and wrong. Then I shall be asked, and what is Right? Right is a conformity to the laws of nature as far as they are known to the human mind . . .

Milton describes himself in his letter to Diodati as enamoured of moral perfection. He did not love it more than I. That which I cannot yet declare has been my angel from childhood until now. It has separated me from men. It has watered my pillow, it has driven sleep from my bed. It has tortured me for my guilt. It has inspired me with hope. It cannot be defeated by my defeats. It cannot be questioned, though all the martyrs apostatise. It is always the glory that shall be revealed; it is the 'open secret' of the universe . . .

It is the soul of religion. Keeping my eye on this, I understand all heroism, the history of loyalty and of martyrdom, and nonconformity of the Dissenter, the patience of the Quaker. (1833)

It is not in the power of God to make a communication of his will to a Calvinist. For to every inward revelation he holds up his silly book, and quotes chapter and verse against the Book-Maker and Man-Maker, against that which quotes not, but is and cometh. There is a light older than intellect, by which the intellect lives and works, always new, and which degrades every past and particular shining of itself. This light Calvinism denies, in its idolatry of a certain past shining. (1843)

Sects are stoves, but fire keeps its old properties through them all. (1861)

In reading these letters of M.M.E. [Waldo's Aunt Mary], I acknowledge (with surprise that I ever could forget it) the debt of myself and my brothers to that old religion which, in those years, still dwelt like a Sabbath peace in the country population of New England, which taught privation, self-denial, and sorrow. A man was born, not for prosperity, but to suffer for the benefit of others, like the noble rock-maple tree which all around the villages bleeds for the service of man. Not praise, not men's acceptance of our point, but the Spirit's holy errand through us absorbed the thought. How dignified this is! How all that is called talents and worth in Paris and in Washington dwindles before it! (1841)

What is valuable in these thoughts is not any system of ideas, metaphysical or even moral, but the spaciousness of heart and mind that comes into expression, the sense of vast perspectives and high aspirations, of self-reliance and reliance upon the impersonal Ideal that transcends special forms and special prejudices. Have we outgrown the need for these things? I hope not.

The sense of human equality is shown at its very best in Emerson's acceptance of political rights of women and in his remarks concerning slavery and anti-Semitism.

You complain that the Negroes are a base class. Who makes and keeps the Jew or the Negro base, who but you, who exclude them from the rights which others enjoy? (1867)

It is the old mistake of the slaveholder to impute the resistance to Clarkson or Pitt, to Channing or Garrison, to some John Brown whom he has just captured, and to make a personal affair of it; and he believes, whilst he chains and chops him, that he is getting rid of his tormenter; and does not see that the air which this man breathed in liberty, is breathed by thousands and millions. (1859)

Mr. Everett, a man supposed aware of his own meaning, advises pathetically a reverence for the Union. Yes, but hides the other horn under this velvet? Does he mean that we shall lay hands on a man who has escaped from slavery to the soil of Massachusetts, and so has done more for freedom than ten thousand orations, and tie him up and call in the marshal, and say, 'I am an orator for freedom; a great many fine sentences have I turned, none has turned finer, except Mr. Webster,—in favor of plebeian strength against aristocracy; and, as my last and finest sentence of all, to show the young men of the land who have bought my book and clapped my sentences and copied them in their memory, how much I mean by them, Mr. Marshal, here is a black man of my own age, and who does not know a great deal of Demosthenes, but who means what he says, whom we will now handcuff and commit to the custody of this very worthy gentleman who has come on from Georgia in search of him; I have no doubt he has much to say to him that is interesting, as the way is long. I don't care if I give them—here are copies of my Concord and Lexington and Plymouth and Bunker Hill addresses to beguile their journey from Boston to the plantation whipping-post.' Does Mr. Everett really mean this?—that he and I shall do this? . . . Union is a delectable thing, and so is wealth, and so is life, but they may all cost too much, if they cost honour. (1851)

This filthy enactment (The Fugitive Slave Law) was made in the nineteenth century, by people who could read and write. I will not obey it, by God. (1851)

If I were a member of the Massachusetts legislature, I should propose to exempt all colored citizens from taxation because of the inability to protect them by passport out of its territory. It does not give the value for which they pay the tax. (1846)

What argument, what eloquence can avail against the power of that one word niggers? The man of the world annihilates the whole combined force of all the antislavery societies of the world by pronouncing it. (1845)

This last quotation shows how well Emerson understood the irrational and unscrupulous forces which, in addition to the well-meant rationalizations, must be encountered by anyone who concerns himself with human equality.

That there was nevertheless a role for quiet reasonableness in such matters he also understood.

I heard last night with some sensibility that the question of slavery has never been presented to the South with a kind and thoroughly scientific treatment, as a question of pure political economy in the largest sense. (1845)

Has the question of segregation been presented to the South with a kind and thoroughly scientific treatment? Probably not. (Written before the Civil Rights movement of the 1960s.) It is worth trying, even though the organs of communication are not altogether open to the effort, and even though none of us can assume in himself an unlimited stock of kindness or of scientific knowledge.

How can Emerson, so right in some ways, say such things as the following, even at the age of twenty-two?

The whole of what we know is a system of compensations. Every defect in one manner is made up in another. Every suffering is rewarded; every sacrifice is made up; every debt is paid. (1826)

The theory is reaffirmed strongly five years later. Was it ever definitely renounced?

The basic objection to it is not that the facts are otherwise. On purely conceptual grounds he should have seen that there can be no such system. In the first place, one cannot conceive an exact common measure for the evils and their balancing goods, or for comparing one person's lot with another's. In the second place, such a system could only work precisely if chance could be entirely excluded from the course of events, and this is impossible if (as is maintained in this book) multiple freedom is the principle of reality. In the third place, why is it necessary that one be precisely compensated if, as one can learn from James and Whitehead as well as the Buddhists, one is in strictness a new entity each moment?

It is only fair to add that the Emersonian doctrine of compensation, to which I have taken such sharp exception, may have been influenced by the East Indian idea of Karma. The openness of this New Englander to Oriental influences is one of the most remarkable things about him. What makes Emerson more vulnerable than Buddhists and Hindus are to the sort of criticisms I have urged against the view that we deserve what happens to us (or obtain our adequate reward) is that Karma has been a vague idea, hedged about with ambiguities and escape clauses. If compensation or punishment do not adequately come in this incarnation, they may in another. Also, it is perhaps not very clear how exact the cosmic justice is supposed to be. Perhaps it is only an approximate or probabilistic affair. But Emerson, being a Westerner, wants more definiteness than that. He thinks of the matter almost as though it were a sort of moral physics, with precise laws and complete reliability. And neither he nor anyone else had yet dreamt of a physics like that of Heisenberg or Dirac.

So, considering the climate of opinion of his age and the influences he was exposed to, Emerson's view was, after all, an intelligible response to those influences.

I suspect that the ardent Emersonian Charles Ives, in composing his music, was somewhat unfortunately influenced by the idea of the cosmos as absolutely harmonious. It follows that whatever combination of sounds the universal harmony permits to occur cannot be wrong. What this shows is only that no pragmatic meaning attaches to such an unqualified optimism as "whatever is is right."

What Emerson really needed was to reinterpret somewhat two of his own sayings.

There is a pleasure in the thought that the particular tone of my mind at this moment may be new in the universe; that the emotions of the hour may be peculiar and unexampled in the whole eternity of moral being. (1827)

He is not to live to the future as described to him, but to live to the real future by living to the real present. (1833)

The point is that the concrete self which is of value to the universe as unique and novel is the self-now. Tomorrow there will be another concrete self, also a contribution to reality. And the final recipient of the contributions? Emerson gives its name, "God." My aim now is to be-now, as a contribution—not to me later, save as one possible step among others toward the ultimate destiny of all value—the enrichment of deity. Just now I can have no greater privilege than to serve God. This is indeed the perfect compensation, but it is enjoyed now. Future happenings to me are not mathematically or otherwise perfectly correlated to what I now do. Indeed, this may be my last moment. And if my aim is to contribute to the divine life, this aim will have been attained, whatever the fate of the later me.

Emerson, like Western thinkers generally, is imprisoned in the jail labeled "substance" or "soul." He objects to the idea that God is a person, because that would "shut Him out of my consciousness," but fails to see that an absolute law of compensation shuts each person up in his own destiny as though only what happens to him can justify his deeds. For if what happens to another can be sufficient reward for those deeds, why demand a self-serving reward too? And if what happens to another cannot be a sufficient reward, then selfishness and not love is taken as definitive. Furthermore, if one's ultimate self is the deity, then in serving deity one sufficiently serves oneself, and nothing further should be called for. Mysticism as the view (taken as the whole story) that ultimately God gives Himself to us is a subtle way of subordinating God to the self; but mysticism as the view that ultimately we give ourselves, humble though the offering may be, to God is the true recognition that God is all in all. Substance philosophies have always stopped short of or compromised this principle. Emerson is merely one of countless examples.

Emerson accepted the metaphysical idealism of Berkeley and Edwards, according to which nature is but appearance ("a picture in the human soul"), the way in which the Over-Soul communicates with the human soul, a system of ideas whose genesis is in God but whose flowering is in man. There is here also an influence of Brahmanism: All is appearance except the divine Spirit. In my opinion this is not the alternative to materialism so much as an inverted form of materialism. The true alternative to the materialism that denies intrinsic value and spirituality to most of nature is to affirm that, on every level, nature involves intrinsic created values distinct from those on other levels and quite independent of the highly special values embodied in humanity. Nature is no mere set of divine-human ideas, but an inconceivably vast ocean of life and feeling whose inner qualities are largely hidden from us, yet nonetheless real and beautiful for all that. Just as the divine power does not consist in monopoly, but in generous sharing of power, so the divine life shows itself in a sharing of life with multi-quintillions of living, sentient forms. Science is more and more convinced that the line between living and nonliving is arbitrary, that all matter is in principle akin. This need not and ought not to imply materialism, but rather the opposite. If all is akin to us, who are essentially feeling, remembering, and loving creatures, then all, in its own way, however different that way may be from ours and however humble, is at least minimally sentient. It is in this direction that speculative metaphysics has developed in our country in more recent times.

On one issue Emerson was on what, in this book, is held to be the right side. "All necessary truth," he said, "is its own evidence." What he had specifically in mind was the Deistic point that reason alone, without biblical revelation, can apprehend moral and religious ultimates. However, "self-evident" is not a simple property of truths. To an idiot nothing is evident. To a clever man taught certain prejudices much may seem evident, or doubtful, or evidently false, that in fact he has not considered carefully or freely enough to judge one way or another. And Emerson had no method for assessing candidates for the status of evident or necessary truths, except the method of earnest and disinterested private reflection. This is indeed an element in the sound method, but it is not the only element. Discussion, careful weighing of criticisms and opposing views, must also come in. And something more.

May Sinclair has said that "logic is the backbone of philosophy"; but in Emerson there are only scraps of logic, and the system as a whole operates, so far as it does operate, without benefit of consistency, following poetic fancy wherever it happens to lead. But even the poetic coherence is only in scraps. Not only is the result little improvement upon Deism, it is in some respects retrogressive, for it affords scanty protection against a quite irresponsible irrationalism.

A flaw in many rationalistic systems has been that logic has been looked upon solely as the means for drawing out the consequences of axioms known to be true from the outset. "Self-evidence" seems naturally to suggest this view. But there is another way of looking at the matter. If nothing is evident to everyone, and if the human capacity for discerning intrinsic necessity is fallible, (and what human capacity is not fallible?), then the mere fact that a proposition initially *seems* self-evident to the thinker is to be taken neither as conclusive nor as insignificant, but as something in between. Deduction of consequences from supposed axioms should then be regarded as a magnifying glass by which the meaning of the candidates for axiomatic status may be clarified. The more we know what a statement implies the better we understand the statement, and the better we understand it, the more likely we are to be able to judge correctly whether or not it is genuinely necessary, that is to say, *undeniable save through misunderstanding.* Philosophical axioms are provisional, not as are laws of science, which must be tested against empirical facts, but as attempted formulations of ultimate but initially obscure intuitions. Language is only relatively reliable; we must always be ready to reconsider formulae, and this rule does not cease to apply merely because one is not dealing with an empirical matter. Premises are to be judged by consequences as well as consequences by premises, and this is so whether the means of judging is empirical observation or the attempt to become conscious of a priori necessity—

or of what is presupposed by any experience or any thought whatever. Emerson admitted that he was "weak" in metaphysical reasoning.

So far as his thought has intellectual structure, it is merely that of theological or Calvinistic determinism, plus Edwards's virtual elimination of physical nature and with a vaguer, less personalized conception of deity (influenced by Hindu mysticism). The creation is somehow embraced within the divine reality; we are not simply extrinsic to the divine life, but somehow are the divine itself, in a particular individualization. Thus the sharp line between "theistic" and "pantheistic" doctrines that theologians tried so hard to maintain in medieval and early modern times becomes almost entirely blurred.

This goes so far that it is doubtful if, for Emerson, God himself is free, since we hear little or nothing of the possibility of a different creation, much less of none at all; it is even clearer that man has no freedom, distinct from that of God, the divine order of things admitting of no free play, all things being completely molded by this order. Of course, it is impossible to apply these doctrines consistently.

It is melancholy, rather than comic, I feel, that a man of genius could have supposed that such views constitute a viable philosophy. Ethan Allen, Jefferson, and Paine, with their simpler, less pretentious statements, were in a stronger position. Allen, at least, roundly rejected determinism.

The Transcendentalists, nevertheless, were a valuable force in that they helped to keep alive the dialectic between churchly religion and detached religion, or between institutionalized traditional doctrines and rational norms, or secular reason and private experience of transcendent values. Each of these sources of insight has its merits; and without the Deists and the Transcendentalists the possibility of utilizing all of them might have been lost sight of, in this country.

On two further points, Emerson and his friends offered something positive. (1) While their version of idealism (or at least, Emerson's— for Thoreau is different at this point) was much too subjectivistic or anthropomorphic to appeal to some of us, the contrary extreme of materialism (or a mere dualism of mind and matter), is not necessarily more intelligible; and it was well that idealism in some form, however inadequate, should be kept alive. (2) Belief that the Over-Soul is inseparable from this very universe leads to the paradoxes we have pointed out; but the extreme contrary belief that God is free not only to create otherwise, but not to create at all, may be just as absurd. Therefore it may have been well to keep alive the view that there is some essential link between the creator and the creation, if not in its particular then in its most general features. Some creation may have been essential, even if not this one. Thus, as balance against the extreme forms of antipantheistic dualism (the world simply "outside" God), even Emerson's pantheism may have been valuable. It will not do to say, "There is God, and there is the World"; for then there must be a third and inclusive reality, which is *God and World*. The resulting dilemma is rigorous: Either this total is God (and then one aspect of pantheism must be accepted) or else there is something which includes God and the world besides; and therewith God is reduced to a mere constituent of a complex total reality, hardly a dignified position in which to place the divine.

We may add that in Emerson's notion of self-reliance there is a precious grain of truth. Each human soul is a unique focus of "creative" action, to use Emerson's own term. But then why toy with determinism and assert the absoluteness of the universal order? Creative action cannot be precisely ordered; for each such action must order itself, and the conjunction of creative acts is in a measure, therefore, unordered. I cannot perfectly and precisely order my act in relation to yours, which is not yet committed, or at least not yet known to me (nor will it ever be perfectly known to me). You are in the same relation to me. As for God, his ordering of us both must leave open some scope for our own self-ordering. This self-ordering cannot be both open to us and yet entirely closed. We alone can close it, but we do this as two, not as one; and this lack of oneness cannot go for nothing in the result. No absolute unity of direction, no inevitable harmony, is possible here. An element of disorder or chaos is inherent in the notion of multiple acts of creativity. Chaos *is* multiple freedom, except so far as the unsurpassable form of freedom gives directives, which cannot be all-determinative, to the surpassable forms. Without God, said Jefferson, reality would be "unmitigated chaos." With God, the chaos is still there, but mitigated. In Whitehead's simple phrase, "disorder is as real as order." Why did not Emerson see all this? The only answer I can give is that most of the philosophers of modern times have failed to see it or to keep it steadily and clearly in mind. And Emerson was not an originator in philosophy. He could only follow, not lead.

A well-known Emersonianism (see "Self-Reliance") is that "consistency is the hobgoblin of little minds." We have seen that Emerson was a determinist, a denier of freedom. But of course there are passages suggesting a different view. Consider the following, from the same essay:

I suppose that no man can violate his nature. All the sallies of his will are rounded in by the law of his being, as the inequalities of Andes and Himmaleh are insignificant in the curve of the sphere.

This magnificent image is tempting, but is it not also misleading? It is a static spatial image, whereas what we are concerned with is temporal. Was it the law of his being that some hopeless degenerate should have gone to pieces as he in fact has? The slight deviations or open alternatives which, the passage suggests, may actually escape rigid determination by heredity and environment can be cumulative, rather than canceled out into insignificance. At a given moment, taking me as I have been up to the moment before, there are only small contrasts between this that I might do and that. But suppose I had done a little otherwise, in a better direction, on many previous occasions; my present range of alternatives might be different indeed. Emerson overlooks another possible image: that of the continental divide, where a tiny difference in position between two drops of water will put one drop (or some of its molecules) eventually into one ocean and the other into another ocean. It may be so with our decisions. We make millions of them in a lifetime. Who knows? Perhaps the very "law of our being" becomes in effect rather different in the long run from what it was at the start!

There is another inconsistency or ambiguity in Emerson. He oscillates between two very different forms of extreme optimism. According to the one form, the whole is eternally perfect. In that case progress is secondary, if not irrelevant. According to the other, perfection lies in the future, when "evil is no more seen." Emerson was influenced by an early pre-Darwinian form of the doctrine of evolution. But neither this doctrine nor any other in which the reality of freedom is taken into account can prophesy the disappearance of evil, for this would mean the complete separation of opportunity from risk; rather, they are inseparable. The slighter the risks the slighter the opportunities. The ascent from invertebrates to humanity did not consist in the reduction of risks, but in their immense magnification. Or, to go farther down, think of the safety of an atom, to which naturally corresponds its meagerness of opportunity, so slight that we cannot easily grasp it as such. We have some difficulty seeing either good or evil in the existence of an atom or even of a worm. Everywhere this relation between possible good and possible evil is found. In a philosophy of creativity, this is no accident, but is inherent in the meaning of good as the expression of multiple freedom, from which discord and evil also spring. The only optimism that is free from illusion is the faith that risks are justified by their attendant opportunities. Those who wish to escape all risks simply wish to turn life over to others.

To link Emerson with Thoreau is in some respects rather absurd. For they were almost as much opposite as alike. Emerson anthropomorphizes nature; like Edwards, he tames it down to a moral spectacle arranged for human edification. But Thoreau wants to escape from mere man, and not simply to encounter God enunciating moral lessons. Somewhere he says of some migrating warblers, "I have taken too little heed of this. I had thought that they were no better than I." Again, "Man is a past phenomenon to philosophy," "the place where I stand, and the prospect hence is infinite." [3] Thoreau loved nature, not himself or his kind reflected from nature "as in a mirror." Humanity, he thought, is but an item, "as a grain of sand," but *a* meaning, not the meaning. And a substantial part of man's meaning is to participate in as many other meanings as he can. True, there are passages seeming to contradict this.[4]

Emerson finds fault with Thoreau for his perverse contentiousness. "Must we always talk for victory and never for truth, comfort, or joy? . . . Always some weary captious paradox to fight you with? " (1856) This fault might be guessed from Thoreau's *Journal*. Thus he calls the cricket's "chirrup . . . wiser and more mature" than the voice of the wood thrush, thereby comparing a tiny-brained creature, quite literally tone deaf, to one with, by comparison, a large brain and splendid pitch discrimination.[5] True, there is method in Thoreau's madness. For he likes, at times, to get as far as possible from "mankind and all their institutions," and the wood thrush's song is, as he admits, more melodious than the cricket's, that is, more like human music—for which, after all, Thoreau yields to no one in admiration.[6] The cricket's monotony, he tells us, suggests "the life everlasting." Thoreau is at once more objective, with a keener eye for particulars in nature, and more boldly subjective, indulgent of personal fancies, than Emerson.

Thoreau in the end was somewhat frustrated. His freedom from mere work and bondage to others that was won by choosing the simplest means of existence at his disposal was not an illusion; it did for him what he planned it should do. But his search for meanings in nature was not wholly successful.[7] I think one reason is that he both was and was not a scientist (a biologist) and also that biology was then not yet, as a science, the intellectual adventure it has since become. Evolutionary theory, cell theory, biochemistry, genetics, eth-

47

ology, ecology, were scarcely conceived as yet, and it is they which have made biology the engrossing subject that it has become. Again, as a philosopher, he was altogether an amateur, and scarcely even that. He called himself "a mystic." He was a literary moralist-naturalist of a delightfully eccentric kind.

The common elements in Emerson and his friend were ethical nobility and a sense of the dignity which may come from the practice of solitude and from economic independence, purchased if necessary by simplifying needs. Both realized, like the old Stoics, that we exist, not merely in a society, but in a cosmos—though it was Thoreau who had the ampler sense of what this means. He would not have called nature a mere "picture in the human soul." Both men emphasize things we are in need of today. And both underemphasize other things, such as the values of organization and community, which we also need.

It was said of Thoreau that no man ever died more serene and happy. And why not? He had lived according to his faith (suffering imprisonment for it on one occasion), and he had caught innumerable glimpses of the sublime and inexhaustible beauty of the cosmos. The diaries of Emerson also show a man who enjoyed nature, who lived with dignity, courage, and kindness, whose sharp eye penetrated many a disguise, but who never lost his sense of the positive values of the life around him. He had everything but a sane metaphysics, and perhaps after all he was closer to that than most men.

How close he was can be seen from the fact that he speaks of human beings as "creators in the finite." But, being a determinist, he must take our decisions as reiterating precisely certain divine decisions. Otherwise the element of "anarchy" that he denies is implied. (Royce, by denying the openness of the future as God sees that future, faces a similar problem.) And so we see why Emerson could write so eloquently in his poem on Brahma.

> I am the doubter and the doubt,
> And I the hymn the Brahmin sings.

Genuine diversity implies multiple freedom and risks of conflict and disharmony as equally genuine.[8]

Emerson rather gives himself away as a metaphysician when he speaks of God as "feigning to divide into individuals." (1845) To some such pseudo-sense does Advaita Vedantism, toward which

Emerson inconsistently leans, reduce. Is there any consistent way of holding the doctrine? With most Westerners, and probably most Easterners, I think not. Our decisions are not relevantly taken either as simply divine or as mere appearances—of what to what? Appearances of appearances to appearances of appearances—let us rather try to talk sense.

Notes

1. Ralph Waldo Emerson, *Complete Works.* Centenary Edition (Boston: Houghton Mifflin, 1903–1904), vol. 6, p. 325.
2. *The Heart of Emerson's Journals,* ed. Bliss Perry (Houghton Mifflin, 1914), 173. See also pp. 180, 206.
3. *The Heart of Thoreau's Journals,* ed. Odell Shepard (Houghton Mifflin, 1906, 1927), p. 125.
4. Pp. 139, 196–197.
5. P. 197.
6. Pp. 191, 259–261.
7. P. 198.
8. Rem B. Edwards (chapter 2, note 3) interprets Emerson as a believer in freedom, though a very unclear one, and as a genuine pluralist, rather than a complete mystical monist. Perhaps as he matured Emerson came closer to these positions. But the unclarity persisted. See R. B. Edwards, op. cit., pp. 186–188, 220–221. I cannot recognize Emerson as a panentheist (a term I sometimes use for my theism's dual contrast with classical theism and classical pantheism (e.g., as in Spinoza). If the sage of Concord ever gave up the determinism expressed in his journals or the mystic monism of his poem "Brahma," it was in an indecisive and confused fashion.

CHAPTER 5

James's
Empirical Pragmatism

In the thought of William James (1842–1910) there are a number of themes, but the central theme, as my former colleague Robert Roelofs once pointed out to me, is this: The brain is the organ standing between incoming perceptual messages and outgoing motor responses; hence, thinking, being correlated with the brain, is likewise mediatory in function—it interprets and combines percepts in order to guide behavior. Charles Peirce had a similar idea, and it was one source of his original pragmatic theory of meaning. James took the idea from Peirce, but without Peirce he might well have arrived at it himself from his studies in psychophysics.

In "Reflex Action and Theism," and also in "The Sentiment of Rationality," James drew a notable conclusion from his and Peirce's doctrine. He held that two philosophical extremes were ruled out by it: sheer pessimism and sheer optimism, the first saying that choice among modes of action was meaningless for, whatever we decide to do, things are bound, at least in the end, to turn out absolutely ill, and the second that choice is meaningless because things are bound to turn out absolutely well. Choice between genuinely possible modes of behavior presupposes that not all of them must or can be equally bad or good in their eventual or total outcome. An atheism which condemns us to ultimate futility and a theism or absolutism (such as Leibniz's or Royce's) that predestines us to forming exactly the right constituents in a perfect or best possible world—these are equally meaningless doctrines from a pragmatic or psychophysical standpoint. Neither gives any guidance for conduct. What does give guidance is a philosophy that tells us that *this* mode of conduct will ultimately give better results than *that* mode, neither being ruled out by the initial conditions.

It seemed to James that in respect to this issue atheism and traditional theism, as often interpreted, were equally absurd. If the world at large is indifferent to values, then in the long run our values are doomed, no matter how wisely and nobly we try to act for the best. The cosmic forces are ultimately decisive, not only because they bring about our own death, but because there is no reason why they should not eventually overwhelm the species also. If, at the opposite extreme, the world at large is providentially determined to the last detail, then what follows for conduct is that nothing we can possibly do will be other than exactly what is required for the perfection of the whole. But "anything you do will be futile" and "anything you do will be correct"—these give exactly no guidance for conduct. They are irrelevant to practice altogether. And here we come to a point which both James and Peirce learned from a friend (Nicholas St. John Green), who was fond of quoting Alexander Bain's definition of belief: "An idea upon which one is prepared to act." Sheer pessimism and sheer optimism cannot be acted upon, for they imply nothing as to how one is to act. It follows that they cannot be believed. Only verbally can one accept them. In terms of the proper function of words as expressive of thought, nothing is asserted.

One consequence of these considerations is that determinism is unacceptable. Not because it tells us that what we decide will make no difference (as James well knew, that would be fatalism, not determinism), but because it implies that the difference our decision will make and the decision itself are bound to be realized. True, we cannot in advance know what the decision will be, but the question is, what can one *do* about the alleged truth that there is already some definite decision which "will be?" If one knew the future decision, it would already have been made; so the alleged truth could not be used in *that* way. If one does not know it, then also there is no use to be made of the proposition. Either way, the statement is pragmatically null. When determinists (Jonathan Edwards, for instance), work as hard as they often do to show that the causal inevitability of our decisions is compatible with their being voluntary and so free, what they really prove is that this inevitability is totally empty of significance. It does no harm, perhaps, but it does no conceivable good. So it is mere verbiage and not a genuine candidate for belief.

You may say that we can use the proposition in dealing with the decisions of others. For here it seems that we can know in advance without having decided in advance. Part of the answer is that relative predictability of decisions, rough or approximate determinism, is indeed pragmatically significant and even indispensable. But this James is ready to accept, and as a trained psychologist he could not well do otherwise. Much is predictable, at least with probability and within more or less narrow limits. The sole question at issue between intelligent thinkers is only whether predictability does or does not have limits and, if it has them, what sort of limits. The absolute denial of limits adds nothing to the practical applications and hence is pragmatically null.

Moreover, determinism does in certain ways do harm and is in that sense pragmatically bad and false, rather than merely null. For one thing, if it is supposed that all things are interlocked in causal chains allowing no free play, no indeterminacy or chance whatever, then the only way to conceive a divine providential element in existence is to make this element responsible for the entirety of the world in all its details. Either, then, God does everything or God does nothing. Calvin, or at least some Calvinists, chose the first horn of the dilemma. But this is the absolute optimism which is pragmatically impossible. (It also makes deity a sadist or masochist or both.) Take the other horn and you have absolute pessimism, the total denial of any cosmic factor making for good. In the infinite long run, all is at the mercy of blind necessity or mere chance.

Is there nothing suspicious about the neglect of James's "Dilemma of Determinism" that has characterized most recent apologies for determinism? When one adds that Peirce's "Doctrine of Necessity Examined" is also commonly ignored, suspicion grows stronger, the suspicion that determinists have been making things easy for themselves by slighting the literature of the subject except where it supports their views. Boutroux's *Contingency of the Laws of Nature* and Lequier's writings on the meaning of human freedom in relation to divine knowledge and power are similarly passed over, and much else besides.

Atheism, we have seen, fails to make clear how *in the end* practical decisions can matter for good or ill. A common form of theism equally fails to make this clear. Practical significance belongs, it seems to me, only to a theism which conceives providence as guaranteeing, not that we shall always do precisely the right thing, but that *if* we act in the best and wisest way the probable outcome, taking all the future into account, will be better for the universe than if we do not so act. At least, our efforts will be appreciated. God must have power to appreciate and sustain our efforts and bring them to some worthwhile outcome; but God need not and must not have power to completely determine the efforts or their results.

What sort of divine power would fit these requirements? How far short of omnipotence? Here James is dismally at a loss. He can only reject two absolute extremes, leaving undecided the locus of truth in the seemingly infinite gap between them. He goes so far as to say that, since God must be limited in power, there may even be several Gods, rather than a single cosmic deity. He also cannot decide what degree of knowledge to attribute to his god or gods. Here, too, only the absolute extreme is to be rejected: God must not know everything. "Who can say," wrote Maritain, "perhaps God does not know American pluralism! " It is fascinating to imagine James reacting to this caustic comment.

Thus from James's form of pragmatism he can at most reach the conclusion that there must be a superhuman power or powers. (Or, at least we must think that there is.) However, the conclusion is not proposed solely as a pragmatic postulate. From his study of mystic experience James concludes that there is respectable empirical evidence of the superhuman. But again, the evidence does not suffice to define the attributes of deity, save in the vaguest fashion.

We are reminded of Cleanthes in Hume's *Dialogues* searching for empirical evidence concerning the existence and nature of deity; his arguments prove weak, inconclusive, or hopelessly ambiguous as to their precise outcome. Theodore Parker was right and Hume was right: Taken as an empirical question, this one is unanswerable. James's honesty serves to confirm the verdict, against his will.

I wish to suggest, however, that it is *unpragmatic* to take the theistic question purely empirically. For, in reality, it is an a priori requirement that James is dealing with. If atheism will not do because it cannot guarantee any value difference in ultimate outcome between wise or conscientious and rash or wicked choices, then a merely superhuman power or set of powers will not do either. If, without God, our action, for all we can see, is eventually futile, then with a God defective in power it is equally futile. If the human species may wither away or be destroyed, so equally may a merely superhuman being. The problem is solved only if we impute to deity at least one infinite or absolute attribute, indestructibility, power to survive any possible danger or counterforce. But this amounts to infinite power, at least in the sense of survival power. Nor is even that enough. Deity must not only surely survive, but also must survive mindful of our having existed and able to preserve *forever* the value we have achieved. Whittle away at these requirements, and you might as well adopt atheism and be done with it, so far as James's initial problem is concerned. It is strange that James did not see this. His was the pathos of blanket empiricism. All the trouble comes, he thought, from trying to find truth a priori.

Is it not obvious that no empirical evidence can disclose the reality of the required divine attributes? We cannot subject the immortality of deity, or of anything else, to observational tests. What James gives us is the necessity of acting *as if* our actions were contributory to an eventual good, with the implication that there is (or we believe there is) an indestructible power whose values include ours and always will. It matters not what the facts may be, the pragmatic definition of "fact" as such, any fact which we can take into account as practically significant, by James's reasoning already commits us to God as by no means merely finite in capacities. Our actions— any actions—say this for us, no matter what our words may be and no matter what we observe. No less than this follows from James's analysis, if anything at all follows. By understating his case, James misstated and ruined it. No wonder R. B. Perry, Horace Kallen, and some other admirers were unable to accept James's form of theism. No wonder, too, that Royce was not persuaded by James to give up his identification of deity with the timeless absolute.

James failed, in fact, to distinguish between two senses of the pragmatic criterion, the a priori and the empirical, or between ideas that are pragmatically essential or necessary and those that are merely useful or pleasant but not indispensable. Much confusion resulted from this oversight. A true idea, said James, is a good or useful idea; and this must be so if truth is what we want of ideas, and if what we want is (by definition) the good or the useful. But with empirical ideas this is little more than an idle wordplay. For until we know how far reality is as the idea represents it, we do not know how useful the idea will be. If it misrepresents reality, then no matter how comfortable we may be with the idea at the moment, sooner or later it will mislead us, or others we care about, and thus not be good or useful. With empirical ideas, the avoidance of wishful thinking is a main desideratum. With respect to these ideas, no judgment of value other than that based on evidence, as well as upon considerations of consistency, clarity, and the like, should be decisive.

With a priori or metaphysical ideas the logical situation is not at all the same, though this is often overlooked. For here the only relevant judgment of positive value is that in any *possible* world state the ideas would be useful. And the only way this could be so is for the idea to be true in any possible situation, that is, metaphysically or a priori true. How useful an empirical idea is with special reference to *this* world can only be judged when and in so far as we know (and this may take indefinitely prolonged observation) what sort of world we are in. But a metaphysical idea claims to fit us to the totality of conceivable worlds or world states and hence to be useful no matter what world state we may be in. If we can discern that the value of an idea is thus independent of the particular or contingent nature of the world, then we can (and it is the same thing) discern that its truth is similarly independent. It is idle to complain of wishful thinking if the idea is required for any wish fulfillment whatever. It is wishful to think that one can ride because one would like a horse, but this is relevant only because there are other wishes, which can be satisfied without a horse. For the sake of these other wishes one acknowledges the facts about horses. But honestly facing facts cannot have value if there is no value. And the theistic question is how, from a realistic, comprehensive point of view, there can be *any* value, *any* meaning, *any* significant truth.

James's "will to believe" argument was much weaker than he saw with regard to contingent matters, where we may indeed hope but should firmly believe only upon good evidence. However, his argument was stronger than he saw with regard to questions of principle, where value and truth are indeed coincident. In *any* world it would be good to believe in God—who after all is defined, in nearly all theologies, as infinite in creative ability to respond appropriately to whatever world there may be.

The equivalence of truth and value in nonempirical matters was somewhat ambiguously expressed by the poet Keats in his famous concluding lines of the *Ode on a Grecian Urn:*

> *"Beauty is truth, truth beauty,"—that is all*
> *Ye know on earth, and all ye need to know.*

As I have argued elsewhere, necessary truths cannot be ugly or bad; for the only use of such negative valuations is to suggest things to be prevented or avoided if possible, and only the contingent can ever have been preventable or avoidable. Necessary truths can, however, be positively valued; for their contemplation is satisfying. The beauty of pure mathematics is of this kind. Such satisfaction or enjoyment is self-justifying, whereas suffering, as such, is not. The beauty of necessary, a priori, metaphysical truths is one with their truth. Truth simply by coherence is here in its rightful place. Truth, usefulness, and beauty are here all one. The most beautiful metaphysics is the most true. Historical systems of metaphysics, however, all have their incongruent features, their aspects of ugliness and (in principle) evident falsity. These somehow escape their proponents but not their philosophical rivals.

Keats, of course, does not distinguish between contingent and a priori truth. However, he is partially right even about contingent truth. No truth whatever is simply unbeautiful; for anything we can experience or think at all has some immediate appeal, some inner coherence; its degree of beauty in the broadest sense cannot be zero. In this sense being as such and truth as such are good. But this is a minimal goodness and by itself no guide to action. We are always trying not simply to produce value but to optimally produce it, given the circumstances.

But, you may ask, is not the basis of the entire pragmatic reasoning—the mediating status of human thought and brain—a mere empirical fact? Superficially yes, but basically no. Any reflective creature whatever, other than God, would be in the same position, so far as the argument requires; for it would be a fragment of a world, reacting to other fragments and making decisions about these reactions. The empirical facts are here merely illustrative, and do not enter the argument in their contingent factuality.

It may seem that we have jeopardized our position by talking about *infinite* capacity in God. Must this not imply the complete predestination, the unreality of our apparent decision making, which James begins by rejecting? Answer: No. That God's capacity to have and deal with various worlds is absolutely infinite or unsurpassable does not mean that divine decisions about a world must or can be all-determinative of that world. As some of us have learned partly from James himself, no conceivable God could simply determine a world. To create, according to neoclassical metaphysics, as held by Peirce, Bergson, and others, is not the same as to determine precisely what others shall be or do. Apart from self-creation, which is the heart of all freedom, to create is to influence but not fully determine decision making in others. To create with divine wisdom and power is to inspire decision making in all others in such a way that the chances of harmony and intensity will justify the risks of evil. What world results depends partly upon the chance interplay of the more or less free decisions making up the world. Any world that is possible at all *could* result from some possible divine decision, but no such decision could in detail prescribe the world that results. Thus there is no possible world that God could not have, but the world that God does have cannot have been completely specified by divine decision.

In this way we avoid James's two forbidden extremes without falling into mere vagueness as to what lies between. The mediating position is just as definite as the extremes. Indeed the atheistic extreme is highly indefinite in its positive content; for one could conceive an indefinitely vast hierarchy of superhuman beings none of whom would deserve worship or solve the a priori pragmatic problem. One must transcend this hierarchy altogether and conceive a being that is just as literally infinite, in certain respects, as it is finite in others. It is infinite in capacity to have worlds and to preserve its own identity through all of them, but it is not "omnipotent," as that term is usually interpreted. It has indeed ideal power to influence the world, but a monopoly of decision making is, as I have said before, and probably should say again, not an ideal but a nightmare. The error is not, as James perhaps supposed, one of granting God too much power, but of a mistaken view of the nature of power. To have power over partially free beings (and according to my neo-classical doctrine there can be no other power over concrete realities) is never to determine their actions, but always and only to influence, or set limits to, their own self-determining.

James worried a good deal about the question of God's knowledge. He thought that if God knew all things there would be absolute divine control of all things; also that knowledge of all things would be timeless, and hence we should confront an unintelligible dualism of time and eternity. Worse, we could not contribute value to God by our decisions. How can one contribute to what eternally is what it is? But it did not occur to James that "knowing all things" need not be timeless if the totality of things is itself a growing one. Complete knowledge, omniscience, is to know all past events and to know that certain divinely supported laws make some, but not all, features of future events inevitable; it is to know also that beyond these inevitabilities there are only those real possibilities which are essential to a world of freedom. To know all this would be to know all there is. Since James believed in real possibilities, it is remarkable that this analysis, centuries old, never occurred to him. To know the definite past as definite, and the partly indefinite future as just that, is to know all there is to know, conceiving the temporal process as James himself did conceive it. The argument, there can be no new knowledge where there is no ignorance, is a fallacy of ambiguity. Not to know what "will" happen is a defect only so far as there is

57

such a thing as what will happen. But if the future is as James thought, then the future does not consist exclusively of what will happen, but also of what may or may not happen, the real possibilities. True knowledge knows things as they are, hence the indeterminate future as indeterminate. When the future is past it will be determinate and known as such. "Ignorance" in the proper sense is not implied at any point.

Had James read Fechner more carefully and completely he would have discovered this idea in the German writer, whom he admired. He would also have discovered that Fechner avoided the idea of divine monopoly of decision making, while yet attributing to God maximal or ideal creative power. Once more, it is not that men have attributed too much to God, but that they have attributed the wrong things. Not too much knowledge, but knowledge of all time as a complete totality, which is something time cannot be, so that this would really be error or ignorance. Not too much power, but an unwillingness or inability to bestow power upon others—really weakness, indicative of "insecurity," as the current jargon has it.

It was Fechner and Jules Lequier (of both of whom James was aware) who in the nineteenth century solved the pragmatic problem which James discerned but failed to solve. The grossly neglected Socinians in principle solved it in the seventeenth century; but scarcely anyone in James's time knew that. Jean Wahl (in conversation) implied that Lequier knew it. James evidently did not read far enough or carefully enough in Fechner to come upon this solution.[1] And Lequier's writings were not easily accessible.[2] Such, frequently, is the lag in philosophical communication.

There is a striking analogy between James and Fechner. For both, philosophical questions were existential (as we would now say), involving a person's basic response to life. Both went through a severe personal crisis, more severe for Fechner (he did no academic work for many months), before reaching a decision as to what to believe. Both rejected determinism in its classical form. As Fechner's crisis was the more severe, so was his decision the more definitive, his solution more fully worked out (though ignored by the world). Both men put much of their energies into psychology as an experimental science. Fechner was the clearer concerning the distinction between empirical and metaphysical questions. He was, however, more conventional or traditional in his religious feelings, at least with regard to questions of immortality and of posthumous rewards and punishments.

Let us summarize what we have found. With respect to empirical ideas, James's equation, useful = true, *is not itself a useful formula.* For, although every empirical idea would, *if true,* be favorable to some conceivable purposes and unfavorable to others, until one *knows* that the idea is true one cannot judge the direction and degree of its utility. Thus the pragmatic criterion *of truth in general* is not itself pragmatic. Only in the original Peircean form of a criterion of *meaning* is it serviceable. If and only if we have some notion of what the truth of an idea *would* imply concerning the feasibility of various purposes, do we understand the idea. But an empirical idea, apart from knowledge or assertion of its truth, implies nothing as to what purposes are feasible.

With respect to nonempirical ideas, the problem is different. For a nonempirical idea is one which plays no favorites among possible purposes, but in a certain sense treats them all alike. One cannot ask, "What would such an idea, if true, imply concerning the feasibility of this purpose or that? " For a nonempirical idea cannot be simply false, it can only be necessarily true or necessarily false. If, then, its truth discriminated among possible purposes, this discrimination would be valid or invalid a priori, and some of the so-called possible purposes would be impossible. A priori ideas, therefore, can only have a blanket relation to all purposes, purposes as such. Absolute optimism, as a priori, would imply that all possible purposes whose realization matters at all would be realized, and this is absurd or meaningless. Absolute pessimism would imply that no purposes would (from an ultimate point of view) be realized, and this is even more obviously ridiculous. The proper mean between sheer pessimism and sheer optimism can only imply (and it will be equivalent to) the belief that in particular situations there are some feasible purposes, which are not all jointly feasible, so that selection must be made and priorities assigned. This is the only rule by which we can live; so this position is pragmatically obligatory. It must be taken as true, for its falsity would be pragmatically null. James made a great discovery here.

James, like John Stuart Mill and, more recently, John Hick, has been applauded as a thoroughgoing—or in my phrase, monolithic—empiricist. I submit that the value of these thinkers is that they show so heroically well how *not* to try to solve the essential religious problem. Their points, so far as valid, survive criticism only if taken as nonempirical. The essential religious truth is metaphysical. It is not and could not be a theorem of observational science. If true, it is a philosophical truth of pure reason, a priori intuition, and reflection, or religious faith and revelation.[3]

Notes

1. Gustav Theodor Fechner expounds his idea of God in the long chapter, "Gott und Welt," in his *Zendavesta* (1875, 1922). There seems to be no evidence that James had read that chapter.

2. Lequier published nothing himself, but Charles Renouvier edited some of his writings published posthumously in 1865 under the title *La Recherche d'une première vérité*. A copy of this book was sent either to James or, with his knowledge, to the Harvard Library. How much he read of it remains a question, but he clearly adopted some of the ideas, especially the quatrilemma, accepted also by Renouvier, that one must choose among:

I am determined to believe in determinism;
I am determined to believe in (indeterministic) freedom;
I freely believe in determinism;
I freely believe in freedom.

Lequier and James knew perfectly well the theory of "compatibilism," that deterministic freedom makes sense. They thought it a sophistry, as have Peirce, Whitehead, and some other great minds. The issue is twenty-five centuries old. It is a metaphysical issue, not an empirical one.

The a priori pragmatic test negates not only determinism but also, as Lequier and James both held, the idea of a timeless knowledge of creaturely choices. For nothing follows rationally for conduct from the idea that what we decide is eternally true—rather than becomes true as we decide and thereafter remains so. The timelessness is merely verbal, does no work in our lives. We still have to make the decision as though the truth about it is first indeterminate and then determinate, as though omniscience has yet to acquire the definite knowledge that our deciding alone can make possible. The point is not that God is first ignorant and then knowing, but rather that first there is no definite fact of the kind to know and then there is the fact. Creation is unfinished (not fully definite) and never can be finished. Any God that treated it as finished, exhaustively defined, would be mistaken. And we are part creators of ourselves and of God. Exactly that is our significance. On this point Socinus, Fechner, Lequier, James, Peirce, and Whitehead are in agreement. But James alone of the six completely missed the point that "knowing all truth" is entirely compatible with "acquiring new truths" as new realities come into being. That he did not realize this was not simply his fault. Historians had not told the story of the new tradition among theists that had been forming for nearly four centuries. It has far more adherents now than when, seventy years ago, James died. Since 1600 it has always had more adherents than scholars have in general acknowledged.

3. Of James's books, three, *Pragmatism, The Meaning of Truth,* and *Essays in Radical Empiricism,* though influential in their time, seem to me to give us James at his most confused. In contrast, his great *Principles of Psychology,*

the *Textbook of Psychology* (briefer version), *A Pluralistic Universe, The Varieties of Religious Experience,* and the posthumous *Some Problems of Philosophy,* together with several fine essays ("Reflex Action and Theism," "The Sentiment of Rationality," "The Dilemma of Determinism," and "Theoretical Conceptions and Practical Results"—his first formulation of pragmatism) give us James's permanently valuable message.

I agree with Marcus Ford that if James had a definite cosmology it was pluralistic panpsychism (or psychicalism), not materialism, emergent dualism (often called naturalism), or neutral monism. James was certainly a pluralist of a vaguely theistic sort, and it was experience not mere matter that he took to be real. Nor was he a phenomenalist like Kant, Mill, Spencer, or the early positivists. See Marcus Peter Ford, *William James's Philosophy: A New Perspective* (Amherst, Mass.: The University of Massachusetts Press, 1982).

The lengthy account in *A Pluralistic Universe* of Fechner's life and works may well be the best in English, except for the negative evaluation of the Fechnerian theology. James did not know the history or adequately see the logic of speculations (beginning with Socinus) that tried to revise theism to make it consistent with its religious claims and with the clear admission of genuine creative freedom in the creatures. The change required is the admission of some form of finitude, relativity, or change in the divine reality. Classical theism denied this, holding that God was in *all* respects infinite, absolute, and immutable. James writes about Fechner as though the only alternative were to affirm that God was in *no* respect infinite, relative, or mutable. Elementary logic tells us, but theologians often forget, that *S* is *P*-and-not-*P* is contradictory only if *P* is affirmed and denied of *S* "in the same (or in every) respect." Classical theism assumed that deity is "simple" precisely in the sense that there can be no distinction of respects in the divine reality. In that case one must choose between an unqualifiedly absolute and an unqualifiedly relative deity. But what I call neoclassical theism holds that we must conceive a real distinction between God as infinite or absolute and God as finite or relative. James, like many of his more traditional opponents, allows the classical view to beg the question between itself and the neoclassical form by neglecting entirely the possibility of the distinction in question.

Because Fechner says that the divine power does not simply and unqualifiedly make (fully determine) its creatures, therefore (James holds) the Fechnerian God is "finite" and hence there must be something outside it. This is doubly erroneous. First, James neglects the question, "Finite in what respect?" Second, the whole of finite reality may itself be finite spatially, and yet by definition there will be nothing outside it. Physics had not then perhaps clearly conceded, as it does now, that the spatial whole may be finite. The totality of finite reality may itself be finite, for all James has shown. Our nerve cells are not simply "outside us," yet we interact with them. So, in an eminent fashion, may God with the creatures. As I understand words, infallible knowledge of all reality (free from the possibility of error or ignorance) can have nothing simply outside it; yet it cannot be the emptiness of sheer infinity either. Fechner may have been somewhat unclear, but he was much less crude or confused than James's criticism of him. Even

Hegel and Schelling knew that the merely infinite or merely eternal can have no knowledge of the finite and temporal, and Fechner knew it also. He also knew that a *merely* finitistic idea of God is idolatrous, a changing of the subject, as all high religions conceive deity.

CHAPTER 6

Royce's Mistakes
and Achievements[1]

In what sense can a philosopher be mistaken? If philosophy is, in ideal, a critical and well-reasoned view of reality, then it is a mistake for a philosopher to adopt any tenet without careful consideration. I believe that parts of Royce's doctrine were carefully considered, but that on at least one cardinal point he proceeded hastily. This was his belief in the antecedent reality of factual truths. Before an event occurs, he supposed it to be already true that that event is "going to occur." This is a common enough view, generally adopted with as little justification as Royce gave for it. Yet long ago Aristotle defended an alternative position,[2] as Royce implies by his phrase, "despite a well-known remark of Aristotle's."[3] Quite apart from Aristotle, the issue should not be settled in haste. If truth is agreement of a proposition with reality, then *either* propositions can become true that were not previously true, *or else* nothing can become real that was not previously real. For, as the Stagirite implied, no statement can be true of a thing unless there is that thing; hence, before there was event E, nothing can have been true of it, for there was no such "it." To say, then, that the truth about E was there all along is to say that E was there all along. Royce, to be sure, believed just that; for he held that all events are real, once for all, in the eternal consciousness. But his task was to justify this belief, not to assume it in the disguise of a supposedly self-evident theory about truth. Furthermore, he entertained other beliefs that were jeopardized by this one, and, for many of his readers, were even made incredible by it. Had he proceeded with more caution at this point, he might have avoided some of his worst difficulties.

63

What reason did Royce offer for the theory of antecedent factual truth? He gave an illustration and seemed almost to rest his case upon it. A prisoner is about to be sentenced, the judge being supposed to act with freedom. The prisoner does not know what the sentence "is to be," yet he trembles with apprehension. Surely he could not make so much fuss over a mere nonentity; hence the future sentence must be real, even though a reality belonging to the future. Is this a respectable argument? There is, we may grant, a real possibility, perhaps probability, of an unfavorable sentence by the judge. This probability is not blank nothing, but neither is it a fully defined event. Fear is directed at just such partially determinate outlines, or potentialities, of the future. I see no sound argument here for Royce's contention.

What other evidence did he offer? Only this, so far as I see: He did, and this I grant, offer justification for the notion of an ideally adequate—or (as he called it) an absolute—experience, one definitive of "reality" or "truth" as such; and this definitive experience must, he held, be "complete," that is, free from unanswered questions or unfulfilled purposes, and hence, Royce inferred, there must, for it, be no open future, no truth as yet in the making.[4] Here I find a double ambiguity. First, an open future does not imply unanswered questions, if this means properly formulated questions the true answers to which are unknown. "How will the judge decide? " If his mind is not yet made up, if there is real indeterminacy, then there is no way in which he *will* or is *going* to decide, but only possibilities of decision none of which is marked as *the* decision. Of course, *some one* of the possibilities *or other* will be selected; but this no more implies that there is a possibility already marked for selection than the command, "Make up your mind," is a command to make it up in this way rather than in that. Just so the passage of time enforces a change from irresolution to resolution, and insofar this change can be truly affirmed beforehand; but there need, for all that, be no particular form of resolution constituting the fact in advance. Resolution is to be achieved somehow, that is all.

The second ambiguity in Royce's argument is this: The requirement that, in the Ideal Experience, all purposes must be fulfilled slurs over the distinction between cognitive and other purposes, and it is only the cognitive which Royce's arguments can show must be fulfilled in the experience posited as definitive of reality. Cognitive questions concern the *de facto* totality of accomplished events, including the real causal determinations already in being for the future. If the events of my next birthday are not, as yet, fully determinate, but are a set of more or less limited or "real" possibilities, then the Ideal Experience envisages these possibilities in the precise degree of indefiniteness which is their very nature as possibilities.

The foregoing implies that even the Ideal Experience has in some sense a future as well as a present. And why not? The reason for positing an Ideal Experience, on Royce's own showing, is that there must be a coincidence somewhere between reality and the content of experience. This would require a purely eternal experience in which all events are once for all present *only* if truth or reality must similarly be a timeless totality, the same whenever referred to, rather than a partially new totality every moment. One cannot reason both ways at once, cannot argue that truth must be above time because ideal knowledge must be so and then also argue that the ideal knowledge must be supertemporal because truth is so. And the whole point of Royce's procedure is that the nature of experience explains the meaning of "truth" or "reality," and not vice versa.

Let us consider this nature of experience. The effectively given content of our perceptions does not coincide with reality; but how do we know this? Because, says Royce, our experience is infected with doubt, unclarity, inconsistency, and unanswered but genuine questions. Suppose, then, a conscious experience free from doubt, perfectly clear and consistent in its meanings, and without any unanswered questions. For such an experience, no distinction between what is given and what is real would be relevant, and we can only conceive the two as coincident. With this I heartily agree. But how does it establish the timelessness of truth? To face an open future with full awareness of its kind and degree of openness is not to doubt, but to know surely a character of the given universe, namely its potentiality for further determination. There need be no confusion, no inconsistency, and no genuine question without an answer. For the query "What is going to happen? " has a valid meaning only so far as the future course of events has outlines that are real now.[5] The tense of "is going to happen" says just that. Insofar as determining tendencies that are now in effect leave certain details to be settled later on, the only valid question is "What *may* or *can* happen? " and the true answer (apart from degrees of probability) is, "Any one of several things."

Royce uses the term "fragmentary," or incomplete, for the nonideal modes of experience. There are two radically distinct conceptions of this incompleteness: We may view it (1) as the failure to experience clearly the entire *de facto* reality, or (2) as the failure to include as actual all that ever can be actualized. This second "failure" is properly

65

so called only if the correlative form of success is logically conceivable, and this in turn requires that possibilities of experience be *not* inexhaustible, and this requires that there be no incompossible possibilities. For if there be incompossibles (and Royce admits that there are[6]), then the absolute actualization of possibility is not itself possible, and if possibility is inexhaustible by actualization, then *any* totality of actual experience leaves unactualized potentialities open for actualization. What justification could there be for refusing to actualize further possibilities?

There is a pathos in Royce's insistence that in the Absolute all goals are eternally attained. Be serene, he says, about the impossibility of banishing open possibilities for yourselves—for in reality, that is, in the Absolute Experience, there are no open possibilities. It seems the more remarkable that Royce took this illusionist way out when we reflect that his treatment of suffering deliberately took just the opposite tack. Be brave, he said, in your pain and grief, for the Ideal Experience shares in all your suffering and sorrow.[7] Very well, why not also say that it faces with us an open future of inexhaustible potentialities? If suffering cannot be excluded from the all-inclusive consciousness (and I agree it cannot), then neither can the inexhaustibility of possibility fail to apply to it. Can it be doubted that Royce was deeply at odds with himself here? Had he seen the conflict, in which way would he have resolved it?

We need not hesitate, I think, in answering this question. He would never have given up his insight into the love that shares in all the joys and sorrows of the world, in favor of the medieval concept of a divine self-enjoyment to which neither the joys nor the sufferings of creatures contribute anything whatever, nor make the slightest difference of any kind. In this regard Royce knew clearly what he believed and why.

Our philosopher betrays his secret a little more clearly, perhaps, than Leibniz did, when he says that, although abstractly and for mere thought other universes were "possible," yet in view of the all-wise decision to will just this universe, the others are exhibited as not "genuinely" possible.[8] Thus an eternal act excludes all but one infinitely complex cosmic possibility from actualization. Moreover, since in eternity nothing can happen, or merely happen to be so, the alleged voluntariness of the divine choice collapses. There never really was an alternative to this world, and its mistakes or misfortunes are all necessary ones—or rather, since it is the divine essence which requires them for its perfection, they are not mistakes or misfortunes, and the very distinction between better and worse is contradicted. No more than Leibniz could Royce argue away this inconsistency. The impasse was not due to the attribution of perfection in some sense to deity, nor to the combination of this with the affirmation that the divine life includes the world, with its sufferings and evils. For Fechner had shown how this affirmation is compatible with a well-defined concept of divine perfection.[9] But he had done this only by granting an open future to God, whose perfection consists in the ideal fashion, unsurpassable even in possibility, in which he deals with each *de facto* state of the world. Perfection of will is meaningless, Fechner points out, where there is nothing given for the will to deal with, no problem to solve, no impulses to control. A will simply *is* the control of something that itself, so far as that will is concerned, is involuntary.

Let us now consider more closely Royce's evidence for an Ideal Experience. The best statement of this is in *The Conception of God*. His contention was that we cannot understand the fragmentariness of our experience, its ignorance and confusion, except in its contrast with an experience whose conscious ideas are fully adequate to its perceptions and whose perceptions fully justify its conscious ideas— a very brilliant and profound formula.

Suppose we try to conceive *all* experience as more or less ignorant and confused. Then, first, this supposed fact itself must be unknowable absolutely. For how can any incomplete survey of reality constitute evidence that there is *not* a complete survey? I question if this challenge can be met. Atheism, if true, is empirically unknowable. It cannot be known by pointing to the evils in the world, for as Royce shows, I think irrefutably, a world exclusively harmonious and happy is meaningless, or self-contradictory.[10] This point is quite separable from the dubious contention that each evil is divinely chosen; indeed, the inevitability of some evils or other, in spite of the divine perfection, is much more intelligible upon the Fechnerian conception of the divine will, as facing an open future, and having something involuntary (not its *own* volition) to deal with.

For Royce's purpose, we must now note, it does not suffice to show that atheism, since its truth is purely unknowable, is meaningless. One still has positivism to deal with, the view that the very notion of an Ideal Experience is meaningless, whether its supposed referent be affirmed or denied. Royce is equipped to deal with this position also. There is certainly a conception of nonideal experience, infected with doubt and error: Such are our experiences. Now try to suppose that *all* experiences are such. What then constitutes the truth which this or that ignorant or erring experience misses? There are three possible answers.

(a) The truth is known in some other experience, itself ignorant, though not in the same respects. But then the totality of these partly ignorant experiences—who knows the truth about that? [11] Obviously no one of them.

(b) The unknown truth is such that some experience *could* know it. Royce considers at length the view that unknown facts are defined by the possibility of knowing them.[12] He has two objections: The total truth, which must be a single complex truth, could not possibly be known by experiences all of which are deficient in conceptual clarity and perceptual adequacy; and furthermore, nothing is really possible unless something, itself not merely possible, makes it so. Possibility is not a self-explanatory idea.

(c) One may hold that the unknown truths are made true by reality as independent of all knowing. But this implies that we criticize our knowledge by comparing it with bare reality. On the contrary, the comparison is between experience as idea and the content given in perception. The criterion of knowledge is and must be an *internal* character of experiences, namely, the adequacy of ideas to what is perceived, and vice versa. This implies that the truth is precisely a definite internal harmony of concepts with perceived objects, and this formula defines Ideal Experience. We should not say that Ideal Experience is bound to conform to reality; rather, we should say that Ideal Experience, with its content, must *be* reality. If an opponent now objects that we have shown only that we must conceive Ideal Experience, not that it must exist, Royce replies that possibility must have a foundation, and, if the experience definitive of reality is only possible, then instead of reality we have only the possibility of reality, a possibility itself not real.

I am persuaded, in spite of the fashionable counteropinions of our day, that all this is essentially sound. But there is an apparent and gross fallacy in the form which Royce (in *The World and the Individual*) gave the argument.[13] He asked, What relates an idea to its object? According to "Realism," as he defined it, the object is quite independent of the idea. In that case, must not the idea be likewise independent of the object? Then there can be no reason why it should even partially correspond to it, or be able to single it out as *the* object it is trying to be true of. Formally, the argument is fallacious. A relation between subject and object can very well be external to the object but internal to the subject, just as, in many cases, P entails

Q, though not vice versa. But, says our author, it is "contrary to the whole spirit of realism" to admit *any* internal relations. This is correct of some forms of realism, such as Hume's, with his dictum, "What is distinguishable is (symmetrically) separable." Nevertheless, no logical rule is violated in holding that a mental state depends upon what it knows, though not conversely.

To concede to realism that particular objects are independent of particular subjects does not weaken, but rather strengthens, the case for idealism, properly defined. If the object is internal to the subject when the latter knows the object, then first, the more we know, the more the world becomes constitutive of ourselves as knowers, and thus, at the ideal limit, "reality" coincides with "content of experience." But second, how can the thing known become a constituent of experience—which, according to Royce's self-observation (and mine), is a unity of feeling, purpose, valuation, meaning—unless the thing has some feeling, purpose, valuation, meaning, of its own to contribute? The argument is simple; I have not seen it refuted.

There is an additional argument. The subject, according to realism itself, is relative to, connected with, its object, though the latter is, in this relation, independent and insofar, "absolute." Very well, but the object, though not relative to the particular subject in question, must nevertheless be relative somehow; for it is an effect of antecedent causes, and effects are relative to their causes. Yet each effect becomes in its turn a new cause, and in this regard an absolute, since effects cannot influence their antecedent causes. Thus every causally relative term is, looking to the future, an absolute, a condition to be accepted just as it is by all further process. Suppose, then, that every subject, as such relative, becomes object for other subjects, which themselves become objects for still further subjects, and so on. The logical structure of this supposition is identical with that of causes which produce effects, themselves in turn causes of further effects. Just so, a subject may derive its possibility from antecedent subjects which it objectifies, and be itself in turn objectified by new subjects.

In this reasoning I have, of course, passed from Royce to Whitehead. The former never quite saw that for his idealism, according to which subjects are the only concrete objects, he needed both internal and external relations.[14] (What indeed could we mean by internal relations, if there were no other kind?) Similarly, he did not see that he was combining two logically distinct propositions in his idealism: the doctrine that reality is ultimately eternal, with exclusively internal relationships, and the doctrine that reality and content of experience somehow coincide. Not only is the eternalistic doctrine not deducible from the second, more plainly "idealistic" doctrine, it really contradicts it. For, though experience is a response to data, and as such requires the data, yet to say that the data in turn require just this or that response to themselves is to say that the data logically contain the response, and that, in effect, they respond to themselves, which is nonsense.

I am able to agree with Royce that all things must be data for an Ideal Experience only because I think, or hope, it is possible to conceive this experience not as a single all-inclusive and eternally determinate affair corresponding to all events throughout time, but rather as a progressive and free process of adequately experiencing each *de facto* state of the universe as it is actualized. In this view, freedom belongs not alone to the divine experience; rather, all experiences have their degree of self-determination, of creativity, and this implies that the results of creative action are in part divinely accepted, rather than willed or decreed. What such a result requires to gain its place in reality is not precisely this, or precisely that, divine acceptance, or response to itself, but only *some* divine, that is, ideally adequate, response *or other*. We have here the same distinction as that between "Some decision or other must be made" and "Just *this* decision must be made." It is analogous also to the distinction between "A universal must, in order to exist, be embodied in *some* concrete individual or other" and "It must be embodied in just *this* individual." Royce, I fear, missed this point.

It was a merit of Royce to see clearly that the relation of experience to experienced, or of knowing to what is known, could not be a merely external one. It is logically impossible that a knowing experience should be one entity and the entity experienced simply another, additional one. For then there would be no reason whatever why the knowing should agree with the known; in other words, why the knowing should be—knowing. However, Royce failed to see that the knowing could very well be additional to the entity known. For while the knowing must agree with the known, there is no necessity for the reverse agreement. Plato could be Plato without our knowing Plato, or our existing at all. We, not Plato, are the dependent factor in the relationship. Of course a known entity could not be that, a known entity, without someone knowing it. But for this no particular subject is required, only any subject able to know the entity in question. Royce, like others before him (for example, Berkeley) was insufficiently clear about this distinction, and hence about the essential asymmetry of the subject-object relation. A particular subject requires its particular object, but the object as such requires only some subject or subjects able to know it. Royce neatly and absolutely missed the asymmetry of the most fundamental of all relations. Did his teacher Lotze, or his object of meticulous study, Hegel, do much better? Even Peirce and Bergson were not entirely clear at this point, and Whitehead, though his technical doctrines conform to the principle, never announced the principle itself in unequivocal terms. He unequivocally implies that his "prehension" is an asymmetrical relation, but does not explicitly say that it is. And some of his rhetoric about internal relations and dependencies among actualities seems to imply symmetry in their dependency relationships. So far as I know, I am the first to be explicit and consistent on the point.

Royce's merit remains, and it is that he was the one who forced the issue so sharply (in *The World and the Individual*) that the fallacy in the symmetrical view could scarcely be overlooked. No one had ever committed the fallacy so glaringly, not even Berkeley or Hegel, though I think they committed it. I am one of those who think that clarity, even clarity in fallacious reasoning, can be a high achievement. My immense admiration for Leibniz is partly based on this belief. Where Leibniz was wrong, he was more sharply and unambiguously wrong than his predecessors. It was not for nothing that Royce was a symbolic logician.[15] He could be very definite in his mistakes.

But Royce was only half wrong. He was simply right in rejecting the kind of pluralism, derived from Hume, that fails to see the asymmetrical dependencies that make the universe a universe, constituting the irreversibility of causal relations, temporal relations, and experience-experienced relations. Moreover, Royce saw equally vividly that the dependence of an experience or subject (he usually said "idea") on its objects is significant not only in theory of knowledge but also in ethics. A theory of motivation based solely on self-interest is an absurdity and not a harmless one. "Community" is basic to any understanding of ethics or religion. Only through confusion or ignorance can we suppose that altruism is a mere derivation from the interest of an individual in that very individual. To be a person at all presupposes interest in others, and Royce knew the genetic psychology that supports this statement. He taught psychology as well as philosophy.

Alas, Royce weakened his case here by proposing a demonstration for personal immortality in the conventional sense, which opens the door to an ultimate self-interest theory: In the infinite long run all goodness will then, perhaps, come home to one in personal advantage. It is my fervent belief that it is only God who will inherit all goodness, all value, only God who has no possible personal advantage in doing anything but good to others, only God in whom there is complete harmony between self-love and love of others. As for Royce's demonstration, it subtly begs the question. His argument is that the individual must "will" and "define" itself and the career in which that self is actualized. But no being can define and will its own termination. It cannot be there as dead to will that deadness! However, from the Buddhist-Whiteheadian standpoint from which I write this book, the final unit-realities are not individuals in Royce's sense but momentary actualities—thus my experience now. This experience does, in a sense, will and define itself, so far as this is logically required; it intends and wills its own temporal finitude. And this must be so in the last experience before death in a given personal series of experiences. There is no need for that experience to will that there be no more in its series. Future actuality, including divine actuality, will define the termination of the series so far as this is a logical necessity.

In whatever sense the concrete actualities die, are temporally finite, they more or less unconsciously will this death or finitude. They intend their own supercession by other actualities. Whitehad has elaborated what is involved here in his theory of "initial aim," "satisfaction" and "subject-superject." In spite of the inconclusiveness of Royce's argument, however, I again salute him for his candor, his earnest forcing of an issue, thus helping his readers to come to a clear decision in an important matter.

Santayana was one who chose his words carefully. His suggestion of something "sublime" in Royce is appropriate. I for one would be intellectually poorer if I had not encountered one of his works, *The Problem of Christianity*, at the age of nineteen and had not read much more of his writing a few years later. Although Royce was the most traditional of our classical thinkers, he has the merit of summing up a good deal that is great and noble in the tradition. His *Lectures on Modern Idealism* is a profound study, and his *Spirit of Modern Philosophy* is an eloquent historical introduction to its subject. Peirce's tribute to Royce, "our American Plato," has its justification in view of Royce's keen awareness of mathematical and logical structures, his eloquence, and lofty vision of human and superhuman actualities. There was also a noble concern for the future of humanity, especially with reference to the terrible problem of war, for which he tried to find a solution in an international insurance scheme.

Royce (1855–1916) produced few disciples who went even nearly all the way with him in his speculations. The times favored James and Dewey. Nevertheless, countless students and readers have felt themselves privileged to encounter his high earnestness and candor, his ingenuity, learning, trust in human reason, and complete good will.

Notes

1. Revised from a paper read at the annual meeting of the American Philosophical Association, Eastern Division, December 29, 1955.
2. *On Interpretation* 19a, 21b–23a; *Metaphysics* 1026b–1027b; 1065b.
3. *The World and the Individual* (1920), Vol. I, pp. 403–404.
4. Ibid., pp. 340ff.
5. See my "The Meaning of 'Is Going to Be'," *Mind* 74 (1965): 46–58.
6. *The World and the Individual* (above, note 3), pp. 296, 573.
7. *William James and other Essays* (1911), p. 183; also *The Spirit of Modern Philosophy* (1892, 1920), pp. 470–471, and *The World and the Individual*, Vol. II.
8. See *The Conception of God* (1909), pp. 269, 293; *The World and the Individual*, pp. 572–574, 588.
9. See *Zendavesta*, chap. XI; also C. Hartshorne and W. L. Reese, *Philosophers Speak of God* (Chicago: University of Chicago Press, 1953), p. 243.
10. See especially "The Knowledge of Good and Evil," *International Journal of Ethics* (1893), republished in *Studies of Good and Evil* (1898), pp. 89–124; also *Sources of Religious Insight* (1912), pp. 250–254.
11. *The Religious Aspect of Philosophy* (1885), p. 425; *William James and Other Essays* (1911), pp. 218–221.
12. *The World and the Individual*, pp. 258–261.
13. Ibid., pp. 118–119, 133.
14. He seems to affirm the latter in *The Conception of God*, p. 314, but to deny them flatly on p. 302, and in many other places in his writings.
15. Bruce Kuklick, in his excellent study, *Josiah Royce: An Intellectual Biography* (Indianapolis and New York: The Bobbs-Merrill Co., 1972) points out that Royce was the leading symbolic logician in this country after Peirce and before C. I. Lewis.

CHAPTER 7

A Revision
of Peirce's Categories

Although Charles S. Peirce (1839–1914) was born three years before
William James and sixteen years before Royce, there are several
reasons for considering him after the others. Because of their success
and efficiency in publishing and teaching and their popular style,
James and Royce achieved wide influence before Peirce, whose publications in his lifetime (apart from book reviews and highly special-
ized scientific essays) were scanty and mostly severely technical.
Peirce could know the thoughts of James and Royce more easily and
correctly than they could know his. They took from Peirce a few
hints and used glimpses of his ideas for purposes mostly rather
different from those he had in mind. It is even possible that Peirce
learned more from his brilliant younger contemporaries than they
did from him. He was a person who learned from everyone. And
finally Peirce was farther ahead of his time than they; his influence
is growing and will grow while theirs diminishes. His grasp of the
exact sciences was far beyond theirs, yet he was as creatively imaginative in speculative philosophy as they, with a vivid sense of
ethical and religious values. It is he who comes closest to summing
up the combined wisdom of one of the most remarkable trios of
thinkers that history has to show.

Like most writers, Peirce sometimes indulged in exaggeration. To
emphasize the importance of his novel theory of philosophical categories, he once termed it "my one contribution to philosophy." But
perhaps this is only a simplification or elliptical summary of what
is arguably true, that what is good in Peirce's system is in some
way grounded in the theory in question. If so, it seems unfortunate
that the three categories, Firstness, Secondness, and Thirdness (de-

rived by a process Peirce called phenomenology or phaneroscopy) have not given his students any complete satisfaction. Martin Gardner, a former student of mine, writer on mathematical puzzles, author of a novel and other books, has gone so far as to say that Peirce's categories are taken seriously only by Eugene Freeman and Charles Hartshorne. (When Freeman wrote his dissertation on the subject, the *Collected Papers* were not yet available. He is now more critical of Peirce than he was then.) I believe that the "one contribution" as Peirce gave it to us is neither so definitive, powerful, and correct as Peirce hoped nor so weak and mistaken as Gardner, Murray Murphey, and, apparently, a good many others suppose (to judge from the rather general neglect of it by contributors to the *Transactions of the Peirce Society*). I cannot doubt that, though partly misconceived, the doctrine brings us closer to the truth in certain respects than any previous doctrine and, when freed of certain errors, can be of great value.

Murray Murphey, student of the development of Peirce's thought, objects to Peirce's categories that they are held to presuppose only mathematics but not logic; indeed, logic is said to presuppose ethics and aesthetics, and these three to presuppose phenomenology and the categories—yet in fact logic is employed in deriving the categories. In my view this is not a crucial objection. All of the disciplines mentioned are, in their first principles, like mathematics, nonempirical, and among a priori truths the relations are symmetrical, the criterion being that of mutual coherence. Hence I take Murphey's point, so far as cogent, to turn against Peirce's classification of sciences or branches of knowledge rather than against his theory of categories. The order of priority indicated by the classification has at most heuristic value and does not mean that the categories stand or fall by whether they are supported, without circularity, by mathematics standing alone. A priori truths have no unique linear order. Each is given support partly by direct intuition or illustration in experience and partly by its congruence with other intuitions on the same ultimate level. How far, if at all, I could claim Peirce's support for this view I shall not further inquire in this chapter.

A. The Numerical Clue: Dependence and Independence of Phenomena

Early in his career Peirce (1839–1914) set out to revise Kant's categories—and they needed revision. I have tried, through most of my long career, to revise Peirce's categories—and again, revision was needed. I believe that, at last, I have had some success. My two previous attempts were not acclaimed by Peirce scholars, and I was myself not satisfied with them.[1] The present version is in part substantially different.

Instead of seeking a wholly "presuppositionless" stance from which to inspect the given (a search I distrusted when, before I had read Peirce, I encountered Husserl in 1923–24) Peirce sought to limit his explicit presuppositions to some elementary formal mathematical insights. He did not try to completely "bracket" the physical world, an attempt which, as Husserl goes at it, presupposes that the physical world is not genuinely given, but rather is only intended or postulated. In other words, Husserl assumes that an experience is logically self-sufficient, independent of any world of realities other than itself. Not only is this a presupposition, it is one in conflict with the given. Our being "in the world" is an irrreducible though more or less vague datum. To anticipate, this is implied by Peirce's Secondness (also Whitehead's prehension).

Let me state some points of agreement with Peirce. (1) He was right to consult *phenomena* from the outset in philosophy. (2) He did well to look to *relations* among phenomena as crucial, since all analysis must employ them. (3) He did well also to see both *dependence* and *nondependence* as equally basic forms of relatedness. Without dependence there can be no inference from one phenomenon to others; without independence anything would in principle be inferrible from anything else, which is illogical. In logic $P \rightarrow Q$ is significant only because it does not hold universally. It is the same with dependence and independence among phenomena. (4) Peirce was brilliantly original in seeing in the process of *counting* some formal clues to dependence and independence. To say "first" is not to imply any definite or actual second, but to say "second" is to imply a definite first. The first person to make a certain statement could be the last and only person to make it, but the second person could not be the only one. Firstness thus does model independence and Secondness, dependence.

True, the second person might not know or be influenced by the first, but in that case, and insofar as the apparent non-influence can be taken as absolute, the secondness is extrinsic, or relative to spectators or historians of the sequence. It is also obvious that in counting there may be arbitrariness in the order of items considered, as in counting votes. But even in such cases there is real dependence, for the conscious or felt *act* of assigning secondness presupposes and depends on the act of assigning firstness. And Peirce is seeking relations among experiences.

Peirce did once put the question, Is the *basic* secondness or dependence the form in which the dependence is one-way only or the form in which it is mutual? [2] Most oddly he failed to give a sharp answer to his question. Clearly "*y* second to *x*" is the principle while "*x* second to *y* and *y* second to *x*" is the special and indeed degenerate case, since it destroys the distinctiveness of the dependent and the independent factors as such. And in the clearly analogous case of propositional implication, Peirce saw this. Equivalence is not the principle of which one-way implication is a special form. $P \rightarrow Q$ is basic, $P \longleftrightarrow Q$ is a complication derivative from the other. So also with one-way and two-way Secondness.

What misled so fine a logician here? It was some apparent phenomenon of interaction, such as two persons trying to push a door in opposite directions. The symmetry appears a given fact, each man's force opposing, second to, that of the other. Perhaps the physics of today, better than prerelativity and prequantum physics, helps to clear up this confusion. In any case, it was not wise to trust an example involving two besouled bodies, not to mention the door, to establish an elementary categorial point.

Far safer is Peirce's example of immediate memory, or the experience of surprise as dependent on a previous expectation (or lack of it). Present awareness feels the contrast with previous awareness that was innocent of the contrast. The innocence is essential to the previousness. Had Peirce only seen—or did he see it?—that in perception as well as memory it is always *independent and previous* events on which present experience depends, he would have almost reached Whitehead's concept of prehension, which by definition is one-way. Peirce does say that feelings tend to "spread" and, unless this spreading is instantaneous, Whitehead's concept, "feeling of (past) feeling," is implied.

Another question that Peirce seems to answer unconvincingly is this: Is the basic idea modeled by Secondness that of dependence on one and only one other thing, or is it that of dependence on other things, regardless of how many or few others? Peirce regards the single other as definitive of Secondness, and dependence on two others (Thirdness) as essentially different, while dependence on more than two can, he holds, be reduced to cases of Thirdness. Thus he *counts the number of items* on which a phenomenon depends, defining Firstness as dependence on zero others, Secondness, on one other,

Thirdness, on two others, and dismissing all higher numbers as reducible.

My suggestion is that Peirce here misapplied the numerical model and thereby incurred needless trouble. In the first place, no actual phenomenon, and he virtually admits this, depends on *nothing* else.[3] God, as classical theism defined God, would depend on nothing else (similarly, Whitehead's primordial nature of God, or my "abstract eternal essence" of God); but an actual feeling or phenomenon can be independent only of *some* other phenomena while being also dependent on some. The number of items on which a phenomenon depends or does not depend is, I suggest, categorially irrelevant. What counts are the *kinds of relations* of dependence or independence. Thus in a visual experience, for example, countless stimuli (most directly, probably, neural discharges or the like) condition the experience in essentially the same way.

B. The Temporal Clue: Futurity as Thirdness

Stimuli come from the past, not the future; experiences depend only upon the past.[4] Peirce's own view of time (he speaks about "the indeterminate future," "the irrevocable past") implies this, as indeed does his whole basic philosophy.[5] Counting the number of past items on which an experience depends, or future items on which it does not depend, is idle. Why not an infinite or indefinite number in both cases?

But now we seem to have only two categories, Firstness or independence (of some other things), and Secondness or dependence (on some other things). And Peirce insists that there are three and only three categories in the set. Moreover, in this he is right. Sheer dependence (in relation to some) and sheer independence (in relation to some) do not exhaust the forms of dependence and independence. As we shall see, Peirce's own philosophy, more than any previous one, makes this clear. But the third category is not found by adding one more item on which a phenomenon depends. It is found by noting a third relation, in addition to simple dependence and simple independence, in which one phenomenon can stand to others (no matter how many others). This third relation is also exhibited or modeled by the process of counting, though not in the way Peirce has in mind. To say "first" is not to imply a definite, actual second, but it is to imply one or more *conceivable* further members of the class in question. We do not count wholly unclassified items.

78

Moreover, relations of an experience to other experiences or events are not adequately described by saying simply that particular past events are implied as conditions of the experience, while particular future events (Peirce being an indeterminist) are simply not implied. Were that the whole story, we could foresee nothing of the future and there would be no causal laws at all, however statistical or approximate. Future events in their full particularity are indeed unpredictable and matters of chance, as Peirce says, but the approximate *kinds* or *classes* of such events are predictable and determined. Like countable items, events later than a given event are not unclassified; they all share the relational property of having that event in their past as among their necessary conditions. Peirce rightly insists that, while the past is the "sum of accomplished [meaning fully particularized] facts," the future can only be conceived in more or less "general" terms, through laws or "real thirds." The past is what happened, the future is what (within certain limits of probability) *may* happen. Thus there really is a third relation among events beside or intermediate between simple dependence and simple independence, and this third relation is real possibility, probability, or law. Here precisely is where nominalists, whom Peirce likes to scold for this, are most wrong; they have no proper view of the future.

Before Bergson, Whitehead, and others, but helped by Aristotle, Peirce saw sharply and profoundly the categorial distinctiveness of futurity. "Time is a species of objective modality" is one expression of his insight. Given a particular past, all later events are, in their full concreteness, arbitrary additions to that past, but certain abstract, more or less general, features of these additions are settled in advance. Because of the reality of chance and (the same thing from a different aspect) the partial openness of the future, no event is a necessary successor to its predecessors, which are thus Firsts with respect to all their successors. But there is, nevertheless, a positive relation of an event to the intensive class of its possible successors.

Thirdness, then, is neither sheer dependence nor sheer independence but an intermediate relation: nondependence with respect to definite particulars, dependence with respect to more or less general outlines. Futurity, or real possibility (causality in the forward direction), contrasts alike to sheer necessity and pure possibility. Analogously, abductive arguments introduce hypotheses not strictly required by, but implying, the available evidence, somewhat as events are not required by but imply their predecessors, to which they are second. Deductive arguments require—are second to—the truth of their conclusions as events require their antecedent conditions.

79

It is time to ask how the necessity relating premises to conclusions differs from that relating experiences to predecessors. To say that the one necessity is logical, the other causal or ontological, labels but hardly analyzes the differences. The difference is in *degree of concreteness*. Premises are abstract, simplified outlines, and so are conclusions, while experiences are concrete and completely particularized. Hence, while our knowledge of a premise can be quite clear and adequate, so far as its relation to a deductive conclusion is concerned, this is never the case with our knowledge of experiences as requiring their necessary conditions. Concrete events, which actual states of experience are, exceed our powers of clear intuition. For example, we may seem, in an experience, to remember such and such a feature of previous experience, and if we remember it, then necessarily it occurred. But the line between remembering and imagining or guessing is more or less hazy for introspection. The same sort of difference occurs with perceiving and imagining, and many aspects of an experience are not definitely introspected at all, even incorrectly. Experience is incomparably richer than our understanding can clearly grasp. Leibniz and Democritus knew this; Peirce (also Whitehead) asserts it. (Husserl is uncritical here.)

If logical necessity is only between propositions, then causal or ontological necessity is not logical. However, propositions are significant only as elements in awareness. The ontological necessities of a state of awareness, a single experience, are those whose conscious detection more and more adequate introspection approaches as a limit. The Firstness of an experience is what ideal awareness, say God's awareness of the experience, would disclose as its independence of (some) other experiences; the Secondness is what ideal awareness would disclose as its dependence on (some) other experiences. The common aspect of logical and ontological modalities is, then, awareness or experience.

The foregoing is in partial agreement with Leibniz, according to whom each monad (individual sequence of experiences) mirrors or expresses every other, but only God can grasp the vast or infinite complexity involved. The Peircean version is: Each momentary experience expresses and has as necessary condition all previous moments but no subsequent ones. It also expresses certain limitations on its possible successors. Somewhat as Leibniz thought, only God can distinctly intuit the necessary (or the contingent-probabilistic, qualifiedly necessary) relationships.

Mahāyāna Buddhism (as in Fa Tsang in seventh-eighth century China) had a view like that of Leibniz with a similar (though possibly less complete) neglect of the asymmetry between strict dependence on past and partial dependence on future becoming. Delightfully relevant to our topic is Fa Tsang's declaration that, not only can there not be a second without a first, or a third without a second, there also cannot be a first without a second or a second without a third. He neglects the distinction between definite actual terms and indefinite or possible ones. Here Peirce is right and Mahāyana Buddhism is infected with sophistry. Hegel (in the *Logik*) and Blanshard repeat much the same error. They (this is most clear in Blanshard's case) miss, or unjustifiably deny, the openness of the future, modeled even in the abstract matter of counting.

It was always mysterious to me how Peirce arrived at the idea of generality simply by adding a third term to the relational situation. I now see that he did not actually arrive at it in this way. His real point was that one-way independence or Firstness is unqualifiedly so only with respect to future *details*. Although there are no particular successors that an event must have, it does have to have successors, and some *general* features of these are settled in advance. The independence of events from their successors does not mean that any sort of event could follow a given event, any more than we count totally unclassified entities. A world in which the future was completely unforeseeable and without even probabilistic or approximate laws is not what Peirce would have regarded as more than verbally conceivable. Its existence would be entirely "unknowable," a notion he (rightly) took to be a non-concept. It follows that there are indeed three forms of dependence: (1) the positive form, strict dependence; (2) the negative form, strict independence (both holding asymmetrically among definite particulars) and (3) dependence that leaves the final particularity open and can be stated only in more or less general terms.

With the above revisions Peirce's scheme achieves far greater clarity. His Secondness is then equivalent to Whitehead's prehension, or feeling of (previous) feeling. His Firstness is any such feeling as bound to be felt by suitable subsequent subjects as feelers. His Thirdness includes Whitehead's "symbolic reference" or, more generally, "mentality." Whitehead is in some respects clearer than Peirce, in others less clear.

The central role of asymmetrical dependence is better seen using Firstness and Secondness as models than Whitehead's language consistently suggests. On the other hand it was Whitehead who clearly asserted the asymmetry of perception and the perceived, the data of which are never strictly contemporary with, or influenced by, the perceiving. Whitehead thus brings out the common temporal structure of perception and memory. He was aided here by relativity physics. Whitehead also, thanks probably to quantum physics, avoids Peirce's confusion between continuity as order of possibility and continuity as (allegedly) the order of actual becoming. Thus the excesses of what Peirce called synechism are escaped, with the advantage that we can speak of events in the singular as well as in the plural, of definite actual entities that become rather than continuously change without ever achieving singular definiteness. Synechism confuses pure geometry with physics or psychology. Quantum physics supports a nonsynechistic ontology, but, as Von Wright (by implication) has shown, logical analysis should have led philosophers to reject synechism.[6] Here Peirce erred.

C. The Logical Clue: Relative Predicates

Peirce's phenomenology explicitly presupposed mathematics, including mathematical aspects of logic. Peirce was one of the chief inventors of the mathematico-logical theory of relations, or as he termed it, with penetration, the "logic of relatives." This superseded for him the old "subject-predicate logic," as Whitehead and Russell later called it. They regarded it as the source of some traditional errors. Whitehead spoke disparagingly of "the urge to say, 'S is P'." Not that there are no entities with properties that logically correspond to subjects with predicates. The point rather, as Peirce saw clearly, is that what describes an entity is not simply its predicates. Thus, S *is surprised.* The description is incomplete or somewhat indefinite— surprised by what? Or, S *perceives*—perceives what? We must divide predicates into those which seem complete in themselves and those requiring one or more particular entities beside the one being described. The essential predicates are relative ones and imply dependence or relativity. There are relations because there are relative or dependent things. An elementary proposition of the most important kind refers to more than one subject, if that means concrete entity; it is the predicate that is single.

Yet normally there is in a sense but one primary subject, the one being described; the other entities that the proposition refers to are not being described but are merely used in the description of the primary subject. In medieval logic the entities forming part of the description (e.g., the entities that a perceiving subject perceives) are termed objects, in contrast to the subject, of the relation. This usage, which seems to me appropriate, I very likely acquired from Peirce.

Anyway, he certainly was aware of the distinction it expresses. It means that the Aristotelian ideal of a subject that requires no other comparably concrete entities for its description but only repeatable forms, predicates, is not an ideal at all but a basic mistake. There can be no such subjects or substances. Predicates ostensibly complete in themselves as descriptive of the primary objects are pure Firsts, monadic predicates. They are mere possibilities, as Peirce says, abstractions from the actual properties of things, which are always (with respect to previous events) relativities, examples of Secondness, or (with respect to future events) of Firstness and Thirdness.

Russell took over the logic of relatives, largely from Peirce, and neatly missed its ontological point. For him the primary subjects or actualities are not relative but absolute. Logically they require only themselves and their private predicates. For Russell, as for Hume, reality consists in an array or succession of momentary states each of which is what it is in logical independence of the others. Thus Aristotle's supposed ideal is taken literally once more. True, there are relations among the states; the relations, however, are "among" or "between" states, belonging to none of them in themselves. Given two states, S^2 following S^1, it is only the pair that really has the relation of following. The pair thus is a third entity or pseudo-entity, and it alone is genuinely relational. S^1 and S^2 are logical absolutes. Each is first to the other, but there is no Secondness. Moreover, to pair items is to relate them. Thus in the Hume-Russell view relatedness is not accounted for ontologically, is given no proper place in reality.

Secondness, taken as primarily asymmetrical, excludes two contrary extreme doctrines: absolute pluralism, as in Hume, Russell, and many others, and absolute monism, as in Bradley or Sankara. Granted Secondness and Firstness, there must be many actualities, but each actuality is a unity of itself with others (its predecessors). There is no actuality inclusive once for all, since no actuality is the last, Thirdness being the requirement that there shall be *some* suitable successors to any given actuality. The noninclusiveness of actuality with respect to successors is Firstness. A first has no definite future second, but is destined to be seconded—as one may put it. There are no future seconds which definitely *will be;* what will be is that the "indeterminate" future will be progressively replaced by additional constituents of a partly new determinate or "irrevocable" past. Thus the three categories do imply ontological consequences. They really have the importance that Peirce ascribed to them.

It seems close to obvious that without Secondness there can be no understanding of what it is distinctively to be a caused or conditioned phenomenon, that without Firstness there can be no understanding of what it is distinctively to be a cause or condition, and that without a third and intermediate relation between sheer dependence and sheer independence there can be no understanding of time's arrow, the contrast between the already settled, decided past, and the not yet decided, needing-to-be-decided—yet not merely indeterminate—future. The past is "the sum of accomplished facts"; the future is the set of real or limited possibilities for future accomplishment, a determinable seeking further determination. The nominalistic error is not to see that futurity and generality are inseparable, as are pastness and particularity. Time is indeed "objective modality." Of the critics of nominalism I regard Peirce as second to none. But he should not have been so fascinated, almost hypnotized, by the idea of counting "One, two, three."

D. Peirce's Obsession with Continuity

The other basic source of confusion (already referred to) in Peirce was also a fascination, that with continuity. He expressed this feeling candidly, and one finds it also in Benjamin Peirce, his father. Neither father nor son—it appears—seriously considered the reasons for taking unqualified continuity as the order, not of actualities but only of possibilities, not of events but of thinkable abstractions. Charles (and doubtless Benjamin, too) did see that possibilities form continua, thus all possible hues and shades of color, or all possible sizes or shapes. But actual colors or sizes or shapes are a selection, involving discontinuities. All the animals that have lived on earth, being finite in number, could not form a continuum of size, shape, color, or anything else. Only all thinkable creatures, being infinite or indefinite in number, may be conceived as forming continua with respect to various properties. Yet, although Peirce saw how possibility and continuity belong together, he wanted actuality also to be continuous. This was his "synechism." He held that when we experience first red and then blue we pass through a continuum of intermediate colors, each present for an infinitesimal time.

Peirce rationalized his overindulgence in the admiration of continuity by the specious argument: "Since continuity is a totality of possibilities, we should approach phenomena with the hypothesis that they are continuous, since in that way we avoid excluding anything a priori." Not so. We are excluding any and every one of the infinite forms of possible discontinuity—in spite of the a priori truth, which Peirce himself made clear, that continuity is the order of possibilities, a meaningless truth if it is also the order of actualities. Our initial hypothesis should be that actuality is discrete, but with our minds open among the unlimited, mutually incompatible, possibilities for discontinuity. The totality of ways in which a continuum of possibility can be broken up into discrete actualities—what is that but the continuum over again? So I think Peirce really missed the target here.

The consequences of his uncritical love for continuity were substantial and not fortunate. It immediately meant that though he had an ontology of relations in the idea of relative actualities, he lacked any definite terms or subjects for the relations. There seems to be a succession of experiences, but (if the succession is a continuum) there are no single experiences. In any fraction of a second, however small, we have an experience, but this experience is not really "an" experience, since it has parts, each of which is an experience. In any fraction of a second, Peirce held, we have infinitely many successive experiences. Hence his denial of direct intuition (or what Whitehead calls prehension).[7] Some have praised this Peircean doctrine. I think it was a mess. There are, to be sure, no conscious intuitions both entirely distinct and infallible; but there are direct intuitions. They are the key to relations of dependency or secondness and to all causality.

Another consequence was that, though Peirce talked about the "logic of events," and saw what physicists have been seeing lately; that science deals with relations of events, not (in last analysis) with relations of things or persons, he could not, in the continuum of becoming which he posited, give meaning to the idea of a definite single event. Hence he failed to clearly transcend the old Aristotelian pattern of reality as a set of things and persons, individuals, taken as ultimate terms of analysis. Even James came closer to anticipating our present recognition of quanta, objectively single happenings. Yet it was Peirce who wanted to guide the future development of physics. That he never dreamt of something like quantum theory is a defeat for him. He did anticipate the idea of indeterminacy, or real possibilities, and of laws as statistical. But the idea of discreteness that we tend now to see as essential (though Einstein struggled against it to the end) did not occur to him, except that he once admitted (perhaps thinking of James's "drops of experience") that our experiencing *may* occur in discrete units, saying only that we do not know this to be so.

E. Peirce on Individuals

Peirce did say that individuals can hardly be regarded as entirely definite. After all, each moment they receive new determinations not prescribed by causal laws and initial conditions. The secret lesson of Leibniz's theory of genetic identity, an open secret since Whitehead, is that only the past (not the future) careers of individuals are wholly definite. Aristotle knew this, Leibniz denied it and thereby burdened his doctrine with serious paradoxes, of which his idea of pre-established harmony was one. Peirce agreed with Aristotle, not Leibniz, but like Aristotle he failed to clearly draw the conclusion, that each moment there is a new determinate actuality, the individual-now. It is a continuation of the individual career as it has previously been, but, since the less cannot contain the more, the indeterminate the determinate, if we are looking for concrete definite unitary wholes of reality, we should recognize that the individual-now is always a new such whole. The Buddhists, whom Peirce admired, saw this. But the assertion of the continuity of becoming makes it impossible to conceive definite single wholes in the succession of such wholes constituting an individual career.

I shall never forget what Bochenski once said to me, apropos the thesis that "reality consists of events": "Aristotle said so. He did not dot all the i's and cross all the t's, but. . . ." So when I encounter writers who defend Aristotelian substances against Whitehead, who did dot the i's and cross the t's, I am not immensely impressed. They all fail to see what Bochenski did see, that Whitehead's "societies" are nicely tailored to do what "substance" was primarily intended to do, and that is to furnish identifiable features of reality sufficiently definite for ordinary purposes but not necessarily so for science or metaphysics. To suppose them entirely definite is to commit oneself implicitly to the paradoxes of Leibnizian laws of succession unique to each individual and equally determinate for past and future.

How right Bochenski was, in comparison to extreme opponents of Whitehead who yet appeal to Aristotle, may be seen by considering how Aristotle explained the identity of an individual through change as the actualization of potentialities inherent in the individual all along. Aristotle's point is translatable into process terms. Of course an individual event-sequence or career, once begun, has the potentiality for its later prolongations. But the actualization of a potency is not contained in the potency; rather the potency is contained in the actualization. The present is more than the past; there is a new whole of determinations. This is the creationist view of reality. Events are capable of being superseded by what is more than they are. An infant "self" does not contain the adult phases of "itself." There is a numerically new concrete reality with each new determination.

Andrew Reck (in an unpublished talk) complained that such a view makes things much too fragile. The reply is that it leaves them exactly as fragile as they are and not a whit more. All individuals are destructible (except God), for all Reck can show; and if he wonders why they last as long and well as they do, I remind him that calling something a "substance" tells us nothing as to what enables it, for a limited time, to maintain the "defining characteristic" of its career. The explanation of causal stability, of which individual endurance is only a special case, by self-identity is merely verbal, since the criterion for being a substance is precisely the kind of causal stability in question. The explanation is circular, as Buddhism realized long ago.

That self-identity is a special case of causality is obvious enough; for causal influence relates members of two careers as truly as members of one and the same career. Buddhism generalized the problem of causality better than Aristotle did and came much closer to modern physics in this respect. Process philosophy has a definite theory of causality, not adequately taken into account by some critics.[8]

As for Peirce, his admiration for Aristotle was extreme ("by many lengths the greatest intellect"). Coupled with his fondness for continuity, it may have helped to prevent him from dotting the i's and crossing the t's, from anticipating quanta and process metaphysics. Yet his three categories, freed of one-sided synechism and a kind of numerology, harmonize happily with those twentieth-century doctrines. I agree with several writers who have said that Peirce could have been an even better thinker had he not spent so much of his life in solitude, far from colleagues and students who could have forced him to see the limits of certain of his convictions. As it was, he did wonderfully well. Besides many other achievements he started ontology on the track indicated as the right one by the logic of relatives. Russell and many other famous logicians never got on that track at all.

F. Application to the Theory of Signs

Peirce's uses of his categories in the theory of signs are not diminished in value by the proposed revisions. *Indices* are signs insofar as dependent upon, second to, their objects, hence yielding knowledge of the latters' existence. *Icons* are signs insofar as they are independent of, or first with respect to, their objects. They give knowledge not of existence but of quality of more or less definite possibility, whether or not any other instance than the sign of the quality exists. By what they are, simply in themselves, they stand for whatever may or could resemble them. *Symbols* are signs insofar as they give information through some probability, law, rule, convention, or habit—some real Third—governing behavior. Symbols are terms, propositions, or arguments. Terms—for example, 'human'—are symbols standing for what there may be, thus analogous to icons; propositions are symbols, analogous to indices, standing for what there actually is; and arguments stand for certain relations of symbolized meanings and thus are symbolic on a higher level. Terms must be understood through perceived or imagined icons, and propositions through both icons and indices. A photograph with a proper name is a "dicisign," a proposition saying what a certain existing person, place, or thing looks like. An argument is a proposition relating propositions. All signs as such are more than merely iconic or indexical, since neither similarity nor dependence suffices to make an object a sign; some interpreter of the object must so use or intend it, and this requires *purpose*, of which reference to the future as partially indeterminate is an essential aspect.

It appears that my tinkering with the three categories has not deprived them of their relevance. Another confirmation of my revision is that it strengthens Peirce's use of categories to test philosophies. Hume, Berkeley, and Russell lack genuine Secondness and indeed so does Hegel, who also has no really clear form of Firstness. Extreme nominalism has no clear distinctions among Firstness, Secondness, and Thirdness; extreme monism also lacks such distinctions. Classical determinism makes causal requirement symmetrical, analogous to a logic limiting implication or logical dependence to equivalence. Many a philosophical error is avoided if the distinctiveness and ultimacy of the three modes of dependence are adequately realized. Peirce pointed the way to a great discovery without altogether arriving at it.

Peirce called the inquiry which led to his categorial theory phaneroscopy, also phenomenology. His use of the second term did not, so far as I know, precede his reading of Husserl and may have been suggested by this reading. But the idea and practice of basing all philosophy on an inquiry into the given, the phenomena, was Peirce's before it was Husserl's.

G. God and the Categories

Peirce inherited a tradition which sought to exalt deity by what was called "the negative way," by denying to God various adjectives applicable generally to the creatures, such as finitude, contingency, dependence, change, and the like. Peirce saw difficulties with some aspects of this procedure. He did object to the idea of a divine purpose completely immutable and determinative of the changing details of the world. He was critical of the idea of changeless divine knowledge of all change. He expressed skepticism of "the latest patent absolute" and had more faith in a less pretentious, vague notion of divinity the mere contemplation of whom inspires worship. In spite of all reservations, however, he was still somewhat under the spell of the medieval tradition in thinking about God. Thus he employs the term "necessary being" in what, for neoclassical metaphysics, seems a rather uncritical fashion, as though the denial of contingency or dependence to deity can safely be taken as absolute or unqualified. Similarly, he denies the applicability of "exists" to God, since this term implies dependence, interaction with other existents. And so the category of Secondness has no divine or eminent form. But without Secondness, Thirdness is unintelligible, and so, after all, is Firstness. The three categories form a system, the minimal content of any concrete actuality.

In one passage Peirce seems to apply the three categories to God. God before all creation is First, during creation is Second, and as the infinitely remote completion of creation is Third. The world is a poem whose poet is God. (The same metaphor is found in Whitehead.) But Peirce's tychism, or spontaneity of feeling, implies that the words of this poem to some extent determine themselves, so that the better analogy is of a play whose actors, rather than the playwright, give the final form to the details of the performance. (This analogy, too, is in Whitehead.) None of this is really intelligible unless all three categories apply to deity as well as to creatures. So God can exist as well as having mere being. Peirce's denial of divine "existence" anticipates Tillich's similar denial; and in both cases the influence of classical theism with its one-sided exaltation of independence, necessity, eternity, and being at the expense of responsiveness or sensitivity, free creativity, becoming, and existence, is at work. God is both being itself in its eternal aspect, or as the ultimate universal, and the concrete, individual actuality which is in perpetual further creation and becoming as the creatures exercise their freedom.

Deity is the form of forms, the ultimate universal, and the individual of individuals, the individual with strictly universal functions, relevant everywhere and to which every thing is relevant, changing with all change, permanent with all that is permanent. This is not Hegel's concrete universal, if I understand that (to me) confused idea, but it does what Hegel was attempting to do. There must be eminent or divine Firstness, Secondness, and Thirdness. Only in this way can Peirce's system really complete itself. The playwright must enjoy, and thus be influenced by, the actor's performance, rather than merely by the play as planned in the divine thought. That is a mere outline compared to the beauty of the concrete creation.

Finally, I claim that my revision of Peirce's categories makes them more, rather than less, Peircean. For they really do, as revised, sum up Peirce's contributions. They imply or express his tychism and superb insights into the difference between past and future and into the primacy of relations of dependence and independence, his synechistic theory of possibility (without blurring the distinction between possible and actual); they clarify and strengthen his somewhat vague and wavering theology; they do no harm to his objective idealism or psychicalism; they agree with his form of realism of universals and preserve its subtle distinction from Whitehead's doctrine of eternal objects, so far as I understand that difficult doctrine. If by trying for fifty years I have succeeded in improving somewhat the basic outlines of his system, standing on the shoulders of Whitehead to look down slightly on Peirce's thinking, and in seeing a few things not visible to Whitehead, standing on the shoulders of Peirce, this only shows the value of studying these two thinkers of rare knowledge and wisdom.

Notes

1. "The Relativity of Nonrelativity: Some Reflections on Firstness," in *Studies in the Philosophy of Charles Sanders Peirce*, ed. Philip P. Wiener and Frederic H. Young. (Cambridge, Mass.: Harvard University Press, 1952), pp. 215–224; "Charles Peirce's 'One Contribution to Philosophy' and His Most Serious Mistake," *Op. cit.*, Second Series, ed. Edward G. Moore and Richard S. Robin. (Amherst: University of Massachusetts Press, 1964), pp. 455–474.

2. On the symmetry or nonsymmetry of Secondness, see *The Collected Papers of Charles Sanders Peirce* (hereafter CP), ed. Charles Hartshorne, Paul Weiss, and A. W. Burks. (Cambridge, Mass.: Harvard University Press, 1931, 1934, 1958), paragraphs 1.322, 324, 327; 5.45; 7.531; 8.330.

3. For Peirce's attempts to illustrate his definition of Firstness as zero dependence on anything else, see CP, 1.302–313, 357; 5.44.

4. According to some physicists, quantum theory implies that events may be dependent upon particular future events, but this interpretation of quantum experiments my metaphysics forces me to reject. See John Archibald Wheeler, "Genesis and Observership," in *Proceedings, University of Western Ontario Series in the Philosophy of Science,* ed. Robert Butts and Jaakko Hintikka. (Dordrecht and Boston: Reidel Publishing Co., 1977). There is also a problem about contemporary events, which relativity physics takes to be mutually independent, whereas quantum theory casts serious doubt upon this. See my essay "Bell's Theorem and Stapp's Revised View of Space-Time." Also essays by Henry P. Stapp and Wm. B. Jones in *Process Studies* 7.3 (Fall 1977).

5. For Peirce's view of futurity, see CP, 2.86; 5.458–461.

6. G. H. von Wright, *Time, Change, and Contradiction* (The Twenty-second Eddington Memorial Lecture, delivered 1968). Cambridge: Cambridge University Press, 1969).

7. For Peirce's denial of direct intuition, see CP, 5.258–263, 265; 7.536, 674–675.

8. See my "Creativity and the Deductive Logic of Causality," *Review of Metaphysics* 27, 1 (Sept. 1973): 62–74.

CHAPTER 8

The Down-to-Earth
Activism of John Dewey

Probably the most influential (in his own time at least) of the philosophers dealt with in this book was one of those who were least closely associated with Harvard University. He was also, in his early phase, the one most influenced by Hegel. It has been said of Dewey (1859–1952) that he lacked a sense of form and a sense of tragedy. The first lack is perhaps shown by his somewhat unappealing style and his deficient appreciation of mathematics and symbolic logic, the second by his failure to face squarely the basic evils and dangers of human existence, especially war and the population-pollution problem (both evils indefinitely aggravated, rather than alleviated, by technology and modern hygiene). Also, as Heidegger noted (when asked how he differed from Dewey), there is Dewey's neglect of death, of our mortality. James, Peirce, and Whitehead are very different and had little to learn from Heidegger on that score.

It is difficult, perhaps impossible, to deal with John Dewey in the course of this inquiry without doing him injustice. For Dewey was little interested in theoretical problems, except so far as they seemed relevant to the theory of practice. In Aristotelian terms, "practical sciences" were Dewey's concern. Not what are mind and matter, but what can we best do with our minds and bodies, was the question. "Doing" here included scientific investigation, especially in psychology and the social sciences. His form of behaviorism was a relatively astute and subtle affair. And of course no one made more important contributions to educational theory. That these contributions had certain unfortunate effects some of us are convinced, but anyone who denies that they had also some good effects knows little of the history of education.

Although they were scarcely his primary concern, Dewey gave some consideration to the five speculative problems listed in chapter 1. To the first, or theistic, problem, his direct contribution was essentially negative or critical. He attacked with a good deal of effect the notion that loyalty to an ideal either requires, or is even (in strict logic) compatible with, the belief that the ideal is exhaustively actualized in an eternal and immutable deity. The whole point of an ideal, he reminds us, is that it defines possible, but not wholly actual, achievement. If God actualizes all possible value without our efforts, then He cannot represent the ideal for our striving. Our poor second best would by definition add nothing to the perfection already and eternally in being. This means, Dewey thought, that we must forget about God so conceived if we are to have a relevant and genuine ideal for our conduct.

On a broad front, and at times with great eloquence, Dewey argues that actual value, actual achievement, is by its very meaning temporal, not eternal. It implies genuine risks and uncertainties, open possibilities rather than predestined outcomes. The soothing influence of terms like "eternal" derives from the contrast they imply with the conflicts and hazards of the temporal process.[1]

Taken by itself, eternity would be wholly empty. I regard this as profoundly true. Mere fixed being is (as Nietzsche said) only an abstraction. Disregard all differences between situations, and what is left is identity; disregard all novelties, and what is left is the primordial and everlasting, the eternal. The eternal perfection that many have worshiped as God is but a contrast effect, an abstract residuum illegitimately taken for a superior version of the concrete fullness of existence. Dewey expresses this thought in a rich variety of ways. The tradition of condescension toward becoming, finitude, and relativity which constitutes what I call "classical" metaphysics or theology is here given a critical examination such as it has not often received.

What Dewey never, or almost never, seems to suspect is that another metaphysical tradition, the neoclassical, which has been growing up for some centuries, is free from the condescension in question but yet is definitely theistic. Instead of deifying being or eternity, this other tradition speaks of a divine becoming and a divine finitude or relativity. This view was represented in Barnard College, in Dewey's own institution, Columbia University, by W. P. Montague. I asked Montague once if Dewey had ever paid him the compliment of careful criticism. His reply was, "I think it is fair to say that he has not." This is also my impression from Dewey's writings. If a

93

scientist were, in so glaring a fashion, to neglect colleagues who differed from him, he would be judged negligent. But such, alas, is philosophy.

Dewey's complaint that those who have not deified being have deified becoming instead may be pertinent enough, at least to the first of his two examples, Hegel and Bergson. But it is less so to Montague, to the much earlier Socinians, or Lequier, Whitehead, and some other neoclassical metaphysicians. These have asserted a divine being and a divine becoming, but not the divinity of either being or becoming as such or in opposition to the other. Nor have they sought to make change "universal, regular, sure." For Whitehead, change is merely the succession of events in some sequence exhibiting a persistent character. The character itself, in so far, does not change, nor do the events change; they merely become. But there is no absolute and inevitable regularity in change—on the contrary, "disorder is as real as order."

Dewey seems to be trying to force the theist into a dilemma: either mere being, eternal self-sufficiency, or mere becoming or change, is God. But the division is not exhaustive. In assuming that it is, Dewey is exhibiting his bias, his will to rule out belief in God, if not by one means, then by another.

Neoclassical metaphysics does not substitute "prescription" for "description," or mere metaphysical "glorification" for the "toilsome labor of understanding and control." This metaphysics does not explain away risk or opportunity; rather, it tries to show why the risks and opportunities for action that confront us are at least significant, even in view of all the future, including our death and the presumptive death of the human species. This is the only "security" it asks for, security against the meaningless optimism or the black pessimism that James rightly judged pragmatically null.

If we grant to Dewey that eternity is only an abstraction, it does not follow, and he realizes it does not, that immortality is equally abstract. That something never becomes is a negative trait of the something, and negation is the way to the abstract. But that the something endures forever is a positive idea. If the something endures unchanged, this indeed is relatively abstract, since it means that the something does not acquire anything from the incoming novelties. But the question is, "Can something which has become real subsequently become unreal? " Can what becomes, afterwards de-become or un-become? Is there a kind of destruction correlative to creation? If so, process seems futile. We achieve a certain quality of life, for a time, but then our life turns into death. What has really been accomplished? Put in another way, each of us is a finite stretch of space-time process, and this stretch is a fraction indefinitely small of the totality, since the denominator of the fraction is as large as you please.

At this point Dewey admits the relevance of the concept of infinity. He offers a solution: We are not simply finite realities in an infinite whole; we are in a sense infinite elements in that whole. For each of our acts sets up an endless chain of consequences. This is a brilliant thought. But there is one flaw. The beginning of the chain is a human act or experience, and this has its intrinsic value or satisfaction. However, if life is a mere emergent (and Dewey holds this view) from insentient matter, and if the duration of our species is not to be infinite in time (and why should it be supposed thus infinite?), what assurance is there that all the later links in the infinite chains of causes and effects which we initiate will involve any *value* whatever? So, in terms of value, which is all that matters, human achievement may after all be purely finite, apart from some assumption that Dewey fails to specify. Here Dewey gives up. The issue has become too theoretical to hold his interest. Can he blame those of us whose interest persists? At what point should a human being renounce the human privilege of thought?

Dewey nobly declares that one should think of oneself as contributing "to the whole," rather than just living for oneself and one's fellows. But he never inquires what sort of whole could intelligibly be thought of as profiting from our contributions. Had he done so, he might have arrived at neoclassical theism. Indeed, I know not what other genuinely appropriate solution to the problem is possible. Dewey's own suggestion for interpreting "God," a suggestion confined to one book, *A Common Faith*, is that God is the universe in whatever aspect it offers ideals and enables us to realize them. The suggestion is not wrong; it is only so vague as to constitute for those metaphysically inclined the merest starting-point, not the outcome, of religious inquiry.

Concerning freedom, Dewey does conceive the human being as creative in a sense transcending complete causal determinacy.[2] Moreover, he generalizes the idea of situations with indeterminate outcomes. This is, he holds, a universal or metaphysical trait of existence as such. In human life this pervasive indeterminacy is maximal, for intelligence is operative only where outcomes are far from inevitable. Action wholly according to habit or past conditioning is not consciously thought about at all. The function of causal prediction is not to foretell the actual future but to make conditional predictions as to probable or approximate outcomes of various responses to situations. There can be such predictions, for indeterminacy is a matter of degree, and much of the time human action is roughly inevitable, while even more nearly inevitable are the actions of subhuman creatures.

Dewey was forever deriding the "spectator" view of knowing. So far as the future is concerned, the ridicule was deserved. The future is for us to make, not to behold coming toward us. Science is creative power above all, rather than a mirroring of a world as it once for all is and will be. Determinism is a purely spectatorial view of reality, and this, as Dewey saw, is enough to condemn it. But he held a fine balance here; he knew the power of habit and the automatic in life and the futility of trying to do everything by sheer will power, taken as deciding freely. Would that his followers were all as clear concerning both sides of this contrast as he was!

As to mind and matter, Dewey really has no fresh insight to offer. He agrees with James's analysis of thought as intervening between perception and action and deriving its meaning from this mediatory role. Hence the validity of behaviorism as a method. Not a little of Ryle's *Concept of Mind* could be derived from Dewey's working out of this thought. Nor would all the differences be to the advantage of Ryle. But still, the ultimate theoretical question is left as it was.

Dewey says there is no need to admit a dualism of two substances, mental and physical, since the reality consists, in both cases, of events. Certain stabilities or causal patterns in events are what we refer to by "matter," and certain other patterns, by "mind." But is feeling a mere pattern in something else? Or is an entire experient occasion (to use Whitehead's phrase) a unity of feeling? We have events whose overall quality seems to be that of a kind of feeling; we have, it is supposed, events whose unity is not that of feeling but—what? A bit of matter? Does that explain anything? Dewey objects to Whitehead's contention that all events feel. The ground for his objection is never clearly stated.[3] I once wrote him about this; his answer was as opaque as his other remarks on this subject have always been for me. If some events are experiences or feelings and some are simply insentient, then we have dualism, say what you will. Two kinds of becoming (or, as we will see in a later section, of quality) replace ordinary dualism's two kinds of substance, that is all. On the issue, Dewey differed from Peirce as Roy Wood Sellars and his son Wilfrid have from Whitehead.

If Dewey was justified in generalizing indeterminacy or precariousness into a "metaphysical" universal, why is it less legitimate to do the same for feeling? The total absence of indeterminacy or creativity, like the total absence of feeling, could not posssibly be observed; and any reason favoring the universalizing of one will have its parallel for the other. Dewey could not see this, partly, I suppose, because of his notion that it is "romanticism," the substituting of metaphysical glorification for honest study and effort to control, to view nature as intrinsically valuable or beautiful. Yet to attribute feeling in lowly forms to elementary constituents of nature is not to say anything about how rich or harmonious these feelings may be, or to offer any guarantee that particular events will turn out according to our wishes or needs. It does not imply that "whatever is is right." Indeed, if to recognize the universality of feeling is romantic, so is Dewey's tenet of the universality of indeterminacy. Accordingly, many of Dewey's admirers refuse to make this assumption. But the grounds for both negations are illegitimate. There is no a priori necessity that absolute noncreativity, or absolute deadness and intrinsic valuelessness, must characterize some parts of nature, any more than there can ever be empirical evidence of these negative absolutes. Hence they serve no purpose other than that of shutting off inquiry in a certain direction. I suggest that this, too, is not a matter Dewey thought out, but one that did not interest him as a subject of inquiry.

Concerning the status of "things" versus events, Dewey also appears to have wavered and not thought the problem through. He speaks of events as the basic realities, but then he also speaks of organisms and environments, and "transactions" or interactions between them, as basic. This is the language of things or enduring substances. Once more, pure theory is subordinated to more practical or methodological concerns.

As to empiricism, Dewey holds that "metaphysical" universality is attainable but only by the "denotative" method. We may point out what is pervasive in experience. But the question is unavoidable: Pervasive in experience we happen to have had or noticed, or in all possible or conceivable experience? The sharp criterion of "empirical," namely, conceivably falsifiable by observation, is not applied. Therefore, I think that one cannot claim that Dewey has dealt adequately with this fifth problem discussed in chapter 1.

On the whole, the ontological content of Dewey is to be found in James and Peirce (but not vice versa). Dewey's achievement is to have formulated a working philosophy for modern living in a world of science and technology, drawing upon a minimum of speculative or religious commitment but yet embodying wise and noble attitudes.

In this, his equal is not readily to be found. I can think of no adequate European counterpart. But, concerning highly theoretical issues of philosophy, he used the discoveries of others rather than making any of his own. Or, if he did discover something, it was in his wonderfully lucid criticisms of the depreciation of change, uncertainty, and conflict, without which (I believe this as much as he did) there could be no value whatever.

Dewey did strike some shrewd blows at the classical metaphysical bias, but his ignorance or lack of understanding of neoclassical metaphysics makes his arguments against theism as such altogether inconclusive. He never isolated the real issue, which is not whether there is a purely self-sufficient and nonreactive, once-for-all perfect and complete being, but whether there is a primordially and everlastingly reactive being, perfect not in its concrete content (for a final perfection in that sense is meaningless) but perfect in its generic mode of receiving from and making possible contributions to the world process. Against this view Dewey's objections are irrelevant. Not even his complaint that theologians have never seriously considered, much less satisfactorily dealt with, the discrepancy between the evils in the world and the perfect power and goodness attributed to deity is justified against the neoclassical view. For in that view, the perfection of the divine reactions to the world does not imply that what happens in the world is fully determined by God's decisions. No God that this philosophy admits as conceivable could simply determine a world. All concrete reality, even divine, must be reactive, and one cannot react simply to one's own decisions. Not the particular evils of the world need to be philosophically explained, for they arise from the aspects of chance inherent in creaturely creativity, but only the scope of the risks of evil.

Why, for instance, was our species not made a little less creative so that we could not have attained quite such dangerous powers as our species now has? But remember, this species is partly made what it now is by its past members and they by members of earlier species, all having some freedom. Are we in a position to judge how far the opportunities made possible by the human type of freedom are worth the risks inherent in it? If we could make such judgments, would we not be as wise as God? This is very different from saying that God deliberately chose our sufferings for us, for reasons we cannot guess. Instead, the reasoning is, God refrained from setting laws of nature, or from acting miraculously in setting aside these laws now and then, so as to limit our freedom more narrowly than it has actually been, because (presumably) the terrible risks are not too high a price for the vast opportunities inherent in that freedom. In a vague way we can understand this. What we cannot even vaguely understand is a benevolent tyrant deliberately dealing out blows and rewards to "creatures" (really nonentities) wholly without freedom in the creative sense. If our theory is not a solution to the problem of evil, there is nothing in Dewey's writings to show why it is not. Yet the theory existed in his lifetime, and in several representatives. It had partial anticipations in the seventeenth, eighteenth, and nineteenth centuries, though these anticipations are scarcely to be found in histories, encyclopedias, or textbooks, such being the ignorance of the learned in our difficult civilization.

In one respect Dewey continues the tradition begun by Edwards, continued by Emerson and Peirce, and brought to a remarkable fruition by Whitehead. This is the recognition of the absolutely basic relevance of aesthetic principles. Intrinsic values are the values of experiences themselves. Utilitarian and moral values are derivatives from, or special forms of, aesthetic values, the values of experiences as such. We live partly for the sake of the future. Any pragmatist is aware of that. But, as Dewey shrewdly remarks, our interest in the future also contributes value to our present experience. It will not do to simply postpone value to the not-yet. Dewey sees that aesthetic principles are far broader than those directly connected with the fine arts. In all living there is immediate satisfaction and dissatisfaction, harmony, discord, relief from (or falling into) boredom, humor (but Dewey is hardly strong on this aspect)—all related to the values that artists are trying to create.

In his rejection of traditional religious ethics, Dewey retains the ideal of love (partly expressed as "shared experiences"); but for the hoary virtue of "obedience to God" he substitutes such principles as, "Use your (creative) freedom so as to increase that freedom" and "Aim at the 'release of human capacities'." My own pious mother, knowing nothing, I believe, of Dewey, used to praise this or that individual she knew by saying, "So and so has *developed*." T. V. Smith once wrote an article in the Deweyan spirit for the *Ladies Home Journal* entitled, "Be Always on the Grow." In Europe Nikolai Berdyaev (in his *Destiny of Man*) gave a religious version by stating as his categorical imperative, "Be creative and foster creativity in others," understanding that God is supreme creativity (and by no means an unmoved mover) and that individual creativity can "enrich the divine life itself." But never did Dewey clearly acknowledge the existence of this transformed theism.

The risks of our thinking-animal existence derive partly from two aspects of animal existence in general: the evolutionary origins of species in previous species and the development of adults from infants. One may verbally speculate that animals could conceivably be created in a nonevolutionary way and adults be produced immediately from parents. But this is mere speculation and may not express any genuine insight into ultimate conceptual possibilities. I incline to think that in its most abstract or general terms evolution is the only way there could be life and that adulthood on a conscious (but noncosmic, nondivine) level requires naive, scarcely conscious immature phases.

Consider the latter aspect, the necessity of a preconscious or naive phase in the life of a vigorously thinking creature. Whether or not a child develops a healthy emotional life depends greatly on how it was treated when its emotions were not under control from the child's own ethical ideals or rational rules, because it was not yet able to form such ideals or grasp such rules. This provides a partial modern scientific equivalent of "original sin," and while it is not exactly the same idea, it has perhaps equally tragic implications. With bad or bungling parents, we will have defective children and thence again defective adults as parents and teachers. With good parents and teachers we can have a probability of good infants, and so eventually (always with the risks of freedom) further good parents and teachers. Thus better education (especially of infants and small children) is the remedy for society's ills—if only we can conjure up or somehow create the educators. But the primary conjuring must be emotional and spiritual, not just intellectual, or through mere inquiry. The whole person must, by human or divine grace, be transformed—as it were, born again. This is where religion comes in.

Dewey sees the need, but yet he does not see it. For to really see it is to be unable to take the theoretical problems of religion as lightly and to offer solutions as casual and neglectful of other men's reflections as is done by Dewey and many of his followers. The tragic dangers of life, and the religious resources to meet them, are alike underestimated.

It is, I suggest, no accident that topics almost ignored in Dewey's writings are death, war, and the Malthusian population problem, expanded to take pollution into account. For these are the really ugly questions for a modern philosopher. No honest practical solution exists for the first, but only a metaphysical interpretation; and the practical solutions for the others are so monstrously difficult even to imagine that all the faith, good will, and intelligence we have must be mustered if we are to find them. Religious resources cannot safely be left out of the reckoning. Nor does Dewey's *Common Faith* begin to sum up those resources. For that we must look elsewhere.

Whatever his defects, for those without a taste for metaphysics and with a strong bias against traditional religion, Dewey does offer a relatively sane and enlightened view of human existence in the age of science. I wonder if in this respect he is equaled anywhere. He pointed out that we entertain goals for the future not merely for the sake of future results, but also to give content to the present. Children do not grow in wisdom merely for the sake of being some day wise adults; any interest they have in adult possibilities is first of all an enrichment of their lives in the childish present. The way to learn to live is to live. Life is always partly for its own sake as it goes along. This is no hectic practicalism, but is akin to an ancient wisdom, "Sufficient unto the day is the evil (and the good) thereof." Dewey is rich in such insights into life's meaning. But he is chiefly a philosopher of middle-sized ideas, not of the largest or most strictly universal ones. He is not quite a philosopher's philosopher. And he tends to starve the religious sense of his followers and not fully to prepare them to see life steadily and see it whole, with its greatest risks and its noblest opportunities.

In some respects the nearest anticipator of Dewey in Europe is Nietzsche. There is in that unhappy thinker a similar disillusionment with traditional ethics and religion and a serious attempt to suggest new values. But Dewey is free from the German writer's hatred of (or, if you prefer, inadequate respect for) women. He profits by the critical view of classical determinism initiated by the late nineteenth and early twentieth century thinkers (Boutroux, Lotze, Fechner, Bergson, Peirce, James, and others) and is able to avoid antiquated monstrosities like the "eternal recurrence." He is also closer to science and sees more clearly the importance of technology in changing the conditions of life and posing new ethical challenges. Here there is some analogy with Marx. Dewey, too, wanted to "change the world." He is, so far as this is possible without belief in divine love, a wise and sane counselor of struggling humanity.

Notes

1. See *The Quest for Certainty* (New York: Minton Balch, 1929) chapter 2. Also p. 39. See, too, the essays "Time and Individuality," and "The Subject Matter of Metaphysics," both reprinted in *On Experience, Nature, and*

Freedom, ed. R. J. Bernstein (Indianapolis: Bobbs-Merrill Co., 1960), chapters 10 and 11. Dewey's most elaborate dealing with religion is in *A Common Faith.* Another characteristic discussion is the essay "The Precarious and the Stable," chapter 2 of *Experience and Nature* (LaSalle, Il.: Open Court, 1923, 1929).

2. See *The Quest for Certainty,* pp. 248–249.

3. See below, chapter 21 for another discussion of this issue. Dewey's essay, "Peirce's Theory of Quality," (*Experience, Nature, and Freedom,* chapter 9) has some relevance here. Dewey takes Peirce to distinguish between quality as Firstness or pure "immediacy" (what something is apart from relations to other things) and quality of feeling. "A feeling is of some immediate quality that is present as *experience.*" Dewey recognizes Peirce's inclination to panpsychism, but holds that this is not entailed by the logical analysis central to Peirce's doctrine of categories. Thus he quotes Peirce as proposing his psychicalism as "a guess." I had not noticed this remark in Peirce. I think it an extreme concession scarcely representative of his basic attitude. And I do not really see how, considering that when any quality is present in our experience it becomes a feeling, we can give meaning to the notion of quality as not that of a feeling. Consider the pain quality of some sensations, or the pleasure quality of some others. What would these be if not feeling qualities and not present in any experience, human or otherwise?

CHAPTER 9

Whitehead's Revolutionary
Concept of Prehension

A. Prehension and Peirce's Secondness

The philosophy of Alfred North Whitehead (1861–1947) is not (at least among philosophers) the most widely popular one of our time. But then, metaphysics, or, as he sometimes called it, speculative philosophy, is also not especially popular. However, interest in this type of metaphysics seems to be slowly but steadily increasing. To me it is really obvious that as metaphysician Whitehead has in this century had no superior, and I question if there has been even a close competitor. Moreover, the most plausible candidates, for example, Peirce (at the beginning of the century) or James, Bergson, S. Alexander, Heidegger (who claimed to have made metaphysics obsolete), or, among the living, Paul Weiss and John Findlay, have all had positions with considerable similarity to Whitehead's. What is called process philosophy (or something significantly like it) is found, with various distortions or qualifications, in all these writers; but, unless I am badly mistaken, none of them equals Whitehead in conceptual clarity and relevance to our total intellectual situation.

My own philosophy (expounded in my doctoral dissertation of 1923) before I had heard Whitehead lecture or knew any writing of his except *The Concept of Nature* and his and Russell's *Principia Mathematica*, I now see as a more or less systematized and energetically defended, but on the whole somewhat naive and best forgotten, form of process philosophy. And while I was assimilating Whitehead's metaphysical works, beginning with *Science and the Modern World*, I was also assimilating and, with Paul Weiss, editing the writings of Peirce. In all this concern with two men of genius

I was also working out my own view. Indeed, I began writing my first book, in which there was rather little of Peirce or Whitehead. With or without their influence I would probably have had beliefs somewhat like theirs, but much less well articulated and argued for.

Metaphysics as it has developed in this century is something rather new. It is ironical that, although criticisms of metaphysics as such are fashionable enough in our time, they rarely deal with the most characteristic twentieth-century forms of metaphysics. I rate this as cultural lag.

Process philosophy takes creative becoming rather than mere being as the inclusive mode of reality. Hegel had done this, and insofar he could be called a process philosopher. But the disciples of Hegel either went back to a philosophy of "being" (as Heidegger verbally, though I trust not really, also did) or else, with Marx, proclaimed a materialism that short-circuits speculation in the interest of a particular economico-political and, alas, military program.

Process philosophy takes becoming as creative in precisely that sense in which classical determinism denies creativity. Creativity is the production of *new definiteness*. It is the ultimate or universal form of emergence. For strict determinism, the definiteness of the world throughout all time is already settled and the future seems indefinite only because of ignorance. The notion of timeless truths about particular events has the same implication. For Whitehead, as for Peirce, James, Dewey, Bergson, or W. E. Hocking (who was influenced by James and, presumably, Bergson), reality is in the making and classical determinism is false. We human beings (in some degree all creatures) are helping to define a reality otherwise not fully definite. Ours is the freedom of partial indeterminacy. On this issue Weiss and Findlay are process philosophers. Here Hegel was at best unclear, and most Hegelians were if anything worse than Hegel. Nietzsche was a determinist.

Of all Whitehead's conceptions, perhaps the most original is 'prehension,' or "the most concrete mode of relatedness." [1] No standard philosophical term current before his work is even roughly equivalent to it. 'Perception' will not do, for several reasons. First, prehension is as much involved in memory as in what is normally called perception. Second, 'perception' tends to refer not merely to what in Whitehead's sense is prehended but also to what is understood as signified by the prehended data (as in, "I perceive that you are unhappy."). Third, before Whitehead the temporal structure of perception was either left ambiguous or mistakenly taken to be that of simultaneity, whereas Whitehead holds that in principle the prehending experience temporally follows the prehended actuality.

To prehend is to possess or intuit a datum, a given. The metaphorical root meaning of 'grasping' is relevant. We could think of a ghost, even believe we were seeing a ghost; but for anyone to grasp or prehend a ghost there must be one. To intuit or in this sense possess, however, does not mean to consciously think or know *that* one is doing so. If we prehend (in any case, as we shall see, somewhat indirectly) something not a tiger, taking it to be a tiger, this seeing *as* or hearing *as* is a character of the prehending, not of the prehended. Hence the current fashionable denial of a *cognitive* given—meaning an absolutely secure grasp of truth *about* what is given—is compatible with Whitehead's doctrine. There are no infallible bits of cognition; yet there is direct intuitive grasp of reality. To intuit or feel (a favorite word of Whitehead's here) is one thing, to think or know that and what one intuits or feels is another. The value of the doctrine of prehension is not that it gives us infallible cognitions of reality but that it gives us reality in a subconscious or nonconceptual fashion. This is what some call the precognitive given.

Peirce's Secondness, as I argued in a previous chapter, is one-way dependence of phenomena on other phenomena. As I remarked, Peirce hesitated between a symmetrical and a one-way form of dependence as the primary form, whereas logically the symmetrical form, *like all symmetry*, is a special or derivative case. Whitehead never, I think, labels his prehension as a one-way relation; but his definitions and explications of the term imply this. Even where the prehended is inside the subject's own body, as is most obvious in aches or pains, Whitehead says that the prehended physiological process occurs just "before," not simultaneously with, the prehending experience. Moreover, Whitehead takes the subject-object relation in prehending to be an effect-cause, not a cause-effect, relation. Effects follow their causes, which are always in the past of the effect. Also Whitehead as a relativist in physics denies interaction or symmetrical causality between contemporary occasions or experiences.

How did Whitehead come to this theory of a one-way causal and temporal relation of experience to things experienced? There was obviously the fact of physics that what we see or hear outside the body must already have taken place for the stimulus to have reached us. For science it is a truism that the perceived is in the past, except perhaps when the perceived is in the body. Whitehead decided not to admit this exception. Partly, I think, he was following his bent, as imaginative mathematician, to try to generalize wherever possible.

But there were other reasons. For Whitehead, perception is only one form, and in a way not the most significant form, of intuitive possession or givenness. The other form is memory. To my mind it is not Whitehead whose thinking is odd here but nearly everyone else's. What is memory if not our present experience of our own previous experiences? It is experiences prehending previous experiences in the same personal succession or stream of awareness.

Whitehead implies that we should take the experience of past experience in memory as the paradigm or privileged sample of givenness even more than the experience of physical realities in perception. He does not argue the point, but arguments are not hard to supply. In perception we have a relation of experience to what seems as different as possible from experience. The vast gulf between human subjectivity, an extremely exceptional form of reality, and apparently inanimate nature must be spanned if we are to understand perception. The whole mystery of "matter"—which physics, after twenty-five centuries of inquiry, still presents as a mystery—is included. Moreover, in taking perception rather than memory as the paradigm of givenness, we are likely to fall into the illusion of simultaneous relations where the exact sciences strongly suggest that the relations are really those of before and after.

Generalizing from physics and from the temporal structure that is most obvious in memory, we arrive at the idea that what is experienced is always temporally prior to the experiencing. This opens the door to interpreting the givenness relation as causal. We can even define the prehended as that which comes before and in principle (though sometimes to an insignificant degree) causally conditions the prehending experience.

Whitehead's prehension is then unambiguously, though not emphatically or in these words, explicated as *asymmetrical dependence.* The dependence cannot be symmetrical since only the past is definitely prehended and "there are no occasions in the future" to be prehended. The future is prehended only as the necessity that the actualities already given must come to be prehended by some suitable successors or other, where 'suitable' means, "able to prehend the given actualities." This necessity is a metaphysical principle, or law, and is part of the meaning of Whitehead's "creativity," the "form of forms."

If subject X prehends an earlier subject Y, then Y does not prehend X; Y is insofar independent. But only insofar. For Y itself as subject or actual occasion prehends, and thus depends upon, still earlier actualities, and these prehend even earlier ones. Thus all prehension embraces an unlimited number of actualities. Only by arbitrary abstraction can one speak of prehension of a single presupposed actuality. Peirce's stress on the number of items on which something depends seems rather unimportant to a Whiteheadian. What is important is the asymmetry inherent in Secondness as well as in prehension. But a Whiteheadian can also see, with Peirce, that the nondefinite necessity of future occasions is neither simple dependence nor simple independence, neither Firstness nor Secondness. It is a Third: creativity as the presupposition of all thought and all objects of thought, the beginningless and endless "creative advance" that (as Bergson said) "is reality itself." Peirce's tychism and "spontaneity" have similar implications. Relations to the future express the necessity of approximately definite kinds of events rather than altogether particular events or sets of events.

As we saw in a previous chapter, Peirce defines Firstness too abstractly or absolutely, and indirectly he admits as much. He implies that no actual phenomenon is literally a First. Rather, Firstness is for him an ideal limit, for instance, of a series of experiences in which Secondness (or reaction or dependence) approaches a minimum, as in an experience where there is almost no memory, thought, or object felt. He says that a First is a pure possibility. But this is to lead away from the professed phenomenological goal of the whole inquiry. We are looking for instances of the categories in actual experiences, not in some hypothetical extreme possibility. Given a (for our knowledge at least) beginningless series of actualities, it is arbitrary to select a certain actuality as first, if that means absolutely first. It is not arbitrary but literally correct if it means, first so far as a directly following second is concerned. Relative firstness can be perfectly definite and actual rather than merely possible.

Peirce says that we cannot think about Firstness without tarnishing it, making it dependent upon our thinking. This frustrating conclusion recalls Bergson's doctrine that logical discourse cannot be applied to immediate experience. Whitehead's view is that in all prehension other than divine there is limitation, partial abstraction, from the fullness of the prehended. He calls this limitation "negative prehension." But this does not mean that the prehending tarnishes the purity of the prehended. The prehended is a First, absolutely independent of its prehendor (though not of actualities that it does itself prehend).

Two other complications should be mentioned. One is that while the prehending depends asymmetrically upon the prehended, the two ideas, prehending and asymmetrically depending, are not simply equivalent. Not all one-way dependencies are prehensions. If proposition *P* entails proposition *Q*, then *P* depends for its truth upon that of *Q*, while the converse dependence of *Q* on *P* may not, and normally does not, obtain. Yet a proposition does not literally prehend; only subjects, which are concrete actualities, do that. Prehension is *one-way dependence as holding of subjects or experiences relative to whatever they have as strictly given*. It is the form that dependence takes when it holds of a subject in relation to other entities. The prehensive relation is "the most concrete form of relatedness," as Whitehead aptly puts it.

The other complication is that if relatedness must be either prehension or a mere abstraction, then there is a problem resulting from relativity physics with its denial, accepted by Whitehead, of influence between contemporary events. This implies "spacelike" relations of coexistence between concrete actualities; yet these relations are not prehensions. The inconsistency, as it seems to me to be, has troubled me for many years. Prehensive relations are one-way influences, while contemporaneity is defined as mutual lack of influence.[2]

Quantum theory has recently been shown to imply a qualification to the limiting of influences to the forward light cone. It seems that there are positive influences, which, though they cannot convey messages, are not limited by the speed of light. This qualification of physical relativity is known as Bell's Theorem, and seems well established. Henry Stapp, a physicist who has studied Whitehead and also Bell's discovery, has proposed what he calls a "revised Whiteheadianism" that removes the difficulty by a bold theory that all events whatever form a single well-ordered series, each member of which is influenced only by its predecessors in the series. In the absolute sense of contemporaries there would be none. If this proposal were able to meet all empirical tests, it would eliminate a great difficulty in process philosophy. It would also partly justify Peirce's view of Secondness as dependence on just one other entity. We need only qualify the dependence as 'direct,' to make Peirce's doctrine compatible with Stapp's revision of Whitehead. Apparently, empirical tests can at best show that Stapp's view is permissible, not that it is uniquely correct. In view of my limitations, I leave this issue for others to consider.

Although, as we have seen, the nearest that traditional ideas come to anticipating the idea of prehension is in terms like 'data' or 'givenness,' the approximation is far indeed from being close. For one thing the term 'given' suggests vaguely an act of the object, or something behind the object, upon the subject, whereas prehending is the act of the subject intuiting the object—the act whereby the subject freely comes into being, utilizing available (past) subjects in its self-formation. The only *action* of past subjects is or was their previous coming to be. Moreover, givenness has had for most writers either no clear, or the wrong, temporal structure. Also, it was thought of as peculiar to perception rather than memory, whereas memory and perception are the two forms of givenness, and both alike give the past. Finally, givenness tended to mean, "consciously detected or detectable so as to furnish indubitable and infallible premises for inference," whereas prehension has no such implication. How far the subject can consciously and securely detect the prehended depends on the level of consciousness an experience attains (low in infants and subhuman animals) and other factors. Only divine prehension infallibly detects its data.

In sum, prehension is one of the most original, central, lucid proposals ever offered in metaphysics. And its meaning can be sharpened by the use of Peirce's insight into the basic contrast between independence and dependence, or Firstness and Secondness. This can be done in such a way as to improve greatly upon the clarity of Peirce's own system of ideas. Thus my analysis pays tribute to both philosophers.

A marked advantage of Whitehead's (or my) form of process philosophy over Peirce's is in the concept of quanta of becoming. Not only is this congruent with the central doctrine of Buddhism and of some Islamic philosophers as well as with quantum theory— which would not have pleased Peirce with his "synechistic" bias— but it also furnishes what the theory of continuous becoming lacks, definite unit-actualities or single subjects prehending and also (subsequently) prehended. A continuum has no definite least parts. Peirce infers from this that we have no immediate, and hence no infallibly given, data, and this is one justification he gives for his fallibilism. But Whitehead arrives at fallibilism in another way, by denying, as Peirce also denies, the absolute distinctness of our intuitions. Such distinctness is a divine prerogative, as Leibniz held. There is no need to derive the principle of nondivine indistinctness from an assumption of continuous becoming.

To ward off a possible misunderstanding, let me say that when Whitehead or I refer to "objects" we are not committing the error, against which Dewey and others rightly warn, of making cognition the essential form of experiencing. Prehension is "feeling of (another's) feeling," and only in special cases is it also thinking of or knowing (another's) feeling or thinking. The objects are immediately intuited or felt, whether or not they are in a pregnant sense known, explicitly judged in answer to explicit questions and with consideration of rival lines of evidence, or the like. Prehension merely as such is not theoretical grasping but just grasping, simply the intuitive having of antecedent realities. Theorizing may be present but does not increase the extent of what is prehended. It only explicates the nature of the given in verbal or other symbolic terms.

Both Peirce and Whitehead are implicitly committed to the idea of one-way dependence as pervasive in reality, although neither writer directly and clearly says so. Both suffer from this failure. Whitehead has misled many readers by some unguarded assertions, such as that "everything is (he sometimes says, "in a sense") everywhere." He also affirms internal relations and only much more rarely external relations, although each case of prehension involves both, since no relation to particular successors or particular prehenders of a given actuality is constitutive of that actuality. His (also Peirce's) denial of "simple location," if unqualified, seems to imply that an actuality has no localization at all and is indeed everywhere. William Alston in his University of Chicago doctoral dissertation argued that Whitehead's system thus reduces to a monism like that of Bradley. So it does if one forgets the explications of prehension and the denial that actualities can be both definite and future or forgets the account given of "creativity." But thus the system is ruined.

In a way Peirce comes closer than Whitehead to recognizing that one-way dependence is the general principle, and two-way dependence a special case. A genuine Second as such is dependent upon its First, not vice versa. Items in a directional series can of course be *counted* backward. But still the second act of counting gets its meaning from the first. The second edition of a book is influenced by its predecessor. A second offspring suffers or enjoys relations to the first from the outset; not so the first to the second. In another way Whitehead comes closer to clarity. For example, memory (prehension of one's own previous prehensions) shows that prehension is the dependent, later effect, and the prehended, the independent antecedent cause. It was first there on its own, whereas memory as prehension presupposes the prehended.

It was Peirce, not Whitehead, who, to his lasting credit, made the concept of dependence and its negative explicitly constitutive of the very definitions of his categories. A First is what it is "regardless [that is, independently] of any other thing." (He should have said, "of at least one other thing.")

Peirce seems not to notice that both the "in" of 'independence' and the "less" of 'regardless' are privations, so that Secondness or dependence is the positive idea and Firstness, its negation. Obviously, prehending or intuiting is a positive act and one presupposed by the status of being prehended. In this sense, Firstness as such, the concept, is paradoxically second to Secondness as such. Peirce and Whitehead both see that the status of being a given object or datum presupposes that of being a recipient of a datum. Whitehead explicitly and Peirce implicitly make prehension the key to causal efficacy. Both philosophers are psychicalists, not dualists or materialists. And their categories support them in this, in ways too numerous to mention here. But if prehending, the experience-experienced relation, is the only form in which ontological dependencies, or what Hume called necessary connections, are given as such, and if these connections are what make reality a cosmos such that one part has implications for other parts, then what does not prehend, mere insentient matter, cannot be the universal explanatory principle. It is quite manifestly Hume's ignoring of the one-way dependencies found in memory and perception, when he was purporting to look for ontological necessities, that explains the negative result of his search. The experience-experienced relation is "the most concrete mode of relatedness," from which more abstract modes must be derived. This formula of Whitehead's would perhaps have been acceptable to Peirce, though his "ideas tend to spread" is much vaguer and his synechism poses difficulties at this point.

Taking into account Peirce's earlier birth, and the enormous intellectual changes that occurred in the three decades between the culmination of Peirce's mental activity and that of Whitehead, I find honors somewhat evenly divided between the two great speculative philosophical logician-scientists in their treatment of the relation of experience to the experienced. No third writer, including the one who writes this, is comparable to either of them. They are the chief founders of process philosophy as a rational field of inquiry.

I shall now discuss briefly some theological applications of the concept of prehension. Since all knowing has its content from prehension, if we conceive a divine knower we must conceive divine prehending. But this immediately implies that (directly contrary to classical tradition, as found in philosophers and theologians from Augustine and earlier, to Kant) God is influenced by, and something in God derives its actuality from, the world that God knows. We influence God at every moment by furnishing data for the divine prehensions. Startling or even repulsive as this will be to some, it was clearly affirmed long ago, first by the Socinian sect in Italy, Poland, and Transylvania, later by Fechner in Germany and Lequier in France. William James would have gladly accepted it. Peirce somewhat hesitantly and perhaps inconsistently implies it. Bergson would surely have accepted it. There are others. For several centuries a new form of philosophical theology has been struggling to be born. It changes all the fundamental problems of theism, in ways that I have discussed in many writings.

If God infallibly knows all, God must directly prehend all; in addition to direct prehension there is only precarious inference from directly or relatively distinctly prehended portions of the world to the less directly and distinctly prehended ones. Thus, since to prehend something is to be influenced or conditioned by it, not only is God open to influence (precisely what the traditional attribute of *impassibility* was meant to exclude), but also God is the most universally open to influence of all beings. (I have argued elsewhere that this does not contradict the notion of divine 'perfection,' provided we reinterpret this term so as to avoid certain absurdities that are comparable to absurdities in the seemingly innocent phrase, "class of all classes.") If God is the universally prehending Reality, it follows, Whitehead further implies, and I agree, that God is also the universally prehended Reality. The universal subject is also the universal object of experiencing. To prehend at all includes prehending deity. However, as follows from what has already been said, universally prehended does not entail universally known. *All* subjects feel God, but only *some* subjects think or know God.

Why must God be universal datum as well as universal subject of experiencing? Here I will only remark that, in process philosophy, for subject or experience X to be influenced by Y is for X to prehend Y; hence if God is to act upon all, influence all, God must become datum for all. Divine decisions could do nothing to creatures who did not prehend those decisions. Whitehead picturesquely intimates this remarkable doctrine by the blunt statement: "The power of God is the worship he inspires." Both Plato and Aristotle had partly similar ideas of the divine 'persuasion,' and Whitehead learned from them. For this philosophical theologian, God does not coerce, bully, or bribe the creatures. Rather the beauty of the divine love intentionally charms them all into responding (however imperfectly) and derives further value from the responses. There is divine feeling of creaturely feelings. There has never before been a philosophical theology that so clearly and directly embodied the biblical saying, God is Love.

Any number of questions arise, and possible difficulties or objections will occur to many. What I could say about these difficulties or objections is mostly to be found in my perhaps too numerous writings. But in philosophy, even more than in science, the last word on a subject is beyond human competence to utter. We must remain always willing to make fresh efforts to learn or to impart the truth about these matters.

Notes

1. Whitehead's account of prehension is found chiefly in two books, *Process and Reality* (corrected edition, ed. D. R. Griffin and D. W. Sherburne [New York: Free Press, 1978]) and *Adventures of Ideas* (pb. edition, New York: The New American Library, 1955, 1964). *Adventures*, written after *Process*, gives the simpler and in some respects clearer formulation. See "Prehension" in the index of that book. For God's prehensions of creatures, see *Process*, pp. 31, 345–346. In the index of *Process*, see "Prehension," "Causality," "Time." In *Adventures*, see chapter 19, section III, for the reason "process must be inherent in God's nature." On prehension as the explanation of causal efficacy and the factor Hume overlooked, see *Process*, 123, 133–134, 140; also *Symbolism, Its Meaning and Effect.* (New York: The Macmillan Co., 1927; Cambridge University Press, 1928), chapter II, section 1–4. Apart from the theological aspect, part three of *Adventures* is the most readable and eloquent account of the metaphysical system. For the theology, the great final chapter of *Process* is indispensable (Whitehead called this his most important essay). As introduction to Whitehead, his *Modes of Thought* is to be recommended (New York: The Macmillan Co., 1938). However, "prehension" does not occur in this book. Yet see p. 128 for the idea of divine prehension. God is presented as Deity on pp. 139ff.
2. Jorge Nobo has a book on Whitehead's philosophy, to be published by the State University of New York Press, that offers a solution for the problem of contemporaries within the Whiteheadian framework. Nobo is a very scholarly writer.

CHAPTER 10

Santayana's Skeptical Eclecticism

The superb craftsman in words who was George Santayana (1863–1952) was perhaps too eclectic and left too many loose ends to rate as one of the great speculative minds. He was a Humean skeptic and also an extreme Platonic realist, much more extreme than some of us would suppose Plato to have been. In ontology he was a dualist who denied mind-body interaction, admitting "spirit" as an idle accompaniment of matter with no causal efficacy of its own. In philosophy of religion he was an atheist, yet (like Carnap, Quine, and many other logicians of our time) he asserted the reality of timeless truth about all physical and psychical occurrences, a sort of ghost of medieval or classical theism. (Of this relation to medieval doctrine he was quite conscious.) As omniscience survived in Santayana's thought in the form of timeless truth, so (as he himself said) omnipotence did in the form of matter. For, since mind has no causal consequences, all real power is in matter. As in Hume's thought, successive mental states are logically independent of their predecessors and successors, and there are no mental causes or substances.

Reading between the lines of Hume's works, one can see that he did not really believe his theory of reality as a mere arbitrary succession of impressions but was inclined to believe in a physical world of the kind posited by Newtonian science. In Santayana this is explicitly asserted. But neither Hume nor Santayana makes the concept of matter a positively intelligible one. It is whatever makes it possible for us to have our sensory experiences, but which itself has no concretely specifiable qualities, only bare spatio-temporal-causal structures, except where in organisms momentary flashes of "spirit" inexplicably occur with their secondary qualities of pain, pleasure, color, smell, and the rest.

114

Santayana was at first a determinist but later inclined to admit an element of indeterminacy in becoming, not because of the creative freedom of mind but simply because the contingency of the world, its arbitrary particularity, seemed to him (as it did to Aristotle, Peirce, Boutroux, Bergson, Whitehead, and others) better regarded as an affair of piecemeal intrusion into reality than as a single wholesale or cosmic decision (of God?) or throw of the dice (what dice, what thrower?). In so reasoning, Santayana showed his acuteness. He did not need quantum physics to tell him that piecemeal or multiple contingency is more reasonable than wholesale or unique contingency. Basic categories are best viewed as having multiple instances.

A similarly acute remark is that God (freely) creating a possible world would *be* a possible world, that is, a reality that might not have been or might have been otherwise. Here the Spanish-American admirer of classical philosophy disagrees, in my opinion rightly, with the Thomistic dictum (found also in Philo, first century A.D. Jewish theologian) that relations between God and the world are relations for the world but not for God, that is, they are not intrinsic properties of divine, but only of worldly, actuality. Aristotle implies this of his Unmoved Mover. However, Aristotle sees what Aquinas denies, that such an unmoved mover, not genuinely related to the world, also does not know or love the world. To know fully the emotions of the creatures, their joys and sufferings, and be simply and utterly unmoved by them is double-talk. A French existentialist has said that God, if he exists, is "in a situation with mankind." This is the same point as Santayana's. Process theology simply accepts it.

Still another example of Santayana's brilliant intelligence is his rejection of the theory, pervasive of Western thought, that self-interest is *the* motivation from which any aspect of concern for others must be derived and by which it must be justified. The passage shows great insight:

When we apply reason to life, we immediately demand that life be consistent, complete, and satisfactory when reflected upon and viewed as a whole. This view, as it presents each moment in its relations, extends to all moments affected by the action or maxim under discussion; it has no more ground for stopping at the limits of what is called a single life than at the limits of a single adventure. To stop at selfishness is not particularly rational. The same principle that creates the ideal of a self creates the ideal of a family or an institution.

The conflict between selfishness and altruism is like that between any two ideal passions that in some particular may chance to be opposed; but such a conflict has no obstinate existence for reason. For reason the person itself has no obstinate existence. The *character* which a man achieves at the best moment of his life is indeed something ideal and significant; it justifies and consecrates all his coherent actions and preferences. But *the man's life*, the circle drawn by biographers around the career of a particular body, from the womb to the charnel-house, and around the mental flux that accompanies that career, is no significant unity. All the substances and efficient processes that figure within it come from elsewhere and continue beyond; while all the rational objects and interests to which it refers have a transpersonal status. Self-love itself is concerned with public opinion; and if a man concentrates his view on private pleasures, these may qualify the fleeting moments of his life with an intrinsic value, but they leave the life itself shapeless and infinite, as if sparks should play over a piece of burnt paper.[1]

Santayana held a substance theory of reality, but the foregoing passage shows that he does not make substantial self-identity of the person the key to motivation. The "I" which loves "me" does not do so because the I and the me are identical; and it does not fail or refuse to love "you" simply because I am not you. The passage is a wonderful Western parallel to the wisdom of Buddhism which, like Whitehead (and modern physics), asks us to put aside substances and their identities and nonidentities as final terms of analysis and to focus on more concrete realities, such as I-now, or you-now, or I-then and you-then. Santayana, like all the best American philosophers (but what British ones?), learned from the thought of India as well as from that of Europe or the Americas. In that way, too, he was almost one of us, although less so than Whitehead the Anglo-American.

Santayana claimed to have "seen through religion;" but he failed to grasp the new type of religious metaphysics represented by W. P. Montague and Whitehead. He did read *Process and Reality*, and his marginal comments show how powerfully biased he was against the religious aspects of that book. He commented on my own defence of process theology in the volume edited by Paul Arthur Schilpp, *The Philosophy of George Santayana*, with the objection that, granting the freedom of the creatures, God ought by now to have been able to get things under better control than seems to be the case. He failed to understand that each new creature is a new beginning, and that freedom, with its risks, is not a problem to be eventually solved and disposed of; also, that the higher is the level of opportunity, that is, of the scope of freedom, the higher also are the risks. Before humanity there were far fewer terrible risks for life on this planet. It is the price of our escape from the relative tyranny of instinct that we are uniquely exposed to the perils of being able to fall into drastic conflict with our fellows and with the nonhuman animal life around us. And every new achievement of science and technology magnifies both the opportunities and the dangers of our situation. Santayana never really saw the spiritual meaning of creative transcendence of causal determination. Causally conditioned we are, as truly as other creatures, but we are much less completely determined causally.

Epicurus long ago held the piecemeal view of contingency and applied it to atoms as well as to human beings. What he did not see is that creativity is the essence of mind as such, not of mere matter, whatever that may be. Santayana's reduction of the causal efficacy of mind is not the same as the Epicurean, but it shows a similar lack of insight into the capacity of mind to explain itself and matter, too.

Santayana's philosophy is, perhaps, most of all, a sharp reaction to modern idealism, in the form which argues that knowing is creative of its objects. Santayana sees that if the thing known depends upon the knowing, then not even one's own past can be known, since in knowing it we would in part at least create it; but a past event created in the present would not be past. Also, if in knowing I create what I know, then the neighbor's mind that I try to know must turn out to be my own mind, my own idea, not my neighbor's. Thus the logical result of such an idealism is solipsism—one knows only one's present mental state (if even that, as we shall see).

With this *reductio ad absurdum*, Santayana dismisses idealism. He entirely overlooks the more sensible form of idealism that Peirce, for example, represented, according to which the thing known in a particular case is not in the least created by *that* act of knowing, but rather constitutes an independent First to which the knowing is a Second. However, the independence or Firstness of the known is relative only, since the thing known itself (memory is the most obvious example) was also a reactive feeling or experience, presupposing a still earlier one as *its* First. (Reaction was one of Peirce's labels for his second category.) The argument for idealism is not that knowing constitutes its objects, but that it constitutes *itself* as a new object available for being known, and that this self-constitution or self-creation of a potential object is the only model we have for the coming to be of reality in general. No such idea ever dawned on Santayana, for reasons which have as much to do with the errors of idealists as with any blunders of his own.[2] Prior to Whitehead the primacy of self-creation had never been put clearly into the center of discussion.

Memory cannot create the past. It remains to ask whether the past can in a fashion create memory, that is, be present in it as its cause. Unfortunately, Santayana is not content to safeguard the independence of the earlier from the later; he also (illustrating the kind of realism that Royce refutes) asserts the absolute logical independence of the later from the earlier. Memory is a self-contained present state, logically not intrinsically related or relative to the past at all. Thus Hume, in his extremest statement, is reincarnate: Mental events (Hume's "impressions") are mutually independent in their logical being. How then do we know that the remembered ever happened? We have "animal faith" that, in general, this is so. Strictly, we do not know it, even as probable. Given a memory, the past logically could have been anything you please. What ground has Santayana for this view? Apparently only the well-known occurrence of "mistakes" of memory. If memory were intrinsically related to the earlier events themselves, how could it ever be mistaken? We do not—Santayana concludes—intuit the past, but only an "essence," which as such is timeless. We intuit a quality, which *may* have qualified the past but also may not have.

This is a crude analysis, for so subtle a writer as Santayana. There are "memories" and "memories," and all degrees of possible confusion between those referring to a fraction of a second ago and those referring to many years earlier, and above all, confusion between memory intuitions and judgments as to what the intuitions mean. A memory going back millions of seconds will skip over countless intervening experiences, in many of which the earlier event in question will already have been recalled. Therefore, one is in danger of confusing memories of previous memories of the event with direct memory of the event itself. Not only previous memories, but also previous interpretations of previous memories, intervene between the given memory and the event. Thus George III "remembered" being at the battle of Waterloo. What did he really do? Did he merely have a present image that he interpreted as a memory of his own presence at Waterloo? Of course, the matter was much more complicated. Near the time of the battle he may have thought about the possibility of being or having been there; his mind became filled with images of experiences he then would or might have had. Later he forgot that these were only imaginings of such experiences; however, he did not forget the imaginings themselves. Imagined experiences, if vivid enough, being much like real ones, it was easy enough eventually to interpret them as having in fact been real. But this was a judgment based, in a complex manner, on many memories, not a simple single memory. Without the distinction between direct experience and its interpretation, there is no clear meaning for 'direct experience,' and hence "Is the past directly experienced? " ceases to constitute a definite question.

Only by ignoring the two confusions, that between single immediate and multiple remote memory and that between interpreted memory and simple memory, can one prove the lack of intrinsic connection between present and past experience. Santayana is one of legions who have based much in their philosophy upon precisely these mistakes. If present experience is self-contained so far as memory is concerned, the reference to the past associated with memory is only a claim, a postulate, or a faith. Are we to say the same about perception of the world around us? Is that, too, only a postulate or faith? Santayana replies in the affirmative, using the phrase "animal faith." The mistakes of perception, like those of memory, exclude the possibility of direct awareness of any part of the physical world. The qualities we intuit in perception are then given only in their own qualitative nature; whether they characterize anything except our perceptions themselves, however, we cannot know. All experience is but a series of dreams plus the animal faith that there is a real world corresponding to the dreams.

We have here the same two mistakes that were committed with regard to memory: failure to distinguish (a) between the more and the less immediate objects of perception and (b) between givenness and interpretation. In a dream we do not experience real things *outside the body* as they really are. But then, even in waking experience there is no good reason to regard the extrabodily object as the most immediate datum. If we start with some obviously remote object of perception, such as a stellar explosion that took place a light year in the past, it is strange indeed to suppose that the most direct object of this experience is separated by a year from the experience. But there is only a difference of degree between such an event and any perceived event outside the body. In all cases it takes time for the stimulus to reach the sense organ and produce there the activity that in turn produces the change in the nervous system and brain with which the experience is, in temporal terms, most closely associated.

Thus, as Russell (also Whitehead) has cogently argued, the only nonarbitrary choice for the most direct object of the experience is the neural process itself. Anything else is by comparison less direct. Attempts to refute this conclusion seem to turn upon some degree of confusion between experience and judgment. We instantly *interpret* the experience as perception of the external object: This is exactly what follows from the assumption that the internal neural object is more directly given and the fact that, since birth, or even before, we learn how to correlate data from one sense with those of another (including kinaesthetic sensations) so as to survive and prosper in a world full of dangers and rewards that can be avoided or won only if, much of the time, we attend to inner-bodily states only as comprehended signs of extra-bodily events.

Not a single known characteristic of sight or hearing is contradictory of this explanation. The dream theory of experience then takes on the following harmless form: In all experiences, awake or asleep, we experience inner-bodily (neural) states (which are always present), but only when we are awake do the functions of interpretive correlation, or reading of these bodily cues as signs of external events, operate correctly. In sleep and in certain abnormal states realistic interpretation breaks down. But the loci of the direct physical data are in all cases inner-bodily. This theory has not been refuted. It has been smiled at or ignored. I have yet to see an argument worthy of the name against it. (The "sense-datum" theory, or the "causal theory" of perception, as they are commonly defined and criticized, are *not* the theory just set forth; therefore, the difficulties with which they are rightly charged are irrelevant to this theory.)

Having cut off the present experience wholly from its past, Santayana can then triumphantly turn upon the idealist and say, "Your 'mind' is wholly incapable of furnishing the link between successive events. Only the despised matter can do this. The enduring substance and causal connectedness of the world are in matter only, not in mind." How then does "matter" explain identity through change and causal interconnection? Since that is what the concept is invented for, by stipulation it must be able to render this service. Look as you may in Santayana's writings, you will not find more than this by way of argument on the point. I submit that the explanation is pure verbiage and nothing more. As Hume showed, we *experience* no intrinsic relatedness of the present of a piece of matter to its past or future and no causal reference from one piece of matter to another. Santayana verbally postulates that, since he finds no linkages in mind, they must reside in something else, which he calls matter.

The situation then is this. In memory we have at least a claim on the part of mind to relate itself to the past and a similar claim on the part of sense perception to relate itself to other things in space (which need not, in the most direct cases, be outside our skins). The claims are examined hastily by Santayana, with every mark of bias in the mode of examination, and found wanting. It is triumphantly concluded that the unity of the world must be found in matter, although we have not even a plausible notion, comparable to perception and memory, as to *how* states of a body influence their successors and only a notion (the push-pull idea of Greek atomism), now known to be illusory, as to how events in one body causally imply changes in another body.

I maintain that Santayana's procedure has no logical force and that only immense anti-idealistic (partly anti-German) bias could account for his supposing it had. This double bias was undoubtedly real and strong, as I think any reader of Santayana will concede. To take memory and perception as illusions plus animal faith is the most suspect epistemology conceivable. To base an ontology upon it is inadmissible, since all that could really follow is that we know nothing.

If we do not literally experience anything past or contemporary with the experience, we either experience that very experience itself only, or we experience something not in time at all. Santayana sees the absurdity of saying that an experience is merely of itself and chooses the other horn of the dilemma: We experience essences, which in themselves are timeless. This leads to three puzzles. One is, how do we even have the idea of event or of experience, if we experience neither one but only a mere essence? Actual existence is never a datum, Santayana says, but only essence, a form of reality neutral to the distinction between existence and nonexistence. It is all very well to say that we posit existence by instinctive faith. How do we know what is meant by 'existence' if we have never experienced any existent? Our experiences have occurred, but as occurrences they are not data of any possible experience.

The second puzzle is: How can we know that an essence is independent of *all* existence? This is just the old thesis, attacked by Aristotle, of "separable forms." When an essence is known, it at least qualifies an actual experience. By what mode of experience could we find out what an essence or quality would be if it qualified nothing, not even an experience?

The third puzzle is, suppose (which the doctrine implies is quite conceivable) nothing existed, and there were only the realm of

121

essence. In that case, either this realm could of itself produce a world, could function as a creator (or a world could spring into being without a cause, other than the realm of essence, which comes to the same thing), or else not only would there be no existing world but there would not even be a possibility of such a world.

The conclusion seems to be that a simply independent realm of essence explains nothing and is itself unintelligible.

Let us now consider Santayana's treatment of the religious problem. He holds that the medieval idea of God was "eclectic" in that it claimed to combine in a single concept what is really several concepts. There is, first, the concept of essence or pure being, the presupposition of all existence, itself presupposing no existence whatever. This was God as wholly independent of the world, which, however, is dependent upon God. There is also, second, the concept of real power, "omnipotence," capable of producing all sorts of things and actually producing whatever does come to exist. Santayana suggests that it is matter that has this omni-capacity. All things manifest the power of matter. Finally, third, there is the notion of Truth, the total character of existence. Theism identified this with the content of omniscience; but, since a truth is not made by the consciousness of it, this identification is illegitimate. Truth, for Santayana, is merely the immeasurably complex essence which sums up the cosmic development throughout all time.

Thus for God we substitute (a) timeless essence, (b) matter to whose fertility in producing new forms we can set no final limit, and (c) a certain segment of the realm of essence. This is surely very ingenious. Moreover, there is some validity in it. For it is quite correct that God as infinite power, for instance, cannot be simply identical with God as omniscient. To know what power has actually produced out of all that it could produce is to be in a determinate state, exclusive of some of the otherwise possible actualizations. It is to be somehow finite, and not simply infinite. As simply infinite, God would at most know only what divine power *could* produce; but for divine consciousness to register the particular actual productions is for it to take on their determinateness and to be no longer merely infinite. The segment of essence that is actualized is not all essence, and knowing that this is the actualized segment is not having all possible knowledge, for it is not the knowledge that some other segment has been actualized instead. Yet this also was possible. The same duality is involved in the notion of divine will. God *could* will to create all sorts of worlds but does will to produce this sort of world. Hence the actual divine volition is not infinite in the sense in which the possible volition is. As Santayana implies, God creating a certain world is a certain determinate *existing* divine state among the possible ones. I find this a devastating criticism of traditional theism. But it is not so devastating against a theism that admits real distinctions between actual and possible in God.

There is one flaw in Santayana's theory of truth: An essence can tell no tales about existence, and therefore the segment of essence that is embodied in events is, as essence, no different from unembodied essence. Only existence can mark the distinction. Now existence does not occur all at once; it is progressively actualized, and only the present is fully real. What then constitutes truth as a timeless whole? That it is timeless, Santayana does say. Neither in existence nor in essence does there seem to be any place for such a whole. The segment in question is there, all right, among essences, but nothing marks it as *the* segment. Only certain bits of it are marked off by what is going on at a given time in the world as *then* true of the world. But what marks the entire sum of such bits as the comprehensive Truth? Apparently, nothing. Existence never is summed up as a whole; not in the world, for the past is gone and the future not yet realized; not in essence, for it is innocent of the difference between exemplified and unexemplified essences; not in divine knowledge, for this is not admitted.

Has Santayana solved any of our five American philosophical problems? Certainly not the first (God and world) or the third (mind and matter). Concerning freedom, he began as a determinist but eventually decided that this was an arbitrary doctrine. Because of the independence of essence from existence, it is merely contingent that anything exists at all. It seems unreasonable to suppose that this fundamental contingency is combined with a universal conditional necessity of everything within the world. (Here there might possibly be an influence of Peirce, who had argued similarly: Why suppose that the arbitrariness of matters of fact came in a single primordial dose, instead of seeping into the world bit by bit? Determinism taken absolutely implies the "single dose" theory of contingency.) So far, so good. But not having the idea of divine freedom, Santayana has no clear universal principle for the distribution of freedom in reality. And he makes little systematic use of the idea of localized or piecemeal contingency, which for process philosophers is inherent in genuine freedom.

Concerning substances and events, Santayana adds nothing significant to the historical debates about the logic of genetic identity. He does, in one fine passage quoted early in this chapter, imply a wiser view than he ever actually utilizes systematically. He attacks the self-interest theory of motivation on the ground that personal self-identity is not such an absolute thing as the theory assumes. Here he is close to the Buddhist insight, which most of the rest of the world has missed. But the insight is not woven by Santayana into a systematic theory.

As to the a priori and empirical elements of knowledge, Santayana's doctrines are clearly not empirical. Existence, essence, and truth are defined, and experience in relation to them explicated, not on the basis of an inductive inquiry, with the admitted possibility of factual falsification, but on the basis of a priori intuitions or pronouncements. In *any* world, Santayana implies, it would be matter not mind that is the real power; and as for essence, it is even independent of there being any contingent facts at all. I think Santayana is in metaphysics a rationalist, and the better for that, but unfortunately he is one who has failed to find rational solutions for the metaphysical or a priori problems. He has indeed written very instructively about these problems, showing us what results from taking an extreme Humeanism seriously; how this almost forces us to accept also an extreme Hobbesian materialism and an extreme Platonism of essences; and how none of these by itself nor the three together give us much understanding of life or the world.

The fault was not mainly with Santayana. Of imaginative systems he had studied chiefly Greek metaphysics, medieval theology, and German idealism. In his rejection of all these I at least can only salute his good judgment. If he was not a sufficiently creative genius to find a viable alternative, that is chiefly his and our bad luck. His chances might, however, have been better had he been less easily satisfied with the defiant pose of saying something like the opposite of his teachers or contemporaries in America or Germany. He defended Hume and Hobbes (or Epicurus) against Bradley, Fichte, or Lotze; he chose false or extreme against genuine Platonism; he supported all three unpopular extremes against medieval theism. Thus he defied everybody who had irritated him. At the same time, he made a fine show of housing his world and his values in the various realms which he so scintillatingly described. It was a somewhat morose tour de force, in literary elegance and intellectual agility reminiscent of Schopenhauer.[3] Reading him has similar values, except that there is perhaps no element in our American writer quite so concentrated in its effect as Schopenhauer's proof that life is evil or his theory of art. Still the great range of ideas in Santayana perhaps balances the scales.

124

Santayana was a witty man. His replies to my criticisms were scintillating. A letter he wrote to Schilpp was one of the funniest I have ever read. I also admire his character. For reasons that make sense to me, he deliberately left his teaching career at Harvard to live as a writer in Europe. Circumstances did not favor his being happy in a normal career; but so far as seems to be known, he did no harm to anyone, and he never complained about how the world treated him. He did remark that my discussion of his *Realm of Essence* in the volume devoted to him in the Library of Living Philosophers was unduly lengthy and wandered in part from the assigned subject. On both points he was right. He wrote much exquisite, even if disillusioned, lyric poetry.[4]

> *But Morning, with a ray of tenderest joy,*
> *Gilding the iron heavens hides the truth.*
> *[Sonnet number XXV]*
> *or*
> *It is not wisdom to be only wise.*
> *[Sonnet III]*

Notes

1. *The Life of Reason: The Phases of Human Progress*, vol. 5, chapter 8 (New York: Charles Scribners, 1953. One-volume edition), p. 462.

2. I have listed these errors of historical idealists in "The Case for Idealism," *Philosophical Forum*, n.s. 1 (1968): 7–23. Reprinted in *Perspectives in Philosophy*, R. N. Beck, ed. (New York, London: Holt, Rinehart and Winston, 1961, 1975), pp. 277–283.

3. James referred to his colleague's philosophy as "moribund Latinity." James was not the man to appreciate Santayana.

4. *The Complete Poems of George Santayana*, ed. with an Introduction by W. G. Holzberger (Lewisburg, Pa.: Bucknell University Press, 1979; London: Associated University Presses, 1979).

CHAPTER 11

Mead's Social Psychology
and Philosophy of the Present

George Herbert Mead (1863–1931), four years Dewey's junior, was for ten years closely associated with him at the University of Chicago, where Mead taught for nearly forty years.[1] His philosophical training was at Harvard and in Germany. Like Dewey, he was considerably influenced by Hegel, presumably at first through Royce. In Germany he encountered Dilthey and learned about Wundt. He knew more natural science than Dewey but like him was primarily concerned with the social sciences. He is best known for his explication of the development of language and conceptual thinking from primitive gestures, including vocalizations. The gesturer or vocalizer experiences his gesturing or speaking almost as the spectator or hearer does. Consciousness, or the use of concepts, centrally involves "taking the role of the other." One sees one's gestures or hears one's voice as in the same class with a companion's doing so. One internalizes what one experiences others doing or saying and in this way becomes oneself an object for others. This objective self is the "me" in contrast to the "I." The latter is the spontaneous, ever partly new, more or less free, not yet objectified self. Mead is here close to the Buddhist-Whiteheadian view of the momentary self as numerically nonidentical with its predecessors, even though so subtly that for many purposes we can take them as identical.

Mead's famous "significant symbol" is a sign to which one reacts in behalf of internalized others. Imaginative participation in lives not one's own is the key to mentality. David L. Miller,[2] a student and leading interpreter of Mead, and my colleague at the University of Texas, tells me that after Mead had read Whitehead he restated his idea of taking the role of the other by the phrase, "in the perspective of the other."

Distinctive of Mead is a great stress on touch and manipulation. The cash value of seeing something is the possibility of grasping the seen object. So to speak, seeing and hearing are touching or handling from a distance. This focus on literal manipulation is far from Whitehead's primary emphasis on "feeling of feeling," even though, according to both thinkers, a person participates in the life of other persons.

Mead read Whitehead's *Concept of Nature*, perhaps also *The Principles of Natural Knowledge*, and I presume he read *Science and the Modern World*. Miller testifies that Mead had *Process and Reality* and had read it without coming to a definite conclusion about it. He was unwell at the time and never recovered sufficiently to make any further progress in judging that book. One recalls how, not long before he died, Merleau-Ponty in France was reading Whitehead. All three distinguished philosophers had partly common concerns. It is a tragic fact that none of the three had much opportunity to assimilate the ideas of the other two. Mead did once meet Whitehead (in 1926 at an international meeting in Cambridge, Mass.). Whitehead was somewhat unwell at the time, although he managed to read a paper. I recall Mead's speaking briefly to the audience on that occasion. Whitehead recognized Mead's importance, but by the time Mead's writings were being published in book form Whitehead's active career was nearly over.[1]

A difference between Mead and Whitehead, I think, is in the treatment of the mind-body relation. Whitehead analyzed a person as an immensely complex society of societies of societies, whose final singular members are momentary actual entities or occasions, each of which feels (however indistinctly) the feelings of all its predecessors. One sequence of the predecessors is a "personally ordered" series of conscious states, the person's successive momentary experiences, perhaps a dozen per second. The person's body consists of the sentient but not conscious cellular, molecular, atomic societies whose momentary members (many more than the above figure per second) are radically subhuman, but whose primitive feelings are vaguely felt by the person's conscious feelings. The aesthetic richness of a human experience in its sensory aspect is an emergent synthesis of the subpersonal feelings of a huge number of actualities in the body, especially in the central nervous system. The most immediate encounter of human experience with physical realities is not with things seen, heard, or even touched. It is not with the piece of chalk of Descartes (it was said of Mead that he could think freely only with a piece of chalk in his hand with which he would write on the blackboard). The immediate encounter is with sentient actualities inside our skins. These actualities are physical, not mere sense data. But in perception they are the most direct data we have.

The physical world is closest to us in our visceral and other physical pains and pleasures. The world is first of all enjoyed and suffered, not cognized. Knowledge is achieved on the basis of a more primitive layer of socially structured feelings by which we participate in lives not simply our own, but taken into our own by immediate "sympathy," a word also used by Whitehead in addition to "feeling of feeling." Peirce hints at a similar view, as does Bergson, but Whitehead is more explicit in this matter than anyone before him. In a vaguer way I reached some such idea when I knew no philosopher that held it, although I did not at first realize that sympathy with what is outside the body is a less direct relation than sympathy with the physical processes inside the body. Like many others, I was tricked by the marvelous way our distance receptors simulate immediate relations to the distant, although all scientific knowledge shows that the most immediate relations are with what is not outside our bodies but inside them. In his way Spinoza implied this when he defined a human mind as the "idea" (meaning experience) of a human body. Since bodily processes are causally conditioned by processes outside our bodies, our awareness of the former yields knowledge of the latter, as effects are signs of their causes. This is not (either for Spinoza or for Whitehead) the view (mentioned by Mead) that what we immediately intuit are our own *mental* states, from which we infer physical things as their causes. No, we immediately intuit the bodily processes, which, of course, are physical if anything is. Any inference is from physical to physical, from inner-bodily to extra-bodily. The data are already physical and subhuman. True, they consist of feelings, but then for Whitehead so do all concrete realities.

That our mental states are made possible only by our bodily states Whitehead fully grants. ("We think with our bodies," he wrote.) But the reason this is so is a special case of the reason why subjects depend on their given objects. A particular kind of subject requires a suitable class of given objects for its occurrence. The human kind of experience has to be, whatever else it is, the experience of the human kind of body, especially its nervous system. Nerve cells are alive. They are intricately organized. Do they feel? If they do, then our sensory feelings become explicable as our indistinct intuitions of cellular feelings. Our physical pains and pleasures echo the negative and positive aspects of inner bodily subhuman feelings. Mead seems not to have gone this far in extending the attribution of feeling to living organisms. He doubted that plants feel, saying that trees do not "feel thirsty," even though they may need water to flourish. Whitehead would agree, but because trees are loosely integrated. Only microconstituents of such vegetables act each individually as one. "A tree is a democracy."

Dewey and Mead both admired Darwin. One of Darwin's deepest convictions, overlooked by many, was that all life is somehow one and that human attributes, such as sentience, are not to be supposed (as Descartes thought) abrupt supernatural additions to a merely mechanical nature. Darwin was troubled by his inability to see how there could be feeling in plants, thinking that this weakened his evolutionary argument. Somehow he did not realize the importance of the idea of cells, invisibly small individuals making up a vegetable organism and far better integrated than the entire organism. Darwin would have liked Whitehead, I do believe, better than Dewey or Mead, so far as this problem is concerned.

Mead's "mind" is chiefly the capacity to form concepts, to think in the emphatic sense in which most animals can scarcely be said to do so. Whitehead, like Darwin, wished to fully generalize the concepts applied to human beings beyond the specific, high-level forms peculiar to the human species. Specific, complicated, highly refined forms of mind are of course emergent in the higher animals. There must be in all animals, however, some very general aspects of aliveness that are not to be interpreted, even in the most primitive cases, as mere bodily machinery, but are humble, antecedent forms of what in us is the inner quality of living, namely enjoying and suffering, with some sense however minimal of the past and future and of the agreeable and disagreeable, the to-be-accepted and the to-be-rejected.

Whitehead takes a step beyond Darwin and (like Leibniz and Peirce) refuses to make an absolute distinction between living and lifeless things. Many physicists sympathize with this. (Leibniz and Peirce were, among other vocations, physicists, as was Whitehead.) Many scientists today refuse to take seriously the notion that "non-living" vs. "living" is an absolute distinction. Electrons are very "lively" creatures. I know that some scientists reject both materialistic monism and all dualisms of mind and mere matter. If psychologists could take a calm look at the topic they might come to see, as Fechner and Troland (to name two psychologists of note) saw, that even in inorganic nature there are stimuli and responses to stimuli which no non-question-begging criterion shows to be absolutely other than those responses that we take to show feeling or sentience. Leibniz saw the main point here: Nature consists of activities; activities are either collective or singular; what acts as one can be taken to feel as one, what does not so act cannot properly be so taken. Thus clouds, pushed by air molecules, are as wholes insentient, but their invisibly small, individually active constituents are quite different in this respect. So with visibly large plants and their constituents.

I know of no evidence that either Dewey or Mead ever did justice to the problem dealt with in the preceding paragraph. They seem to have followed ordinary common sense as summarized in Aristotle and his countless followers through the ages. Peirce was such a follower, but not on this issue. Ditto with Whitehead. It is modern science that has tended to support Leibniz, not Aristotle or the other Greeks, as to the aliveness or deadness of physical reality. Darwin was even more right than he knew. Life is one, and this goes deeper into nature than he guessed. Wordsworth, called by some England's greatest poet since Milton, was laughed at in the last century for saying plainly enough what Whitehead and a considerable number of scientists are now willing to accept, that no part of nature is simply lifeless or absolutely devoid of feeling. The notion of mere dead matter is a verbal construct, not a datum or a carefully supported conclusion.

When I was in Chicago and Mead was still alive, my colleague T. V. Smith, disturbed by Whitehead's psychicalistic theory, went to Mead for encouragement in rejecting it. Smith's report (in my hearing) on the result was not very definite; but I got a distinct impression that the hoped-for hearty agreement with his dualistic or materialistic prejudices against psychicalism was not forthcoming. He said, "I was surprised." Mead, too late to be sure, was apparently beginning to reconsider this question. Alas, too late.

There is another way in which Darwin is relevant to the understanding and evaluation of Mead and Dewey (founders of what James called "The Chicago School"). Darwin had, while working out his biological theory, changed from a nominal theist (he seems never to have been an enthusiastic one) to a confessed agnostic. This double aspect of Darwin's personal development dealt a double blow to religious believers. However, the way the latter mostly met the challenge did the religious cause more harm than Darwin alone could have done. In both England and America, theists, with a few notable exceptions on both sides of the Atlantic, treated Darwin's personal attitude toward religion as though it were an integral part of his biological theory. (Darwin knew better; the clergyman Charles Kingsley, the American botanist Asa Gray, and historian John Fiske knew better.) Peirce knew far better. Metaphysical issues, such as "Does an eternal (unborn and immortal) God exist?" were not to be confused with questions of temporal and contingent fact, such as how life had changed on this planet. Darwin himself explained his lack of religious belief partly on proper metaphysical grounds, not alone on empirical ones. He accused the clergy of having failed to reconcile divine omnipotence (and timeless omniscience) with human freedom. I say he was right in this; they had not done so. In making God responsible for the details of terrestrial life, they made God responsible for every monstrosity (two-headed calves, animal suffering in general). Also, if detailed human actions are included in the divine plan, actualized with all-determining power, then human wickedness becomes divine action. This problem was purely theological, and theologians had failed to give it a decent solution. Darwin saw this.

What Darwin did not do, and as a biologist was scarcely obligated to do, but some of the best theological or philosophical minds have since been doing, was to go back to the old theological problems and at long last really face them with boldness and freedom, in contrast to the inertia of centuries of repetition of the old evasions, such as that the human mind is incapable of thinking rationally about the divine mysteries. As Berdyaev said, the "mystery" of deity had been "overrationalized"; that is, its received version had been produced by human beings forming injudicious theories about the meaning of religious practices and intuitions. Jesus of Nazareth had been turned into what Heidegger later called "Plato for the masses." It is an open secret that traditional theism was no mere expression of religious faith, but was a blend of the Jewish traditions with Greek metaphysics.

Mead and Dewey came at a time when the issue seemed to be, as today's fundamentalists still think it is, "Either God or Darwin" (and his disciples). As though pre-Darwinian biology and theology together were precisely what Jesus or the Prophets meant by love for God, the all-cherishing parent of the cosmos, or as though worshiping God and worshiping a certain book as verbally infallible were indistinguishable attitudes! Mead and Dewey were not responsible for this situation. The leaders of religious thought were.

In my opinion, fundamentalists are, in some of their effects, promoters of atheism or disbelief. It always was bad thinking to overlook the infinite difference between any book and the infallible, eternal deity. "The Word of God" is a neat little phrase, but what does it express if not one of the many species of idolatry, worshiping as divine what is not worshipful, but human, all-too-human? Whatever we know about human fallibility is writ large in the book in question. Yet religious truth is also there in abundance. "Love God with all your capacities and your neighbor as yourself." So far as words can express the highest truths, these imperatives do so. But that God made woman out of Adam's rib! How can anyone ask us to see that as on the same level?

I recall Mead's saying about Arthur Eddington, "The Englishman always has to get back to his God." Since Mead's death, writers like Ryle and Strawson seem to have shown that the "always" was gratuitous. British empiricism can accept a nontheistic view, under certain circumstances. Mead regarded the idea of God as a version (I suppose an improperly idealized and reified one) of "the generalized Other." After all, the theist Buber said something like this. The issue is not really met by such a move.

A distinctive feature of Mead's thought is his rejection of the view, held by Peirce and Whitehead (and most ordinary people), that the past is immutable, that is, what has happened cannot now or ever be made not to have happened. Events are indestructible and unalterable once they have occurred. Whitehead takes a theistic view of this. Divine "prehensions" immortalize worldly happenings, render them everlasting. As divine possessions they are immune from moth or rust that corrupts or thieves that break in and steal. As a nontheist Mead cannot accept this. The past is nowhere, he thought, if not in the worldly present, in monuments, records, books, traces in rocks, rings in tree trunks, and also in memories of people. But these records and memories are limited, fallible, and keep changing. So past events have no everlasting character. We keep making the future and re-making the past.

I cannot myself see coherent sense in this. Nor could Mead's student Arthur Murphy, who shared Mead's atheism or agnosticism. But I feel the force of Mead's argument, granted the rejection of theism.[2] This is precisely one of about six main reasons some of us have for being theists. I will say for Mead that quantum physicists, some of them at least (especially John Wheeler), are interpreting an experiment (the two-slit phenomenon) as showing that what we must take as an event remote in the past is determined in the present by the way we choose to set up our apparatus now. Mead could have claimed that this supports his view. I am not qualified to attempt a different interpretation of the experimental facts. But I cannot accept Wheeler's interpretation.

It is a satisfaction to an admirer of James and Peirce to note that Mead agrees with them, and with W. P. Montague, Dewey, Hocking, Brightman, Weiss, and some other distinguished American writers in rejecting classical determinism. Incidentally, I disagree flatly with the statement of Murray Murphey and Elizabeth Flower that Dewey's idea of freedom does not imply this rejection. In various places Dewey emphasizes the importance of the idea that situations in nature generally have in advance "indeterminate" outcomes. When I showed him that Clerk Maxwell rejected determinism, he thanked me, and, in *Experience and Nature*, cited the reference I gave him. I admit that Dewey is less clear and consistent on the point than James or Peirce. The latter's criticisms of determinism are ignored in the Murphey-Flower book. Nor does it mention Emerson's determinism.

Why Mead did so little to have his work published is a puzzle. Even Peirce published far more, with his numerous book reviews and scientific monographs on various subjects. True, Mead taught nearly all his adult life and had an interesting family life to which he was devoted. But there does seem to be a puzzle. One wonders how far he believed in the importance of his ideas, other than those about which he did publish. I recall once I said to him, after the one talk of his that I heard, "I begin to see what you mean." "I want to mean it more," he replied with earnestness and vigor. At that moment at least he did believe in the importance of his ideas.

Charles Morris gave probably the best explanation of Mead's relative failure to publish: Mead was more interested in developing his system of ideas and communicating it orally to enthusiastic students than in putting it into writing in the laborious way required to produce books. He was, by all the evidence, more effective in the classroom than Dewey but less effective in books, more of a talker and less of a writer. His personal presence was impressive, certainly more so than Dewey's. The photograph in the volume *The Philosophy of the Act* is most striking: a confident, sparkling intelligence seems to shine from the face and the figure to suggest energy and strength. Then, too, after all, Mead did publish sixty-six articles and reviews.

Whitehead sometimes spoke somewhat condescendingly of "neat and tidy minds" as simplifiers of truth, but, compared to Mead, his thinking is neat and tidy enough. There are the definite singular units of concrete actuality, "actual entities or occasions"; they "prehend" or intuit their predecessors (mostly without conscious dis-

133

tinctness) by feeling their feelings, and through these relationships form groups or "societies" of two basic kinds, "personally ordered" and "corpuscular." There is divine actuality prehending all others distinctly or with full adequacy (without the negative, or eliminative, prehensions that limit all nondivine prehending). Divine actuality is itself prehended, however inadequately, by all nondivine actualities. As in Leibniz, there are countless levels of experiencing or feeling below the human, in many of which there is little more than bare feeling without "symbolic reference" or consciousness of what is felt, feelings that do not judge themselves to any appreciable extent (they feel but do not know that or what they feel). The individual members of the societies on these levels are too insignificant and small to be distinctly discernible by human sense organs, whose essential function is to detect more massive realities, closer to our scale of magnitude.

By comparison, Mead's concept of "the act" appears extremely vague and its relational structure obscure. How many acts are there per second? For Whitehead something like ten, as shown for example, by the number of musical notes in succession that one can distinguish. What is one such act when one listens to music? For Whitehead (as for Leibniz) there are definite multiplicities only if there are definite singulars. In Whitehead's view this holds of multiplicities of succession as well as of those of coexistence in the present, that is, in space. Are there any objectively singular acts for Mead? Bergson says that there are no definite multiplicities of succession. Mead seems to me either Bergsonian or else unclearly somewhere between Bergson and Whitehead.

Whitehead believed that divine actuality invents patterns of order for a cosmic epoch and persuades lesser actualities to conform, at least statistically, to these patterns. For Mead, the patterns somehow are simply there. If they are contingent and if individual acts are spontaneous, free in the creative sense, then there are two kinds of contingency, those expressing what Whitehead calls "decision," and those that are just there, expressive of nothing positively conceivable. According to Whitehead, the transition from pure eternal possibility to contingent fact here and now or in a cosmic epoch is always made by multiple freedom and nothing else, taking deity as supreme form of freedom.

Mead grants that people throughout history have wanted to feel "at home" in the cosmos and to obey some supreme purpose, thereby achieving "salvation." He does not see how we can do this any longer in a world largely interpreted to us through science—except in the sense of seeing society as our home. What is alien to us is the poor organization of our society; "salvation" comes through the vision of a better society. This of course is humanism (recalling Dilthey), a form of deification of our species. That we are social through and through is a Whiteheadian idea. The final society, however, is the cosmos. Mead says that for Jesus the entire species was a family; for Jesus it was also true that the supreme parent cared even for sparrows.

A (merely) "physical object," wrote Mead, is one with which we cannot interact socially. A neo-Leibnizian such as Whitehead explains this impossibility of a social relation with sticks and stones by two principles: the merely collective or unintegral nature of such objects as our senses discriminate them and the low level and insignificance for us of the single members of these collectives, even when, with microscopes and other means of magnification and analysis, we learn of their existence (cells, atoms, particles, or waves). No absolute difference is involved but only immense differences of degree. For deity there is sociality in all relationships. Love (in extreme generalization), feeling of others' feelings, covers it all.

"The act" for Whitehead is prehending, and an actual entity is really a single prehensive integration or emergent synthesis of its relevant data. We know most distinctly and directly only human cases of prehending. The rest are conceived by generalizing analogy. We do know subhuman (cellular) cases directly, but far from distinctly, in our sensations.

It may well be that Mead captured some truths or other that Whitehead misses. But others than this writer must point them out, if they come to much more than the theory of symbolizing in its relation to taking the roles of others as the decisive step in the development of language and concept formation. In this Mead supplements Whitehead more than corrects him.

Whitehead's "eternal objects" repelled Dewey and Mead, and this is a feature of Whitehead that I incline to view as Stephen Pepper did, as an element of unintegrated eclecticism in "the philosophy of organism." Bergson and Merleau-Ponty would have similar objections, as would Wittgenstein.

That a Whiteheadian act, like a Meadian, is emergent means that determinism is not quite true even of "inanimate" nature. No one else, unless Peirce, has ever seen as sharply as Whitehead that the escape from monism into a genuine pluralism can only be through the idea of multiple freedom. Royce's Absolute swallowed up all action into its own acting, all wills into its own will. Royce no more had genuine plurality than did Bradley but was less candid or conscious about what he was doing than the Englishman.

Here then is another reason for Mead's atheism, that Royce's view of God as the Absolute is so incredible. There is still another reason. Royce, like many others, coupled belief in everlasting posthumous human careers with belief in God, confronting those willing to believe in God with the arbitrary choice: God *and* conventional immortality or neither God nor conventional immortality. Like the choice: God with an antiquated biology *or* evolution without God, it puts arbitrary obstacles between a potential believer and actual belief. And this is done ignoring the fact that, as any reader of the Book of Job should see, belief in God need not stand or fall with belief in a supernatural career for human individuals.

Through Mead and Dewey a large number of students and readers were encouraged to seek purely humanistic solutions to human problems. But back of the decision against theism (who knows to what extent? Surely to a substantial one!) was the failure of theologians to put the question of divine existence on its own merits, unburdened with logically extraneous biological dogmas, myths of supernatural continuations of human earthly careers, obsolescent scientific dogmas (Laplace) or theological dogmas (Jonathan Edwards and other Calvinists) of determinism. The time has come to give belief in God a chance, not hamper and cripple it with who knows what absurd or no longer helpful traditional doctrines. Theism is the Great Belief, the others are petty by comparison. To love the all-loving God (not some humanly written book) with all one's mind, heart, and soul means to consider nothing of first importance unless it is logically included in love of God (including love of the divinely loved creatures) !

There is no evidence that Mead was definitely aware of and had reflected upon any form of theism other than what I call classical theism, the doctrine of an immutable, all-arranging, "superwatchmaker" deity, whose intelligence simply imposes the world order. Mead saw that the Newtonian period of science was a natural result. (E. A. Burtt's book on this is a documentation of Mead's idea.) To this extent, Mead thought, the idea had been useful in science.

Darwinian biology suggested a different world view. Animals and plants to some extent arrange themselves and in the long run change their very species, as they respond to their environments. Neither by eternal design nor by the causal past are events fully determined, for there is a "chance" factor—taking Darwin more literally than he intended to be taken. Here Darwin missed a great opportunity and so did most of his religious critics. Suppose there is a chance factor. Is this evidence against theism? Yes, if God is conceived as all-determining Superintelligence. But this is not only not required by the *religious* meaning of God as the worshipful One, it is at best doubtfully consistent with that meaning. If God determines our acts of worship, then it is God worshiping God, not the creatures doing so. The poet Lanier, a pious Christian if there ever was one, said of such an idea:

> *[Ye] Say wrong This work is not of me,*
> But God: it is not true, it is not true.
> . . . .
> Who made a song or picture, he
> Did it, and not another, God nor man.
>
> My Lord is large, my Lord is strong:
> Giving, He gave; my me is mine.
> How poor, how strange, how wrong,
> To dream He wrote the little song
> I made to Him with love's unforced design! ["Individual-
> ity"] [3]

What did Mead know of the form of theism that rejects the absurdity of a merely self-worshiping deity? A long but neglected sequence of thinkers (who have been granted no historian for their achievement) from Socinus in the sixteenth century to W. P. Montague, Whitehead, and others in the twentieth have developed a theism that removes the absurdity, giving genuine recognition to the reality of human freedom and defining creative power in conformity with this recognition. Mead and most other nontheistic philosophers do not know this other tradition.

Nor did Darwin clearly imagine it, although in a letter there is one hint. The reason is found in the power of the classical idea of causality as complete determination of events by their causal antecedents. That was why Darwin did not literally mean *"chance* variations." No, they must, by unknown causes, be determined in advance. Yet Darwin saw definitely that the theological version of this idea was religious nonsense or contradiction!

Mead's own theory of spontaneous action whereby "the future is [or will be] more than the present" (richer in the determinations

137

that, as merely future, it lacked) might have led him into the generalization according to which every truly singular agent (whatever acts as one) transcends, however slightly, causal determination by its past. This contradicts divine governance of the world only, I repeat only, if that governance lacks the largeness, the strength, that Lanier attributed to God, in contrast to the pettiness, or absurdity of wanting to monopolize decision making, leaving to others only the illusion of deciding for themselves. What had been attributed to God was nothing good or great but a meanness or a stupidity. For how dull and nasty, if it were even possible, would be a world such that its supreme consciousness enjoyed no social give and take and beheld no events save those it decided should take place—and yet condemns some of these events as evil or wicked!

Darwinism fits theism better than traditional biology ever could. It shows a world of creatures that partly make themselves and so their descendants—in the long run their descendant species. Why not? Unlike Mead, Whitehead sought a theological interpretation of evolution, attributing decision making to animals generally, not simply to human beings, and conceiving deity as the supreme form of this creativity. Before (or independently of) Heisenberg, he generalized indeterminacy to apply to creatures as such, somehow escaping the iron obstacle to a theory of creaturely freedom set up by Newtonian physics. Perhaps he was influenced (how far was Mead?) by the significance of statistical laws in the theory of gases, Gibbs's phase rule, and entropy theory. Clerk Maxwell and C. S. Peirce had already taken the gas laws as suggestive indications that science gives no unambiguous support to classical causality.

Whitehead, aware of quantum theory in an early phase (years before Mead's death) took it to imply that physical action is in discrete units, rather than strictly continuous. Hence, although he gave additional and more ultimate reasons for the move, he developed his theory of the "epochal" nature of becoming and his doctrine of definitely single actual entities, finite in number in a finite time, offering this as solution of the Zeno paradoxes. Mead's "act" is not definitely singular in this sense. Like Bergson, about whom he reflected and lectured much, Mead has no definite quantum principle. Hence the vagueness of his "act."

From the quantum denial of continuous action, the Peircean principles that possibilities are continuous and that all explanation must consider possibilities as well as actualities (Mead himself holds that the meaning of explanation is its relevance to decision making), finally, from the logical truth that the only way to relate continuous possibilities in an orderly fashion to discrete actualities is by probability, which is a continuous quantity mathematically (Peirce), it follows that the laws we need and, also, alone can know are statistical. So the famous Heisenberg uncertainty principle is not, however often philosophers may say it is, a mere argument from ignorance. It is, as its originator thought, a positive indication of the very nature of things. I had the luck to hear this explanation from Heisenberg's own lips.

A philosopher who believes in freedom should take quantum theory as encouraging a generalized philosophy of freedom, not solely for human animals, not solely for animals in general, but for all singular dynamic agents making up the world. With this, a new era for theology opens before us. The empirical evils that have appeared to so many atheists to support their position are entirely compatible with a theism that views God as giving guidance or directives to creaturely decision making, but to decision making that is genuinely creaturely and not divine deciding unrecognized as such.

Accepting the quantum principle as Whitehead recommends throws light on some of Mead's problems. Thus the distinction between the "me" and the "I" is not merely that between one individual as already settled object for other individuals and the first individual as subject in the act of producing itself. The "I" as the agent for a particular act is the individual now, at the same time as the act. My childish "I," at age five, say, is not the "I" that now writes this sentence. That childish ego could not have done any such thing. Moreover, my childish ego is an object for me as present subject. Its spontaneity, its acting, is not my present spontaneity or acting. Social relations are not merely individual to individual; they are also and finally actual entity to actual entity, whether within the same "personally ordered" series or not. We love ourselves as in the past or future. Self-love involves sympathy, which is *the* principle of motivation, not either selfishness or altruism.

The question of the objectivity of the past is also illuminated by the admission of actual entities. Mead seems to think that the present is given and, on the basis of the given present, we set up "hypotheses" about previous presents, the past. The past, he implies, simply is this class of hypotheses, more or less well founded on the given present. For Whitehead, as for Gilbert Ryle, interestingly enough, it is the past, not the present, of experience that is given. The present self intuits previous presents, it does not intuit, prehend, itself. It is itself; but its successors will prehend it in the future. Moreover, perception also gives us only past events, not strictly simultaneous or contemporary ones. What then is Mead's doctrine, after all, if not a questionable assumption about the given?

Mead says that when the first organisms appeared for whom grass is a food, there existed "a new object, grass as food." Previously there was no such object. If by object one means object-for-such-animals then of course, trivially, there was, before these animals, no such object. But commonsense realism, and to my mind a proper philosophical realism, makes a clear distinction between those constitutive relations of grass without which it could not exist (for instance, temperatures between certain minima and maxima) and those relations that other things have to the grass without these relations doing anything to the grass as such. The physical, chemical, and biological properties of grass can be fully stated without implying anything about its being eaten. Any Whiteheadian 'feelings' that cells of the grass may have occur entirely independently of the grass's future in the stomach of an herbivorous animal. The latter, however, cannot be adequately described without mention of grass. Such an animal really has relation to grass. The grass is indeed "in" relation to the animal, but being in relation to something and intrinsically having that relation are not the same. Plato is now "in relation" to me as I think of Plato, but Plato (unless he did not really die) even now does not possess me as term of "his" relation. I do nothing whatever to Plato by thinking of him; it is only he who does something to me. I hold that these statements are analytic. They are what we should mean by the subject-object relation, whether to the personal past or to any objects whatever, with the sole exception of objects that are merely intentional rather than actually given.

Mr. Micawber was not actually given, even to Dickens, but only imagined, intended. Our basic relation to the past and to nature is quite different. Our picture of the past and of nature keeps changing; neither our past nor nature's past changes in the slightest because our pictures of them change. In the future nature will change in some aspects because we exist, but that is precisely the difference between past and future. Of course, a Mead disciple may say that this is simply my prejudice or arbitrary belief. I can only reply that it is a belief for which good reasons can be given.

The ambiguity just pointed to in Mead's way of speaking was put forth by Arthur Murphy as a deliberate doctrine called "objective relativism." Relative to herbivorous animals grass is food, potential or/and actual. While this is trivially correct, it says nothing constitutive of what grass is that cannot be said without mention of being eaten. Being actually eaten changes the physical and chemical properties of the bits of grass that are eaten, but the properties the grass had while growing remain exactly as they were.

I hold, with G. E. Moore and other critics of idealism, that actually being aware of something, having it as datum, does nothing whatever to the something.

One has to distinguish in this connection between saying that the greenness of the grass, meaning by green here the unitary quality that our visual sensations of it have, would (as Mead grants) not exist without an animal organism stimulated in a certain way and saying that when we see the grass the greenness is merely in our *mental* state. It is also in that of which we are directly aware. But what we are directly aware of may, for all Mead shows, be processes going on in our nervous systems, rather than processes going on in the grass.

I happen to remember Murphy's telling me that he had come to regard his "objective relativism" as a mistake, in no important sense true. This confirmed what I had thought when his article came out. He was a bright man, Murphy, but metaphysics was not his forte. A reviewer once put this unkindly: "Clearly, adventures of ideas are not for Mr. Murphy." His strength, like that of his principal teacher, was in middle-sized ideas and in practical questions of ethics.

The issue, fully generalized, is metaphysical. It is not empirical, a mere question about human or other higher animals. It is a question of the relation of certain ultimate abstractions, such as awareness, to other, comparably general abstractions. In any possible world state there would be distinctions between relations of A to B which are constitutive for A but not for B and those constitutive for both terms, or for neither. And the subject-to-given-object relation is an example of the first type, by the most useful and clear meaning of "given."

The issue can be stated in Mead's terms as follows. "Taking the role of the other" does not necessarily mean changing the other. (One may take one's deceased parent's or friend's role.) Generalizing, one may regard all experience, experience as such, as social in the minimal sense that its givens are feelings of other actualities, including those other actualities that are one's own past experiences. This is a metaphysics of the participation-in-other-lives that some of us think is what all life is and in any possible world state would be. Mead's social view of the human was even more fundamentally true than he thought. As Royce believed, as Whitehead believed, without community in some generalized sense there is nothing, human, subhuman, or divine. We can change others, but only in the future.

Their past actualities we accept, or relegate to the indistinctness of negative prehensions. Change them we cannot.

I find absurd the idea that each time we reinterpret the available data about Caesar, a new Caesar comes into being. It is not the meaning of "pictures of Caesar" to *be* Caesar, or to change Caesar, now that he is dead. That way confusion lies. Murphy reached this conclusion. But Murphy taught *Process and Reality*, year after year, "Each time," he said, "seeing new things in it." *Process and Reality* as what Whitehead wrote did not therefore change. Murphy was, with T. V. Smith and Charles Morris, perhaps the most brilliant of the philosophers produced by Mead's teaching. Of the students who became sociologists I cannot knowledgeably write.

A brilliant teacher Mead certainly was. One has only to read the extraordinary lectures, as noted down by attentive students, on *Movements of Thought in the Nineteenth Century* and on *Mind, Self, and Society* (The University of Chicago Press, 1936, 1934) to see why they made unforgettable impressions upon a host of listeners. The alertness of his mind, his awareness of a vast variety of ideas and historical facts, his ability to enter sympathetically into many contrasting philosophical perspectives, retaining all the while a distinctive individual flavor by his grasp of the social nature of the human animal, make it easy to understand the very unusual power of this professor upon students. Few indeed, if they exist at all, are the books dealing with their topics that rival these two in intellectual qualities. They give an impression of a superior mind interpreting many other superior minds.

Although Mead's sense of how we are what we are only in a social context, apart from which we could at most be no more than subhuman animals, defective as such, is one he to some extent derived from or shared with Dilthey, Royce, Hegel, and Dewey, among others, he certainly made it his own and brilliantly strengthened and applied it. He was a humanist, with certain limitations that this implies, but he was one of the great ones of his kind. What he was not, and did not really try to be, was one of the great metaphysicians of all time, as was Whitehead. That *Process and Reality* was too much for him as an ailing elderly person is easily intelligible. He did not know metaphysics historically as Whitehead did, or in any other way. He was a practicing empirical scientist (like Peirce, but chiefly in different sciences).

It is significant, I think, that, unlike Peirce and Whitehead, also unlike Leibniz, Mead was not a significant contributor to mathematics or formal logic. I connect this with his not being a metaphysician.

142

Mathematical thinking and metaphysical thinking have some common aspects. Neither is empirical in the strict sense of being open to observational falsification. The difference is that mathematical ideas, except where infinity is involved, can be symbolized "diagrammatically" in a sense clarified by Peirce, whereas metaphysical ones (for example, God considered barely as necessarily existent and eternal, even abstracting from all contingent and temporal aspects) cannot be diagrammed. The greater difficulty of achieving consensus comes partly from this. And mathematicians have metaphysical troubles about how to treat infinite collections.

As an empirical scientist (in one of the less "hard" sciences) Mead is impressive. His discussion of scientific method anticipates Popper's slightly later doctrines of "conjecture and refutation." It also had a good deal in common with the views of Peirce. Mead seems to have scarcely noticed Peirce, whose *Collected Papers* came too late to be of help to him. Here, too, Mead and all of us were unlucky. Philosophers, as Plato well knew, should have long lives to learn their task properly. Mead reflected much on Aristotle, less on Plato. Aristotle was a great metaphysician in certain of the aspects of metaphysics that are most readily connected with distinctions of formal logic, above all modal distinctions. Otherwise, he was, like Mead, chiefly an empirical scientist, so far as there was such a thing in his day.

Unlike Popper, Mead seems to have virtually eliminated metaphysical questions and to have been an unqualified empiricist, recognizing only such questions as those the answers to which conceivable experiences might eventually falsify. That falsification is the crucial operation in empirical science he was as confident as Popper.

Take the proposition, "there is something," or "something exists." Does it make sense to anticipate as a possible future occurrence an observation falsifying this proposition? I think not. Hence I take "something exists" as an a priori truth. Metaphysics explores the meaning of this a priori truth and other propositions that fall into the same class, in which, as I have argued elsewhere, "God exists" is included. Hence the theistic question is nonempirical. With Popper (whose remarks on this subject I find obscure if not evasive) I do not equate this with "the theistic question has no cognitive meaning." What Mead did with the question put in these terms I do not know. But then by my criteria Mead was not a metaphysician. It follows that he was a great philosopher only in the sense in which philosophy is not identical with metaphysics. (I believe there is indeed a distinction.) That he was a great teacher seems clear. And a great social scientist.

Dewey, James, Peirce, and Whitehead were greater *writers* than Mead. This difference no amount of editing can render unimportant. What could be done by editing seems to have been done. It is well that we are thus given a chance to experience something of what students and colleagues experienced when those remarkable lectures were being given.

Notes

1. All of Mead's books were published posthumously, edited by one or more of his students. *Philosophy of the Present*, ed. A. E. Murphy, was made from Mead's written versions of his Carus Lectures, given in 1930, and was published in LaSalle, Ill., by Open Court, 1959. The other books, all published by the University of Chicago Press, are: *Mind, Self, and Society*, ed. C. W. Morris, 1934; *Movements of Thought in the Nineteenth Century*, ed. M. H. Moore, 1936; *The Philosophy of the Act*, ed. Morris, J. M. Brewster, and D. L. Miller, 1938.

2. David L. Miller, probably the highest living authority on Mead's philosophy, has given me a vigorous, stimulating defence of Mead's position about the past. He says that for one who thinks, as Mead always did, as a scientist, the past is what evidence in the present enables us to know about. He also says that for Mead the question of the reality of the past had no connection with theism or nontheism.

My position is that scientificism, the doctrine that our only access to existence is empirical, through observational science, is false. "Something exists" states no merely empirical fact (in the Popperian sense), since its negation is empirically meaningless. Although we know that our pictures of Caesar have changed and may change again, it is mere assertion that the past Caesar changes with these changes in us, an assertion that adds nothing to our knowledge.

True enough, God's awareness, unlike ours, distinct and infallible, cannot be used by us to correct our historical hypotheses. But belief in it can give intelligible meaning to our intuition that past people were real people with real feelings and thoughts and that these thoughts and feelings were in no way dependent for their reality on anything that later generations came to think about them. I have heard a distinguished social scientist say approximately the following: For most historians, it is not true that past generations were only whatever we are able to know about them. Rather, for historians generally, it is as if there were a "recording angel, or if you prefer, an electronic recording machine," that accurately registers events as they happen and permanently preserves the record. The record is inaccessible to us, but it is there and divergence from it measures the extent of our failure as historians.

Theism does not give us details of existence. It gives us the meaning of existence—no small contribution. Miller also says that Mead did not argue against theism or for atheism. He was a constructive thinker indeed and accentuated the positive. Basically, it was the cultural situation, rather than any one or two individuals, that produced the atheism or agnosticism of Dewey, Mead, and their students.

3. From Sydney Lanier's poem "Individuality", the second of his Hymns of the Marshes, in *Selected Poems of Sydney Lanier*, ed. Stark Young (New York and London: Charles Scribner's Sons, 1947), p. 12.

CHAPTER 12

Hocking and Perry on Idealism

When I arrived at Harvard in 1919, entering as a Junior, I was already persuaded on two philosophical points: (1) The notion of mere matter, irreducible to mind in some broad sense, is absurd or meaningless; and (2) All minds are included in a universal or divine mind. My reasons for these views were my own, derived from reflection during my two years (1917–1919) as orderly in an army hospital. I had no particular philosophical authority for the beliefs; they were conclusions of chains of reasoning starting from what seemed direct insights into the essence of all experience. Later, much later, I found that my initial reason (eventually others were added) for asserting the reducibility of the concept of matter was about the same as Croce's: the essentially aesthetic character of immediate experience. (Similar contentions are found in Heinrich Rickert, Heidegger, Whitehead, and others.) I still find the argument valid. As for my reasons for believing in an all-inclusive deity, they were perhaps most like those of Royce, whose *Problem of Christianity* was almost the only technical philosophical work I recall having previously read.

At Harvard in the stimulating metaphysics class taught by William Ernest Hocking (1873–1966) I found support for my convictions. I still remember, for instance, his telling indictment of pluralism (or was it dualism?) as "an unfinished thought," and the suggestion that aesthetic values are more ultimate than ethical ones. However, the influences of Ralph Barton Perry (1876–1957) and C. I. Lewis (1883–1964) made it imperative to try to rethink the grounds for and the proper scope and limitations of such convictions.

As I recall, Hocking used to argue, following Royce, presumably, that we criticize judgments by comparing them, not with bare reality, but with other and more adequate judgments. In other words, relations of experience to reality must be found within experience; hence, while the things we are trying to know may be independent of any particular experience or judgment, they are not independent of experience and judgment as such. Some form of idealism is therefore inevitable. Reality is the content of adequate judgments.[1]

Although I was prepared to agree with the basic conclusion (that mind or experience in the broadest sense—the human mind being but one species—is coextensive with reality), Hocking's arguments left me uneasy. Perry's alleged "fallacy of arguing from the egocentric predicament" was not to be ignored. Nor was it enough to say with Hoernlé (whom I knew rather well, although I took no course with him), "It is no predicament; it is an opportunity!" Yet I could not simply agree with Perry either.[2] To me it was (and still is) *directly* evident that physical reality is not merely physical or neutral to psychical properties, but inextricably psychical as well. This was a phenomenological judgment, and (like Croce) I argued that we cannot *think* a dualism of the merely physical and the psychical if only the psychical is given. While I was in the army, Santayana's phrase which I had picked up somewhere, "Beauty is objectified pleasure," occurred to me when I was asking myself, "Is there a basis in experience for a mind-(mere) matter dualism? " It then struck me that (a) sensation itself is through and through a kind of feeling, (b) all experience is more or less aesthetic, exhibits at least a minimal beauty of things, so that (c) physical reality is not first given in aesthetically neutral terms, a certain feeling being then, perhaps, projected upon this neutral datum, but rather the given is pervasively composed of feeling. The notion of neutral stuff, I concluded, is an illegitimate product of abstractive negation, in which low intensities of feeling are mistaken for no feeling. This "Crocean" doctrine (I knew nothing of Croce) has been mine since 1918. It meant, among other things, that I could not accept James's and Perry's theory of pure (meaning neutral between mind and matter) bits of experience.

But what about the fallacies of which Perry and Lewis (and G. E. Moore, whose article, "The Refutation of Idealism" one could hardly fail to read when I was at Harvard) accused the idealistic argument? These were subtle, challenging thinkers. To do justice to their valid points was no easy task. Indeed, it has taken a large part of a lifetime and the help of two intellectual giants, Peirce and Whitehead, to bring it to anything like completion. But what a boon it was to be confronted, as we were in those days at Harvard, with a convinced, imaginative, pedagogically powerful defender, and two powerful critics, of the idealistic tradition!

147

Hocking contended that nature as experienced by us is constitutive of our experience, part of its living unity. (This seemed to me phenomenologically correct.) On the other hand, we do not produce nature, as appearing in our experience, but receive this part of ourselves as a gift. The interpretation given these two points was that in experiencing nature we are being, insofar, "created" by God. This was rather like Berkeley: Nature is a divine language in which Deity speaks to us, by causing us to share in some of His "ideas." The exact differences between Hocking and Berkeley have never been very clear to me.

One difference is certainly that Hocking paid much more attention than Berkeley to the question how we know nondivine minds other than our own. He held that we come as close to direct experience of other (human) minds as would be desirable or suitable, and that less privacy than there is would be disadvantageous, if not absurd.

Nature as experienced is indeed part of the unity of our experience and is of the nature of mind, not of mere matter. This point has been for me a fixed item of speculation, since it is phenomenological, if anything is. But what exactly can be inferred from it? Just where did Moore, C. I. Lewis (on the whole my favorite teacher, more about him in the next chapter) and Perry go wrong, and where, perhaps, were they right, and Hocking in part mistaken? I had a feeling at the time that *everybody* was somewhat in error.

With Perry and Moore one must grant that an act or instance of knowing does not create the things it knows. Of course it creates their being thus known to that knower, but this is all! The existence of the things is another matter. The decisive proof for this proposition was given by Moore. When in memory we know our previous experiences, we are not in the least degree creating these experiences; for this would contradict their status as temporally prior. Hence, to attribute creation of the thing known to an act of knowing is to imply a solipsism of the present moment and indeed, on the assumption, even the present moment cannot really be known, it just is. For this reason, I have long accepted a radical form of epistemological realism. To experience or know is not in the least to create the thing experienced or known.

On the other hand, it remains valid that *when known* the thing known has *become* part of the life of feeling and/or thought of the knower. Here Hocking was right. The task is to reconcile the two points: Knowing finds, does not produce, what it knows, but knowing is partly constituted by the things known. Neither Berkeley nor Hocking (perhaps, directly or indirectly, influenced more by Hegel than by Berkeley) seemed to me to have a clear way of showing the compatibility of these two (to me) evident truths. Yet they are, I am confident, quite compatible.

Let us consider Hocking's proposition that in perception one is being "created." The objects of experience do help to produce what one then becomes. In some sense, they partly create the experiences. However, Hocking seems to regard, not the objects, but God, as the creative agent in the case. But then, what are the objects? Ourselves, so far as created in the manner in question? From this it would follow that, if or when the object is a past event, the earlier event is *merely* a created portion of the present experience, plus God as source. This, I submit, will not do. Or shall we suppose that memory and perception are two absolutely different sorts of knowing? If so, we shall be trying to explain away the evidence that in perception, too, the events perceived have already happened when we perceive them. And there are other objections to a sheer dualism of memory as not constitutive, and perception as constitutive, of the things known or perceived.

The things experienced do, I reiterate, *become* portions of the experiencing, but this status in the experience does not constitute the existence of the things. Rather, it is a sheer addition to that existence. The things already existed, and no particular subsequent act of experiencing was needed for this. It will not do to reduce objects to mere creative acts of God relative to our experiences.

An experience is an event; what is experienced is also one or more events, but these are prior and independent. As such they are, in a fashion, creative of the subsequent experiences in which they are given. The past creates the present. But this is only part of the truth. For, granted freedom as creative transcendence of the causal conditions, the present experience in some degree *creates itself.* Here Lequier, Sartre, James, Bergson, and Whitehead agree. I hold with them. An experience is in a manner self-created. But it utilizes, as materials for the creative synthesis which it is, the antecedent events which have actually happened. The things experienced are not at all created by the experience, but only the being-experienced of these already existing things (or already actualized events). Experiencing or knowing is a more or less free *synthesis* of data already in being. What an act of experiencing creates is, first of all, only this very act itself.

It may seem that not much is left of the idealistic argument. Our experiences find, they do not create, what they know. How then can experiencing be the constitutive agent in reality at large? This was Perry's question, also Moore's. The answer is not so very obscure, yet how many brilliant men have missed it! The mistake is to begin by asking how one thing can create another or how one thing can make another to depend upon it. This is like asking, as Aristotle did, how one thing—itself unmoving—can move another. Plato saw more deeply when he asked, what sort of thing can move *itself?* For "move" substitute "create," and our theory is the Platonic one: Find that thing which can, even in part, create itself, and you will be in a position to ask the further question, "Can it also be at least part-creative of another thing? "

If our experiences are in their overall characters as syntheses self-creative, they are also in part created (or at least made possible, caused) by the things experienced. Moreover, in some cases at least, what is given in experience is itself a previous experience, as in personal memory. Here, then, we have a partly self-creative object which is part-causative of a subsequent self-creative object. The creativity of experiencing as such is here on both sides of the subject-object relationship. (The idealistic camel's nose is already in the tent.) As for experiences other than personal memory, their objects too, by the Crocean principle, are given (though obscurely, vaguely) as of the nature of experiencing, feeling, or thinking—though primarily of other than human types.

Perry's egocentric predicament analysis does nothing to disprove the points made in the previous paragraph. Nor does anything that Moore has to say on the subject of idealism. What Moore misses is this: That blue, for instance, as given has *become* a quality of our feeling or sensing is quite compatible with its previously having been a quality of feeling other than ours. That is, Moore missed the social duality of immediacy, its aspect of participation, *sympathy*, feeling of feeling—the last-mentioned feeling having a different subject from the other. The dogma that A cannot literally feel B's feeling begs the essential question. I challenge this dogma. I *experience* what it denies.

According to Perry, the "cardinal principle of idealism" was the argument, "Whatever I know is known by me, hence all I can know are the contents of my consciousness." Of course, all I know is actually somehow content of my consciousness; but this does not prove that it had no antecedent existence, independent of the status which it has acquired thanks to me, nor that there was any necessity that it ever should acquire this status. Here Perry is right. My childhood experiences that I now know might never have been thus known—for I might have died long since. But there is another, subtly distinct question: Did or did not the occurrence of those childhood experiences entail their being subsequently known by *someone?* There is a seldom-noticed formal analogy between this question and another: An event when it occurs is independent of all subsequent events, but is it independent of there coming to be *some* subsequent events or other for which the given event will be past? Events do not, determinism or precognition apart, have to be followed by precisely the events that in fact follow them. But they do, I hold, have to be followed by some events causally congruent with (though not causally entailed by) their previous occurrence. On that view, to be an event is to be about to become past for some suitable subsequent events. Events must have successors, though not necessarily the very successors they do have. To deny this is to assert that an event might be the last and have no successor at all. This is sometimes said to be thinkable. I doubt that it is, but I will not further argue the matter here. Suppose it is not thinkable and that to be an event entails having successors for which the event will become part of their past. The question then is, "Are there two ways of being successor of an event E, one of which is to experience E as past (in memory or perception) and the other is to have E as past in some entirely different way, say by being an effect of E without in any sense or fashion experiencing it? "

I believe an idealist can make a good case for the view that all instances of having as past are, or involve, forms of experiencing as past—something like memory. Thus, while it is entirely false that to be is to be experienced by this or that particular experience—as it is false that to happen is to be followed by this or that particular subsequent event—yet it is true that to be is to be destined to be experienced by some suitable subsequent experiences, just as to happen is to be destined to be followed by some suitable subsequent events. To be is to be destined to be perceived (or remembered), although no particular percipient is entailed rather than any other. The class of "subsequent percipients" of the entity cannot remain empty, although no member of the class is a necessity. (The concept of class used here cannot, it seems, be purely extensional. This is one of the many reasons why I suspect that much contemporary formal logic is inadequate to philosophy.)

Intuitively I have always felt that Perry, Moore, and many others who similarly criticize idealism miss something at this point, but something seldom clearly expressed. There must be an escape from egocentricity, for ethical and religious, as well as intellectual, reasons. But why need the escape be into a world of mere matter, even as possible? The alternative to egoism is altruism, not mere neutrality or nonsubjectivity. The social structure of experience (and reality) is the answer, not materialism or dualism. "Matter" taken as ultimate is but the shadow of our own will to exploit or use things rather than to sympathize with them or share in their life. I can abstract from my present experience in order to think my childhood experiences in their innocence. I can abstract from my peculiarities in order to think the contrasting peculiarities of another person or animal. But to abstract from all subjectivity, all experience—this is a mere negation, for which the materialists and dualists have yet to furnish the least vestige of positive content.

There is, however, one important qualification. It was first clearly expounded by Leibniz, and was by far his most important contribution, although the one most neglected, because historians did not grasp it. In our perceptions certain quasi-individual objects are presented that no philosopher has ever regarded as experiencing subjects. Indeed, in visual and tactile experience, nearly all distinctly given unities are in the class of more or less obviously *non*-experiencing entities—all except animal organisms. If we perceive an object, either it is an animal, or there is reason to doubt that it is an experiencing individual. Two possible conclusions follow: *(A)* Apart from animals, nature consists of perceived individuals devoid of experience of any kind; *(B)* apart from animals, nature consists of individuals that as such are not distinctly perceived, since what we seem to see or discriminate through touch as individuals are in reality aggregates, masses of indistinctly given individuals, the nature of which, therefore, cannot be known from direct perception. If anything is manifest from the progress of science it is that *B*, not *A*, is correct.

However, many philosophers still follow Aristotle in accepting *A*. I regard this as a species of cultural lag. In addition, I hold, it was always bad philosophy, even apart from science. For perception obviously does not exhibit distinctly the acting agents, the causal powers, of which most of nature must be composed. The Greek atomists insisted upon this. Up to that point, they were right. But they were wrong in trying to deduce the nature of micro-individuals—not one of which is perceived, but which are the primary causal agents in nature—from the confused perceptions of aggregates of such individuals, which, apart from animals, is all that we can have. Leibniz was the first to put these two points together and draw the conclusion: Our experience of animals, first and most adequately of ourselves, is our only definite model for individuality at large. (And the notion of mere stuff, not consisting of individual units, is a confusion, an attempt to get positive information out of the absence of distinctness in our perceptions.) Of course, not all individuals are animals, but the cells of plants and animals can be viewed as self-creative units of experience, and so can molecules, atoms, perhaps particles. The rest of nature consists of masses of individuals, for instance a tree or a cloud, whose active units fall below the threshold of our discriminations.

I do not recall that Hocking gave me any encouragement to follow the Leibnizian lead. It was the Harvard psychologist L. T. Troland, and later Peirce and Whitehead, who most clearly showed the way here, they and Leibniz himself. I suspect that it was Hegel who barred the way for Hocking. Hegel takes the distinction of subject-object "dialectically," treating the two as irreducibly distinct yet in some mysterious way interdependent, though with an equally mysterious asymmetry whereby the subject "overlaps" and is more fundamental. I share the feeling Perry used to express that this mixture of symmetry and asymmetry is never made clear in the Hegelian tradition. Mind "unifies"—but *how*, Perry used to ask? The answer, I hold, is in the social structure of experience. My momentary unity of feeling is a new-felt synthesis of the antecedent feelings or experiences (partly my own earlier ones) in which I now participate. This "unification," however, does not alter or bring into being the antecedent factors; it merely accepts them. They are unified, not in or for themselves, but only in and for me now.

One more step. The unification in question is, in one sense, indeed in and for the antecedent experiences. This sense is that the latter at least unconsciously expected to be taken into account somehow by future experience, and their sense of value and importance entailed this destiny. This is, again, the point made above that while no particular subsequent perceptions are involved in an event's reality, what is involved is "destined to be somehow perceived or remembered" by some suitable percipients. This is the ultimate sociality, that the present, which enjoys contributions from past experience, feels or regards itself as a contribution offered to the future as such. This "contributionism," as I call it, expresses the ultimate meaning of "to be is to be perceived." But note: Only if an event is some sort of experience can it be, in and for itself, constituted by its potential contribution to the future. Thus the real meaning of "to be is to be perceived" is, "to be, as a singular concrete event, is to anticipate as inevitable the status of being appropriated as datum by suitable future experiences."

How, then, does God come in? This question I cannot answer as simply as Hocking (like Berkeley) sometimes seems to answer it. But I can give a hint or two, in closing this chapter. God is entailed as the only unqualifiedly "suitable" percipient to receive the contribution which, relative to the future, constitutes an event. Not that the particular act by which God perceives the event will in any way enter into its already constituted reality. No particular perception ever enters constitutively into a particular object of that very perception.

God's perceptions of contingent things are themselves doubly contingent. All that is destined is that some suitable perceptions will embrace the event in question. But only a divine perception could be unqualifiedly suitable and thus definitively constitute a thing's enduring reality. An event is not "brought into being" by anyone's perceiving it, even by God's perceiving it. For it cannot be perceived until it is, that is, has happened, and then it is already in being. But what is meant by "in being"? It means, I think, "in the treasury of contributions available for suitable subsequent experiencing." Apart from the inevitability of such subsequent experiencing, there would be no difference between "in being" and "not in being." All importance, all value, hence all meaning, is relative to possible contributions to the one Life whose adequate perceivings alone can render immortal the character of an event. What a thing is and what it can contribute to the Divine Life, both directly and (via its intermediate contributions to other nondivine things) indirectly, are one and the same.

I may seem to be saying that God does not create but only preserves reality. However, there is another side of the story. Experiences create themselves, utilizing the things experienced, and these thus can be said in part to create the experiences. Now God is, mostly subconsciously, experienced at all times. (Hocking, I think, would agree.) In this sense God is indeed always creative of us. But there is a distinction to be made. God, as experienced *by* me now, and thus constitutive *of* me now, is God in a certain state S, and this state must in some sense be prior to my present state; while God as experiencing me as I am now can only be God in state S', subsequent to me as I am now. Thus the temporal aspect of God becomes crucial. Otherwise the theory would lead to contradictions. All relations would become internal, although knowing is external to the thing known.

On the issue just touched upon, Hocking met the arch-critics of nineteenth-century idealism at least partway, and it was, I suspect, lucky for me that he did. He rejected the idolatry of the eternal which has poisoned European theology since Greek times, and he convinced me that he was right in this rejection. He held that the all-inclusive consciousness faces an open future and is not in every aspect timeless or immutable. (It seems reasonably sure that William James was chiefly responsible for this. True, there were other precedents in the writings of Fechner, Lequier, and Socinus—but I am not aware that Hocking had these in mind.) Hocking also defended, with James, causally transcendent freedom for man as well as for God. Thus he avoided the "block-universe," the theory of exclusively internal relations, which in England particularly has so often—but illogically—been taken as a corollary of the view that mind is the ultimate explanatory principle. The connection between (a) the rejection of mere matter and (b) the universal denial of external relations and contingency seems to have been the merest historical accident. It certainly does not follow from any conceptual necessity.

I shall never forget the day when, after class, I objected to Hocking's statement of the temporalistic view of God, and he convinced me on the spot that my objection was ill founded. I suggested that if the future were outside God's awareness this would compromise the divine status as the all-inclusive reality. But Hocking brought me, in but a moment or two, to realize something like the following: As "outside" God's awareness the future is really nothing, since, insofar as genuinely open or indeterminate, the future is not a definite object of knowledge. It will be fully definite only when it is no longer future, but then its definiteness will be entirely embraced by the divine experience. I thus saw that my supposed difficulty was unreal. It will scarcely be denied that much—the best-reasoned portion—of the opposition to idealism arose from idealism's apparent denial of the reality of time and contingency, its identification of the real with the rational, necessary, or eternal. From this Hocking did at least as much to save me as did the realists.

Renouncing the block-universe, while it removed certain paradoxes from the idealistic position, still did not suffice to furnish an intelligible account of our perceptions of physical nature. Before exposure, several years later, to Peirce and Whitehead, I was unable to arrive at a clear view of the structure of perception that was compatible with the Crocean principle referred to above, and yet (I hope) defensible against such critics as Perry, Lewis, or Moore.

Many troublesome questions remain: for instance, how the temporal structure of God-and-world can be combined with the relativity of simultaneity so far as this is to be accepted from physics, or how one is to deal with the plausible arguments for precognition.

But one thing seems quite clear to me: The propositions, "experienced nature is part of the felt unity of experience and itself psychical in nature," and "an experience finds, in no degree creates, its data" are perfectly compatible. Therefore, the main point which the anti-idealists wanted to make and the main point which Hocking stressed do not constitute a genuine disagreement. The failure to agree, or perhaps even to understand, rested upon other factors in the two positions as then represented.

Perry was said to have been William James's favorite pupil. There is a pathos in this fact. For in some ways Perry disagreed with James just where James was most firmly convinced of the importance of his views. If James believed in anything, it was our ability to transcend causal conditions by being only incompletely determined by these conditions. Perry was a convinced classical determinist, as I know from having talked to him about it. He thought that scientists would "never accept" any form of indeterminism. He reacted to Heisenberg's famous essay on indeterminacy in this way. His prophecy has proved false. Scientists are not so absolutely committed to any dogma as Perry, an ex-theological student, was to classical determinism. Perry did agree with James in being a pluralist. However, his pluralism was more extreme than James's, closer to Hume's and Bertrand Russell's. The combination of extreme causal determinism and extreme pluralism (lack of any internal relations connecting the constituents of reality) repeated the most bizarre feature of Hume's philosophy. The combination violently connects and violently disconnects the constituents of reality.

In the latter part of his career Perry virtually gave up his efforts to contribute to metaphysics or epistemology and devoted himself to theory of value and to historical scholarship. He developed a curious form of humanistic substitute for theism by defining 'God' as the ideal social organization, in which intelligent altruism and intelligent self-interest coincide. He once even, in a lecture at the University of Chicago, advocated a policy of compromising conflicts of interest as the best way to serve God—"Indeed," said he, "I suspect that, in the last analysis, God *is* compromise." His old age, rumor had it, was not a very happy one. The world (in the mid-1950s) was not compromising satisfactorily, as we all know to our sorrow. It is James's moderate pluralism, or moderate monism, or something not so far from it as Perry's metaphysics, that makes the difficulty intelligible. Free yet interdependent individuals, freer than

156

determinism allows, less free than radical pluralism implies, cannot be guaranteed to be safe from risk of conflict and frustration. We do not live in Perry's supposed world and never can. Indeed, it would not be a world, or anything coherently conceivable.

Hocking was said to have been Royce's favorite pupil. Here there was a deeper affinity between master and pupil than in the James-Perry case. Like Royce in his time, Hocking gave intellectual encouragement to many religious persons. Someone expressed this fact, somewhat unkindly I suppose, by remarking, "Upon William Ernest Hocking has fallen the mantle of 'the genteel tradition.' " The label was Santayana's, and it did have Royce in mind, among others. Hocking was, however, no mere disciple. He tried to do justice to the insights of James as well as those of Royce and definitely made room for the freedom that James required. But he did not emphasize his break with Royce, for instance his admission of an open future even for God. Indeed I have not noticed any passage in his writings where the point is clearly made.

Hocking's writings are more impressive for their eloquence and practical wisdom than for their intellectual acumen. There is more edification than technique in his offerings. I recall a characteristic phrase of his in a (written) discussion of the theological problem of evil: "The great hunter crashes through the world forest." (James would have liked this.) I also recall his saying in class: "Aesthetic values are the most fundamental ones." In this I take him to have somewhat surpassed both James and Royce, who were almost obsessed with the moral aspect of life.

Hocking had, for some, including this writer, a notable degree of charisma. When I first heard him lecture, I felt a somewhat mysterious sense of fascination with the man, his physical presence and manner. He was tall and handsome, with a very serious, Olympian bearing. So, I thought, should a profound philosopher appear. The impression diminished in time, as I became aware of the deficiencies in his argumentation. Like Royce he was capable of presenting a loose, inconclusive piece of reasoning as though it were definitive proof, and (here differing from Royce) of reiterating the same piece of reasoning decades later without essentially clarifying or tightening the logic. (Royce's repetitions added something.) Perry and Lewis seemed superior in this respect, expecially Lewis. Yet it was Lewis more than Perry who saw that mere logic cannot by itself settle philosophical issues. "There are no absolute proofs in philosophy," Lewis said. "But I like a philosopher to half-prove what he believes." Hocking scarcely did that, I came to see.

The presence of Hocking, Perry, and Lewis in one department provided a marvelous opportunity for students to acquire a sense of the nature of philosophical disagreements and the variety of perspectives among which an individual must, in the end, make a personal choice, except so far as he or she can arrive at partly new and (one hopes) better perspectives. I agree with Donald Williams that there was at the time (the early twenties) no better place in the world to study philosophy.

Notes

1. Hocking's philosophical position is presented in his large book *The Meaning of God in Human Experience* (New Haven: Yale University Press, 1912, 1950). See also *The Self, Its Body and Freedom* (Yale, 1928). His other books apply the basic conceptions to various human problems. He taught an interesting course on political philosophy. His *Types of Philosophy*, an introductory textbook, shows his ability to communicate to undergraduates. His son, Richard Hocking, assisted him in revising this book in a later edition.

2. Perry's most controversial book was his *Present Philosophical Tendencies* (New York: Longmans Green & Co., 1912, 1929). His "New Realism" was a radically pluralistic doctrine of neutral entities, mutually externally related, in one form of combination constituting experiences or mind, in another form, matter. Perry is now perhaps best known for his studies of William James and his *General Theory of Value* (Cambridge, Mass.: Harvard University Press, 1954). According to this book, a value is any object of any interest. Three principles for determining comparative values are proposed. Their validity may be somewhat independent of Perry's basic pluralistic ontology. Perry totally misses the participatory structure of experience as a unity of feeling having other such unities as its data. But he tries hard to argue for his doctrines. It is a careful, neat, somewhat dry book. I liked an early book of his called *The Moral Economy* (New York: Charles Scribner's Sons, 1909). Perhaps Perry's soundest judgments were ethical rather than epistemological or ontological.

CHAPTER 13

Lewis on Memory,
Modality, and the Given

Of the teachers in the Harvard philosophy department in the early twenties when I was associated with it as a student, the nearest to a general favorite, at least among graduate students, was Clarence Irving Lewis (1883–1964). He had deeply studied Leibniz, Kant, and some of the post-Kantian idealists, especially Fichte, Bosanquet, and Royce; but he also took John Dewey seriously and appreciated Peirce and James. He was a splendid logician and his systems of strict implication are still relevant and discussed.

Lewis was neither a positivist nor a materialist. It is reported that he said, "I believe in God." He did, I recall, say (or have someone say) grace before meals at home. Yet there is nothing of this faith in his writings. Why? The secret is not very deeply hidden. Lewis in his writings dealt with things he had thought out as a philosopher. He did not claim to have done this with his religious faith. Indeed, he denied having done so. He told me, "There ought to be a metaphysics; but I am not going to make it." He did say that it is "not necessary" to attribute absoluteness in every respect to God. I think it is safe to conclude that William James influenced nim in this negative position. As he put it, James usually reached the right conclusions, "but only God knows how" he reached them. That Royce's absolutism was mistaken, as well as Bradley's or Bosanquet's, he was confident. And he had little trust in Hegel, "in method a poor philosopher." He admired Royce, but did not accept his idealism.

In *An Analysis of Knowledge and Valuation* (1946) Lewis gave his mature view of knowledge and a very fine discussion of intrinsic values. He made a lucid distinction between the relativity or subjectivity of valuations of physical objects or activities (for instance,

159

a painting or a musical performance) and the objective value of our experiences of these things. Who likes what objects tells little or nothing about any intrinsic value of those objects but only something about their instrumental value. (Lewis himself had a great fondness for classical music and opera.) But the liking itself, as a species of satisfaction, joy, or happiness, is in itself good, whatever anyone says. There is much wisdom in Lewis's treatment of this topic. He was a delightful and admirable person and teacher. In his reply to criticisms in the Schilpp volume that was devoted to him, and from which most of this chapter is taken, he showed a generosity and genial tolerance rare in such a context of self-defence.

Lewis's conviction that possibility is not a merely linguistic or merely logical concept was not adequately defended by him and could not be, since he renounced systematic elaboration of metaphysical ideas, although asserting the need for such elaboration. But it is well that he made such a fine technical development of formal calculi for expressing modalities. His former pupil W. V. O. Quine argues against modal logic, but some other logicians have returned to the topic, and the issue is not closed.

Lewis, when I was his pupil, was a determinist (I recall arguing with him in class about this), but later he abandoned the doctrine. However, one reason he gave for doing so was scarcely the best reason. Since he regarded predictions as referring directly not to what happens in nature but to what appearances of nature we shall experience if we make certain experiments, he argued that scientific laws do not furnish strictly sufficient conditions for events. To predict an eclipse is to say that *if* one is at a certain part of the earth's surface at a certain time (with a clear sky) and has one's eyes open one will have certain experiences. But whether one will do all this or not is partly a matter of choice and not of the laws of physics. Lewis never published the lecture (given at the University of Chicago in 1941) in which he offered the foregoing argument, and it expresses a rather odd way of settling the question of determinism. (For a defence of Lewis's argument see note 3 to Chapter 13.) I conclude that Lewis never saw clearly the significance of the Aristotelian view of potentiality as the essence of futurity. Support for this interpretation is given by the fact that Lewis in another talk, at an American Philosophical Association meeting, identified an "individual" with the earthly career of that individual from birth to death (or perhaps beyond death?). Lewis admitted candidly that this Leibnizian doctrine is not the commonsense view. It implies that nothing a person does or that happens to that person could have been otherwise, granted that the person comes to exist at all. If Jimmy Carter had failed to be elected when he was, there would not have been that person at all ever.

For the validity of memory, Lewis appeared to make but one claim: It normally establishes a significant probability that something like what is remembered was really experienced.[1] (Similarly, with perception: It establishes a probability that what is perceived is real, which for Lewis meant that further perceptions will or would conform to the indicated pattern.) These are minimal claims that no one can avoid making, and that indeed every higher animal makes merely by living. The only question is whether we should not go further. Could memory disclose even a probability, if (*per impossibile*—for I hold this to be not genuinely conceivable) it accomplished no more than that? Can we understand the functioning of memory except by seeing that it discloses, not simply probable truth about the past, but the past itself?

Lewis is one of those who hold that not merely is something given as probable, but something is given—period. It is meaningless to ask, how probable is the given? Were there such a probability, then that which disclosed it to us must itself be given, and not with mere probability. I agree with Lewis so far, but I also think that his critics have had some justification. For I do not find that he has furnished us with a satisfactory account of the given.

Is the given temporally present, or is it past, or is it sometimes one and sometimes the other? If it is always present, then in this respect perception and memory are not distinguishable, and the pastness of the thing remembered is wholly due to interpretation, although in some mysterious way there is a probability-assurance governing this interpretation. Was this Lewis's view? It appears to have been unless one reads another conception into his deliberately somewhat noncommittal term 'epistemological present.'[2] If such was his doctrine, then he was accepting a widespread theory, as old as Aristotle, according to which memory consists entirely in something merely present being taken as a sign of something past—a theory that prejudges basic issues in epistemology and ontology. Is it a sound theory?

It does appear to have a certain congruence with some other features of Lewis's general view of knowledge. Thus, were he to hold that hearing, or vision, for instance, is the givenness of events occurring outside our bodies, he would in effect be admitting that past occurrences can be direct data. For example, the physical explosion I hear took place a short time before my hearing it. But

Lewis does not say that such things are given. What he seems to hold is that the given is neither event nor actual physical object, but only the given, a ghostly entity, having no other status than that it is given, a bare 'sense-datum' or *quale.*

There are difficulties with this attenuated view of givenness. Indirect knowledge of nature seems to imply direct awareness of nature at some point. By 'nature' we mean (or ought to mean) an orderly system of events or processes that are not, save incidentally, human experiences. Once we have direct awareness of some portions of the natural system, the rest can be inferred by scientific method. But we are scarcely advanced in analyzing this process by the assumption of nonnatural entities called 'data,' that are nowhere save in our experiences, and in being aware of which we bring into being (mysteriously aided, perhaps, by nature) the very things we are aware of (though not the 'objects' whose probability is thereby somehow established). I still think G. E. Moore's old argument against what he called 'idealism' applied validly to this view. Awareness accepts, it does not make, its data, not even with the help of an object itself not given.

From these, and other considerations, some of which will appear presently, I conclude: Unless something past is given, nothing identifiable is given. Even my seeming to perceive steps before me, to take one of our author's examples, cannot be proved to be given as merely present, since there is a good case, not so far as I know rejected by Lewis, for the view that introspection is really retrospection. Must we not find some escape from the view of memory, central to skeptical philosophies from Hume to Santayana, according to which the past is never literally given? This doctrine seems to drive us to the desperate position that nothing is given, not even the seeming givenness of various entities. (In Santayana, essences are given, but that they are given is apparently a mere inference or belief.)

Why, after all, must memory be thought to have as datum something wholly in the present? Lewis did not, to my knowledge, employ the a priori argument: What is past is gone, nonexistent, hence it cannot be given. This argument seems almost silly, for if there is no such thing as a past event, how can there be historical truths? Or are these truths true of nonentities? Lewis held that all truth refers to the future, but surely historical truth (and historical knowledge) refers to the past also, and not merely to the future. Indeed, according to Lewis, propositions refer to the whole of space-time.[3]

There is one further argument, that from the illusions and mistakes of memory. How could we be mistaken about the absolutely given? The reasoning is the same as Lewis's about perception: Some seen objects turn out not to have been there, hence the seeing was not literal givenness of the objects, but only of the sense data. Similarly, since the remembered may turn out not to have taken place, the remembering cannot have been literal givenness of the past, but only of an 'image' or (Lewis's word) 'surrogate,' in the present. This is the argument that Lewis employs. Let us grant that the reasoning proves something. Does it prove the total nongivenness of past events? I think not. In many instances, a particular event that we took ourselves to be remembering was not, indeed, literally given, for no such event had occurred. But Lewis himself was fond of pointing out how inevitably the given is everywhere mixed with thought; indeed, he suggested that unless the given is thought about, interpreted, it probably cannot become a permanently available item of recollection. Thus, probably all memory, so far as consciously reported upon, involves interpreting the given, and such interpretation is fallible. However, this does not prove that the very pastness of the remembered is supplied by the interpreting process or that the given in memory is not a real part of the past.

The theory I propose is rather this: In conscious memory, for example, verbally reported memory or recollection, certain real past happenings, now given (no, this is not a contradiction!), are interpreted as signs affording more or less reliable information about still other, usually more remote, past happenings that are no longer given, at least not with the same degree of distinctness and vividness. I am convinced that this theory (to be further elucidated presently) explains everything that the other can explain and infinitely more besides.

The objects of memory are aspects of past psychical events. I remember, let us say, C. I. Lewis as my teacher, but really what I remember is how it was for me, in a certain stage of my development, to listen to him and talk with him. I remember him as object of certain experiences that I had of him. It would, of course, be hazardous to impute accuracy to any report that I might make upon the basis of these memories. Conscious inspection and verbal report upon data introduce many possibilities of error. Obviously, the having of past experiences as given is itself nonverbal, except so far as past verbal experience is itself mnemonically had. Consequently, to *say* what we remember involves all the risks that verbalization always involves, not only of failing to communicate to another, but of self-confusion.

Suppose I say that I remember a phrase uttered by Professor Lewis in Berkeley in the summer of 1919, and suppose it could be proved that what he actually said was somewhat different. Would this prove that I am now merely imagining the incorrect words and imputing them to the past? Not at all. If I have (inwardly or outwardly) repeated the phrase to myself or others at various times since hearing it, I may now be remembering, quite correctly, one of these earlier repetitions. And when I thought up the false rendering, I may well have been trying, even consciously trying, to guess, from fragments of memory, what some forgotten words would probably have been. Sometimes I am quite aware of this element of guessing in my recollecting; perhaps never am I aware, with absolute clarity and certainty, where the memory stops and the guessing begins. Thus, when I now recall not so much an original experience of days or years past as subsequent recollections of that experience, I am partly guessing, with respect to aspects not now noticeably given, the import of a blend of past experiences of various dates, only one of which, at most, corresponds to the date of the original experience that I am trying to recall. In two or many steps, usually many, the first experience becomes confused with other factors of imagining and inference, all of them past in relation to the case of memory under consideration. Thus the facts fit the supposition that what recollection utilizes as 'sign' of things past is itself always something past.

As Whitehead says, and there is every justification in the literature for the charge, philosophers rarely consider memory in its primary form, that of the awareness of the immediate past—less than a second ago, say. All remembering of the distant past is probably a mass of *past* rememberings referring to the same, still earlier experience, re-remembered many times over, mostly not very distinctly or consciously. No wonder unambiguous knowledge fails to result! On the other hand, extremely short-run memory, where no intermediate case with the same past datum intervenes, scarcely leaves room for verbalization. Thus nature bars the door to any easy, obvious treatment of memory. Philosophers are mystified, and most of them seem not to suspect the trick, so to speak, that has been played upon them. They hypothetically ask nature to furnish verbalized instances of "certain knowledge" of the past, and then, finding no unambiguous case, they deny altogether any immediate possession of the past. Yet what errors have really been proved against very short-run memory, apart from reports upon it? I begin a brief phrase, or long word, and as I finish it, do I not realize that I also began it? Yet the "specious present" (which Lewis refuses to relate to the "epistemological present") probably does not include this beginning; hence the latter is remembered. (By the flicker tests, for instance, the literal present is shown to be less than a tenth or fifteenth of a second.) I, for one, am sure of no case of error in this sort of thing. It is so little fallible that theorists have scarcely noticed it as a case of mnemonic awareness (I do not say 'knowledge'). Operations that never go astray are taken for granted.

How indeed can anything, any sort of givenness, be more certain than memory in its most immediate aspect? Mathematics is meaninglesss apart from memory of what one just began to say or think about or write down or look at on a page of symbols. To have any sort of datum is useless unless one can be aware that one has just been having it. Lewis seems to see this vividly—yet not quite vividly enough. His "epistemological present" blurs the issue. The "fallibility of memory" is either the fallibility (or merely probable import) of all cognitive functions whatever, and then there are no 'data,' or it is really the fallibility of some types of memory, or more strictly, memory reports, mnemonic interpretations. In our recollecting we are, largely without knowing it, trying to deal simultaneously with many cases of memory, vague or faint enough to blend into an apparently single case.

If it be asked why or how direct possession of data can involve vagueness, faintness, and hence the possibility of erroneous report, I reply: The notion of absolutely clear as well as direct intuition is the classic idea of deity, in one formulation; and we are not divine. The contrary assumption (that we are, in this respect, divine) is implicit in the argument from the mistakes of memory to the conventional theory that its data are merely present, not past, realities. But the divine memory would involve no mistakes; therefore, the argument is inconsistent. I do not wish to accuse Lewis of this inconsistency; but his argument is at least lacking in explicitness.

What follows from the foregoing reasoning, if, for the business in hand, we accept it as sound? One thing that follows is something Lewis himself asserted: To remember consciously that X occurred (that one experienced X) is to establish some probability that it did occur. This is bound to be so, if our theory of memory is correct. For at each step of mnemonic interpretation there is possession (not just imputation) of previous experiences, perhaps even of the most remote past experiences, as more or less faintly, unclearly, or unconsciously re-remembered. This possession of the past imposes limits on the deviation of conscious or verbalized reports from the events reported upon, and the probability of memory reports simply expresses these limits.

Let us inspect this more closely. Although the mnemonic interpretation is wholly in the present, its datum, or what is interpreted, is a portion of the past. Thus the unity of present awareness includes the past. That this is not a contradiction I have repeatedly argued (following Whitehead, Bergson, Montague, and others), but I do find definite contradiction in the idea that there is *not* an inclusive (retrospective) unity in process. For temporal relations of succession must be in some realities or other, and where if not in events as realities? (Or are they in a metaphysical vacuum 'between' events?) And if relation to predecessors is in events, then so are predecessors, for we are not speaking of *relation to*, but of relation to predecessors, P, P', etc. (From what I know of Lewis on relations, he might accept the argument at this point.) Very well, past events are constituent of present events of experience as remembering; further, an experience is one, and this unity colors all its subjective functions, including the interpretive function we are interested in. Hence it is impossible that this function should proceed as though the past events had not occurred or had been otherwise. Their past occurrence, just as they were, must make some difference (for relation to them is constitutive), and the probability of the rightness of a retrospective report expresses the general direction of the range of possible differences. Because of faintness or vagueness and the complexity of the data of memory (all but the just previous experience being re-remembered), interpretation can deviate from the truth more or less widely. But it cannot proceed simply as though the given events were not given, and they could not have been given had they not occurred. For givenness (no matter how combined with interpretation) does not create its data, it merely accepts and uses them. (I regard this as an analytic truth.) Thus we have explained (in some degree) and not merely postulated the validity of memory.

There is another of Lewis's assumptions that we can, to some extent, explain, that of "real connections" in events, causal limitations upon possibility, converting merely logical into "real" possibility—possibility here and now, in a given context.[4] For, as we argued above, it is not possible (meaning, not really conceivable) that a phase of experience should fail to contain relations to previous phases; hence each phase must make a difference to the next one. Insofar, we have causal necessity, the very thing Hume looked for and failed to find. We do not indeed have complete deterministic necessity with respect to the next event (nor, according to Lewis, does science require this).[5] For it is one thing to say that the given data make a difference to the total experience and quite another to say that the total present experience was uniquely prescribed by the data that its past offered for it. Experiences, to be sure, accept their data, they do not make them; but neither do the data dictate their own reception. Were there but one logically possible way to receive the given, it must already be or contain the responses to itself. This is the converse absurdity to the notion that the response creates its stimulus, or the subject its object. Thus, I conclude: The same consideration that explains the probability of the truth of memory reports also explains how there can be probable predictions, at least in one type of case. Because the past is literally had, judgments about it cannot deviate without limit, and with equal probability, in every direction. Also, because future experiences must contain their own unity with their predecessors (to some extent, remember them), and in this fashion literally possess them, there are limits upon what the future, so far as it consists of experiences, can be. (The generalization of this principle beyond anthropomorphic limitations will be touched on later.) Present experience requires its particular past; here there is necessity in the actual structure of the world. Present experience does not require a particular succeeding event, but only some one or other of a class of events, any one of which would fit the requirements. Here there is only probability, whether it is in our knowledge or in the world. I believe this fits the statistical concept of laws that is now—however much some dislike it—the operative one in science. And even the real necessity of the particular past is reduced to mere probability for our conscious knowledge of each particular case, since introspection and verbalization, as pointed out above, are fallible, limited procedures and involve elements of guessing, conscious and unconscious, the effect of which is often multiplied over and over— as we remember, and re-remember, the same incident. Even so, if we make our memory reports unspecific enough, they can approximate in reliability to the intuitive certainty upon which they rest. Thus, "I remember experiences of some sort or other" can scarcely go wrong.

The Generalization of Memory

I wish now to suggest a generalization of memory as I have interpreted it. Assuming some theories of "substance," both one's present and one's past experiences are merely attributes or "accidents" inhering in an identical concrete reality, the individual person. Ac-

167

cordingly, memory, even though it grasp the past itself, cannot furnish an illustration of epistemic "transcendence;" it cannot exhibit an actuality experiencing another actuality. On the contrary, for such theories, memory at most exhibits an actuality experiencing "itself" (as in the past). If, however, one breaks cleanly with such forms of substantialism by taking as the most concrete specimen of reality the event, unit-process, or experient-occasion, rather than the thing or person, then one may find in memory, interpreted as direct possession of past experiences, a clear case of one actuality experiencing, not itself, but another quite independent actuality—for my previous experience owed nothing of its nature to the way I now remember it!

The edge of this issue, unfortunately, was blunted for our author, since he thought of the individual as merely a determinate long-span unit-process, or sequence of events, from birth to death. (Here Leibniz was an actual influence.) The doctrine implies that I should have been another than myself had I just now done or experienced something other than what I did do or experience. Lewis was here looking for the concrete determinate actuality, that which finally "has" properties, in contrast to properties as universals. But the momentary states, experiences, or unit-events meet the requirement; unless one insists (as Lewis, I fear, did) that the truth about all time must be timelessly real, so that a thing must be related, in its own definiteness, to later as well as earlier events.[6] This is a case of what I hold is a failure to do justice to the primacy of asymmetrical, as compared to symmetrical, relations.[7] For this and other reasons I hold that the identity of an individual personality through time is not that of a mere sequence of experiences mutually external to one another, but is that of a "personally ordered" Whiteheadian "society" whose members intrinsically require their predecessors but not their successors. Such a society must be defined in part intensionally, and with a certain indeterminacy, so that alternative possible states, after some initial state taken as given, would equally serve to continue the sequence constituting the life of that individual.

The question I wish now to ask is, "May not something like memory connect us also with past events not belonging to our personal sequence? " No doubt there are limitations on such a possibility. If I could be as vividly aware of your past feelings, or a frog's, as of my own past feelings, I should probably have a very confused sense of my own identity. Thus it is not surprising that telepathy, if real, is rare and scanty. It would be psychologically destructive otherwise. But does it follow that I can have no direct experience of concrete events other than my own past states? Any states belonging to a 'foreign' sequence must be adequately subordinated, in any awareness I have of them. But to suppose them necessarily excluded altogether is illogical, since even one's own past experiences are (a) numerically other than, and (b) only relatively akin and congenial to, one's present experiences. So the way is logically open to admit that there may be direct possession of actualities other than one's own past experiences.

Where shall we look for such direct possession of 'foreign' actualities? Apart from telepathy, and from claims to experience the divine, there are but two plausible candidates for the status we have outlined: physical processes outside the body and physical processes inside the body. To accept the first (the position of naive realism) would involve us in paradoxes because of the elements of illusion and distortion from which there is no good reason to think the perception of extra-bodily events is ever wholly free. Lewis is certainly not a naive realist in the sense in question. Actualities directly possessed are necessary to the experience, so that the latter could not occur without them. But the evidence is that you can have any sort of visual or other sensory experiences you please, no matter what is out there beyond your skin, provided only that certain nerve cells can be suitably stimulated, perhaps by electrodes applied to them. But is the neural process itself dispensable? Can we, for example, have the experience of red unless the optical system is acting in the as-yet-unknown way in which (presumably) it ordinarily does act when we have this experience? For all we know, at least, the neural process is invariably present when the experience is present. It is a good working hypothesis for science that this is so, but philosophically or epistemologically, I suspect that it is more than a working hypothesis. For the only apparent alternative is the admission that when I experience red (say, in an after-image) there is nothing identifiable which must be there besides my experience itself. This, however, would mean that I experience red merely as a quality of my experience—my experience of what? (For a "sense-datum"—as many current writers argue—is a merely verbal entity, which does not furnish an actuality other than my experience to which the red can be attributed.) "Red" is an adjective; but what corresponds to the noun, the entity given as red in its quality? Is it my experience alone, or (in addition) physical processes outside the body, or a physical process within the body, which has the given *quale?* The first would make experience its own object, which I find unintelligible; the second is contradicted by the pervasive elements

169

of partial subjectivity in perception; the third is contradicted by no presently known fact.[8]

Would Lewis perhaps urge, against this neural datum theory, that inspection of direct experience fails to make neurologists of us (the familiar argument)? Such inspection certainly does not give us all the facts of neurology, or of any other science (those who suppose that we directly experience sticks and stones must admit that we cannot read off molecular theory from mere sense perception). Nevertheless, to say that direct experience reveals none of the facts of neurology is to beg the question here at issue. Of course, we do not know the meaning of 'neural system' by direct experience alone, any more than of 'molecule.' Nevertheless, what physiologists speak of as 'neural process' may be found, when more fully known, to include the given sensory pattern in those structural aspects that, as Lewis is fond of saying, are all that science is able to measure and ascertain. We have no reason to think and strong reason to deny that the objects we see in front of us will be found to possess exactly the given structures. The optical system, like all recording or receiving instruments, is imperfect and more or less distorts what it registers. (Only direct experience, apart from inference, does not distort: It merely simplifies, in the sense that much detail is introspectively unavailable.)

No one, whatever his philosophy, denies that the natural and quasi-instinctive claim of sense perception is to relate or adapt us to the extra-bodily environment; but this claim is logically compatible with the view that the direct possession is of the inner-bodily process. We have been learning since birth (or longer) that the practical import of sense experience is chiefly in its power to give information about (not necessarily acquaintance with) the extra-bodily sources of stimuli. But perhaps still more exact information concerning the neural reactions could, if we learned how, be extracted from sensation.

How is all this connected with memory? If memory is the givenness of certain past personal experiences and perception is the givenness of certain neural events, then we confront the following possibilities: (1) the two modes of givenness are alike in that in both the data are temporally prior to the experience having them as data; (2) the givenness of neural events expresses a radically different principle from memory, in that in the former the data are simultaneous with the experience. Such a dualism of principles is never to be adopted unnecessarily. In this respect, the notion, which is apparently Lewis's, that the given is always merely present is preferable to the notion that it is sometimes past and sometimes not. But this unity of principle can also be achieved by holding that to be given means, in all cases, to be past in and for some present. This view has the following additional advantages: (1) Symmetrical relations (Lewis the logician knew this better than I, whether or not Lewis the epistemologist did) are derivative from asymmetrical ones. Consequently, to say that data are symmetrically co-present with the experience and with one another, a mere array of relations in space but not in time, is to assert that experience in principle gives us only what could be inferred, and is insofar superfluous, while withholding the information from which alone both temporal and spatial relations follow: namely, information as to temporal-causal relations of before and after! (2) If, and only if, the datum is past, can we construe the realistic postulate that seems essential to the meaning of knowledge, the postulate that knowledge conforms to the known, not vice versa. This is an asymmetrical relation, which cannot be made intelligible in terms of the notion that the two are contemporary, a symmetrical relation. That only a few neglected metaphysicians have recognized these elementary considerations may show that our treatment of basic epistemological questions, in spite of the subtleties of recent semantics, remains still a long way from adequacy.

In accordance with the foregoing reasoning, we now ask, "May it not be that in sensation we 'remember' (or possess as given) what has just occurred in the nervous system as it received certain stimuli? " Somewhat as many thinkers, including, apparently, Lewis have tended to overleap the primary, most nearly infallible, yet easily overlooked form of personal memory, the sense of what is past by less than a second or two, and have turned rather to the obvious, but not so certain, secondary form of memory, recollection of the more remote past, so similarly have many philosophers tended to pass over the unobtrusive but certain possession of just-elapsed inner-bodily process, the primary sensory givenness, in order to account for the teasingly manifest, but only apparently direct givenness (really 'instinctive' judgment) of extra-bodily objects. In both cases, the oversight has the same source, the lack of ready introspective availability of the immediate case. Some superhuman being may be able to know in all cases that he or she experiences (feels, enjoys, intuits) what he or she does experience, down to the last subtle detail; but should we credit ourselves with such an absolute self-observing power?

Some readers may think that Lewis has, or ought to have, "brain traces" in mind when he speaks of "surrogates for the past" in memory. There are, I presume necessary cortical conditions for our remembering and, by my own argument, they must be data; but (a) I should regard them as immediately past; (b) they are data, not instead of, but along with the personal experiences remembered; and (c) their function is to give memory its selectiveness by their congruity (emotional, aesthetic, intellectual) with certain items in the past and, still more, by their incongruity with all the other items. As Bergson reminds us—and it probably took genius to see something so simple—we have incomparably more "forgetting" than recollecting to explain.

The generalization of memory or sense of the past to include sensation is by no means the end of the story. The further questions arise: Are human, or vertebrate, animals the only remembering creatures, and if not, where is the lower limit of this function? The question may seem to belong merely to empirical science, but this is doubtful. For we have seen that memory, as direct possession of the past, furnishes a clue to the possibility of real connections among events such that probabilities may be objective characters of the world, in knowing which we really do know something other than our knowledge itself. Now, a clue to causality is relevant, not to this or that science, but to all science, and indeed to metascience, to ontology as such. Hume did a good job in showing that there is no other clue to causality. Lewis came closer than Hume to seeing that there is at least this clue.

There are definite reasons why our philosopher did not take the path I am recommending. I shall never forget (my "memory" may, however, somewhat deceive me, since I am in part guessing where I do not exactly recall) his telling me, long ago, how strongly he felt that inanimate physical objects lack any inner life, feeling, or value of their own. They exist, he said, simply to be experienced and used. This anthropocentric position (as I feel it to be) is exactly what prevented Lewis (and so many others with him) from making any really intelligible and more than verbal distinction between phenomenalism and realism.[9] The alternative is to interpret the sense of reality as social through and through. What is it to recognize a process, other than one's own actual experience, as also actual, if it is not to attribute to that process some sort of inner life, value, feeling, and memory (here the causal nexus comes in) of its own? Is there any other way of extracting any real juice, so to speak, from the realist-phenomenalist issue?

It happens that Lewis has, quite explicitly, discussed some such view as the one just expressed.[10] His verdict: If (but only if) we suppose knowledge to require an "analogy of quality," as well as of structure, between our experience and what we know, then the social view of reality properly follows. Moreover, he concedes, for other than cognitive purposes, for instance in ethics, we do need to suppose such an analogy—though only in limited application, that is, so far as other conscious beings are concerned. But (a) even in this limited sense, the social principle transcends all verifiable knowledge and is simply a "postulate"; and (b) insofar as inanimate nature is concerned, it may even be absurd to try to deal with it in terms of "empathy" (the attribution of qualitative analogy to ourselves). Here Lewis is afraid of the pathetic fallacy, and one understands his fear. But there is another fallacy, more insidious among trained minds, which one may call the prosaic fallacy, the error of supposing that what is not, for our casual inspection, obviously endowed with a life of its own is thereby shown to be mere lifeless stuff or bare structure without inner quality. Surely the world is not obvious. Think of the history of science, of the microstructure or megalostructure of things, both different even in principle from what direct perception for ages led people to think.

Please note, too, that we cannot even postulate something as a contingent truth unless we are able to form a conception of an alternative that could be true. But what is the alternative in this case? It is not enough that we have reason to say, "This thing does not feel" (hence does not remember). For a crowd of persons in an elevator does not feel or remember either, although each person does so. Also, a finger does not feel, though it can be a normal finger only as part of a being who does feel. Moreover, its cells may feel. Thus, to be known as a reality whose nature does not in any way include sentience, a thing must be known both not to consist of constituents that feel and also not to be essentially a part of a larger whole, perhaps the universe, that feels. Now I at least cannot conceive how all this could be known by any mind whatever. I incline therefore to suspect that there is nothing here to know, but rather a pseudo-conception.

Wittgenstein wittily says that a teapot is too "smooth" to have feeling attributed to it. But is not this smoothness the teapot's lack of dynamic singularity? The teapot does not "do" things, as a single agent, in response to the environment. However, individual response is in this case masked for our perception, as modern science shows—such response being on the micro-level. And it needs no science to tell us that the only way to experience an object as objectively one, in the causal system of things, is to experience it as an active, responsive agent in the world. I therefore suggest that the notion of a duality of sentient and insentient portions of nature could not be anything but an attempt to generate knowledge out of ignorance, out of a blurred view in which aggregates appear as quasi-singulars, and/or arbitrarily discriminated parts appear as wholes.

If then there is no real alternative to the notion that dynamic singulars feel—and such wit as I have suggests none—then the empathic principle itself is not a postulate, nor does it need verification. The function of postulation, as of verification, is to rule out possible alternatives. Where no alternative can be defined, there is nothing either to postulate or to verify. We are then dealing either with something self-evident, a metaphysical necessity, or with a mere absurdity. But Lewis agrees that the empathic principle, in some instances, is not an absurdity. If, moreover, no alternative can in any instance be offered, the principle must universally apply. The task for empirical knowledge or, in lieu of this, for postulation, is only to specialize the general analogy of feeling to fit particular cases. Here verification is more or less possible. Not only does feeling express itself in behavior, but, as recent British authors have stressed, and sometimes overstressed and overstated, feeling derives its character from its expression to such an extent that there are logical limits to the possibility of deception or mistake as to how another feels. To imagine that any sort of behavior could accompany any sort of feeling, or lack of feeling, is an anarchic mode of thinking that deprives the conceptions of diverse modes of experience or feeling of any clear meanings. Human experience and bodily process are not merely thrown together, but (like all constantly associated things in nature) have intrinsic connections, direct or indirect.

"Verifiable knowledge," Lewis tells us in that very interesting Appendix C of *Mind and the World Order,* is of the physical as such, or of that which is treated as "purely relational, (p. 409). "The directly given quality of experience" is private; the notion that other organisms enjoy experiences qualitatively like ours is "founded only on a postulate." Upon this postulate, whose truth is unknowable, are founded the "sciences of values" and the meaning of "the idea of the good." Also, it is one of the chief elements of religion.

Lewis grants that *if* knowledge were properly to be defined as "coincidence" between subject and object, then of course all objects as knowable must be psychic in nature, and some form of idealism would be obligatory. But this would be a bad definition of knowledge, since such coincidence is utterly unverifiable; and the term knowledge is needed to indicate the verifiable. What can be verified is predictable behavior as publicly observable, not the inner qualities or feelings that individuals may have (pp. 410–411).

174

Obviously, Lewis regards the unverifiable as, for all that, capable of significance; thus he rejects the verifiability criterion of meaning. Still, verifiability is, for him, the criterion of cognitive meaning. The postulate in question has ethical, aesthetic, and religious significance, but it is not capable of any degree of "theoretical assurance." Yet, upon its foundation sciences of values may be erected. And it may be true as well as useful (or so I take him to think).

Lewis expresses a partial agreement with idealism in its argument that if an object is

something more than what it means for me, something in itself, then it must mean something *for* itself; it must, in this respect, be of a nature fundamentally like my own. Insight into the true nature of a reality which is independent of me—which has more than a 'for me' character—is possible only if that nature is spiritual [p. 410]

In the case of other conscious being, empathy has a meaning. In the case of the inanimate, it is dubious whether such meaning is possible at all. But in any case . . . genuinely verifiable knowledge cannot thus interpret things on any analogy to spirits. On the contrary, it can grasp other minds only as things, revealed in the patterns of behavior of certain physical beings. The rest is postulate. [p.411]

Lewis wrote of the "loneliness which is the fate of self-conscious beings." He refused categorically to exorcise this loneliness by identifying the experience of another with the other's bodily structure and behavior. He once called such behaviorism "telling damn lies." Behaviorism was for him a correct methodological program, but not an ontology. It is likely that Lewis was influenced here by Peirce, who was perhaps the very first to define psychology in behavioristic terms and yet was by no means a materialist in ontology.[11] But Peirce did not regard the social principle as noncognitive or a mere postulate. The reason is that he saw no alternative, nothing else that could be true in its stead. Nor do I, nor did Whitehead, Bergson, or Leibniz.

I question whether so strong a conception of privacy as Lewis's has genuine meaning. Can we define the concept of reality—or truth—except through the idea of knowledge of some kind? It will not do to say simply, "The other mind knows *itself* to have its qualities, or at least, it enjoys these qualities," for this presupposes that we have a meaning for the notion that the other mind in its private character is real, is "there," by which we mean that it, in a public sense, exists.

I suggest that the existence of the private, if it can be affirmed in a public language, is somehow not merely private. I hold that the adequate understanding of this publicity of the private is impossible apart from the concept of participation. Not "empathy" only, or what I have been calling imaginative participation, but direct perceptual participation. I go further and argue that the full understanding of this idea requires a contrast between the best animal or human forms of such participation and the highest thinkable (if it is thinkable) form, the idea of an eminent participating agent or mind "to whom all hearts are open," that is, for whom all privacies become fully public matters. Reality is definable, as Royce held, as the contents of a mind fully open to all that it is connected with, that is, a mind in which there is no distinction between clear and unclear participations, because all are clear. For such a mind the real and the directly experienced coincide. However, I shall not argue for this view here.

Lewis persistently takes as "objects" extra-bodily things, and no doubt this is the sort of object we most frequently want to know about. And, of course, the natures of such objects seem very different from our own nature. Nor have we distinct and direct participation in these extra-bodily natures. We must take roundabout paths through mathematical formulas, predictions, and attempts to falsify predictions, to get at them, even in the abstract way of physics, which is limited to mere spatio-temporal geometry, broadly conceived (position, shape, velocity, frequency, and changes in these). But from the fact that most objects do not coincide qualitatively with the directly given it does not follow that no objects do so or that we could have any knowledge were that the case. The immediately given object is the body (or the nervous system) itself, and here there must be some qualitative identity, since nothing is "between" the body and the mind. To be aware of something is not to be aware merely of our awareness; and the quality of that which we are directly aware of cannot be merely a quality of our experience as such, but must also be a quality of that of which we are aware. This is not, by all the evidence, an object external to the body, but certain aspects of the body itself. Is it meaningless to hold that the subhuman cellular life is somehow qualified by certain traits found also in our immediate experience? It cannot, on Lewis's philosophy, be meaningless simply because unverifiable, for he admits that (partial) qualitative coincidence between different minds is significant though unverifiable. According to Lewis, knowledge is predictive or nothing. It is awareness of the connections between our experiences. Immediacy does not of itself give such awareness. Apparently, Lewis believes it could not possibly do so. But here, I suggest, he exaggerates. Suppose one really felt immediately some of the feelings and apprehended immediately some of the desires and purposes of others. Would one then have no inkling of their future behavior and hence of our own future experiences of them? If behavior depends in part at least upon feelings, desires, purposes, memories, beliefs, then to be aware of such factors in our neighbors is to be aware to some extent or with some probability of what the future will bring forth. This can be generalized if the conception is metaphysically ultimate; for then all the individuals in the environment, all the real active agents to be taken account of in making predictions, would be such that their probable future activities would be revealed to a sufficiently inclusive and accurate empathy. Thus perfect immediate empathy would leave nothing for indirect, discursive knowledge to do, unless there can be real singular and concrete objects which could not be empathized. And this the social metaphysics denies.

Epistemology and Ontology

Our philosopher (or one of his disciples) might say that I have been discussing science, ontology, or metaphysics, whereas he has dealt with epistemology. If, indeed, the theory of knowledge is to be sharply separated from the theory of nature, then Lewis's way of doing this is my choice. But how much isolation of theory of knowledge is worthwhile? Perhaps a good deal, if the aim is merely defensive, to ward off skepticism and dogmatism. However, the following considerations suggest (they may not prove) that epistemology is essentially an aspect of ontology, not a separate and prior study.

If we know some actual cases of knowledge, then we know certain samples of actuality, in something of their true nature. Our cognitive experiences are real, and if we can theorize effectively about them, then we know at least these instances of reality. And quite possibly these are the most accessible and illuminating of the samples available to us.

A final argument against the attempt to purify epistemology from ontological commitments is the general principle of intellectual method, according to which an ultimate test of ideas is unexpected applicability, so-called fruitfulness. This is shown when ideas chosen to explain one region of facts or one aspect of experience illuminate also quite other regions or aspects. Our theory of memory does this, for it exhibits certain epistemic relations as making not only the possibility of knowing but the structure of reality in general more intelligible.

Lewis urges that to explain probable knowledge no special contingent fact needs to be assumed beyond those facts already involved in the mere existence and continuance of experience and thought themselves. Let us grant this. Let us grant, too, that in no possible world or state of affairs would there not be probabilities to discover. Such probabilities are already included in any meaningful concept of "world" or "state of affairs." But two questions may be distinguished: (a) Do past events impose limitations on possibilities for the future?; (b) *How*, or by virtue of what real connections, do they do so? The first question answers itself. Even animals 'know' that the past discloses information about the future. The second question we are not indeed forced to answer. It is not defensively required. But why be defensive here? Curiosity has done much for our species. Perhaps we might indulge it here. Memory (and perception interpreted by analogy with memory) may be (Bergson, Whitehead, Peirce, and others think it is) our best key to temporal structure in general. That the present is potentially past is, they hold, that it is potentially remembered or retrospectively intuited. In any case epistemic relations, such as those of memory, are also facts in nature. Having been carried across these bridges to certain parts of nature, we should not forget that the bridges also are parts of nature. Moreover, if the very concept of reality involves probability as objective, as a system of limitations actually obtaining with respect to possible modes of succession, and if such limitations are intelligible only in terms of the mnemonic structure of experience, fully generalized, then this suggests that the notion of a state of affairs not constituted by forms of experiences or the notion of experiences whose data are all confined to the temporal present are alike devoid of coherent meanings.

Need it be said that to speak of "memory" is not to speak of something necessarily human? Amoebae have been shown to learn, and there is no good reason why all the forms of memory must be detectable by us in the foreseeable scientific future. Memory might operate in millionths of a second, or over millions of years, to mention only the most obvious dimension of variability.

Summary of Questions

Now that my point of view has been stated, some of its differences from and agreements with that of Lewis can be summarized and documented as follows. Lewis holds that there are "entirely certain" data.[12] However, he seems to think that no such data are temporally past and that all cases of "present-as-past" are, as such, probable only,[13] the sheerly given being "surrogates" of the past in the "epistemological present."[14] I hold, on the contrary, that the given is never something temporally present, but always consists of antecedent events literally "present" epistemically, though past temporally. Lewis seems to reason to the surrogate theory from the errors of memory.[15] But this, on his own showing, looks like a non sequitur, for in the case of the sensorily given, he admits that it is always difficult to put the given into words or judgments without error, that the data are more or less "inexpressible."[16]

It is also clear that the errors of memory he has in mind are not taken from instances of immediate or short-run memory, concerning which there has been no time for verbal or other interpretation; rather, they are recollections of relatively remote past occurrences, such as we have in mind when we judge the future on the basis of conjunctions observed in the past.[17] Such recollections are needed in induction, but they do not suffice to show us what memory in principle is. That they can err no more shows that nothing past is intuitively possessed than do the errors of sense-perception show that nothing is possessed in sensation.

Lewis has a long discussion of how memory judgments, none of them certain, can, without vicious regress, by their congruence achieve substantial probability greater than that possessed by any of the judgments taken separately.[18] Congruence is held to be weaker than the "coherence" (everything internally related to everything) of absolute idealists, and stronger than mere "consistency." This discussion I find admirable and for all I know entirely correct. I am only concerned about the question: Does not the probability of nonimmediate and interpretive memory rest on a sheer givenness of the immediate past in immediate memory (and as element therein, of the more remote past), just as the probability of sense perception rests on the sheer givenness of something not simply my present awareness?

Lewis is eloquent and cogent on the subject of those who would claim to know (or even to conceive) that the past is unknowable. Is it much better to claim to know or conceive that the past is present exclusively as probable? We may say to any partisan of Lewis's view, "if certainty is 'only an ideal' with regard to the past, is it not an ideal in any reference, and are you not then left with the vicious regress of probability of probability which you seek to avoid? " (That we have memories at all is itself known by retrospection.) Why should not the "epistemological present" include the past itself, and the "surrogates" (giving only probability) be a mixture of the given past with fallible interpretive processes? How could one possibly know that this is not true? And since it helps to make the probability that we must take for granted intelligible, while leaving the errors of memory also intelligible, can we not reasonably know it *is* true? Does not admitting this strengthen, rather than weaken, Lewis's basic scheme?

Confronted by my complicated queries (somewhat simplified in this republication), Lewis understandably chose not to attempt an answer beyond saying that if he ever undertook to reconsider his view of memory he would take my essay into account. I think he felt that he had done what he could in one lifetime with epistemological questions.

Notes

1. This chapter is largely an edited reprinting of "Lewis's Treatment of Memory," in *The Philosophy of C. I. Lewis*, ed. P. A. Schilpp. The Library of Living Philosophers (LaSalle, Il.: Open Court, 1968), pp. 395–414. It is based largely on chapter XI, "Probable Knowledge and the Validity of Memory," in Lewis's *An Analysis of Knowledge and Valuation* (LaSalle, Il.: Open Court Publishing Co., 1946), hereafter cited as AKV.
2. AKV, pp. 330–332, 334, 338.
3. "Some Suggestions Concerning Metaphysics of Logic," *American Philosophers at Work*, ed. Sidney Hook (New York: Criterion Books, 1957), pp. 99–100.
4. AKV, pp. 226 ff.
5. AKV, pp. 228–229.
6. AKV, pp. 54 ff. See also above, note 3.
7. See "The Prejudice in Favor of Symmetry" in *Creative Synthesis and Philosophic Method* (SCM and Open Court, 1970; reprinted by University Press of America [Washington, D.C., 1983]).
8. Not even, I think, by such facts as are cited by W. R. Brain, in *Mind, Perception and Science* (Oxford and Toronto: Oxford University Press, 1951), pp. 8, 70–71. See my essay, "Professor Hall on Perception," *Philosophy and Phenomenological Research*, 21. 4 (June 1961): 563–571.
9. For his last attempt to do this, see his fine article, "Realism or Phenomenalism? " *The Philosophical Review* 64 (1955): 223–247.
10. *Mind and the World-Order* (New York: Charles Scribner's Sons, 1929), appendix C.

11. *The Collected Papers of Charles S. Peirce* Vol. 7, ed. A. W. Burks, section 376.
12. AKV, pp. 182–183, 321, 333, 335.
13. AKV, pp. 332, 334, 338.
14. AKV, pp. 331.
15. AKV, pp. 331, 334.
16. AKV, pp. 321.
17. AKV, pp. 326, 328.
18. AKV, pp. 338–362.

CHAPTER 14

Morris Cohen and Wilmon
Sheldon on Polarity

A. Morris R. Cohen's Agnostic Rationalism

Cohen (1880–1947) was influential as teacher, author, and lecturer.[1]
He was perhaps most enlightening in his reflections on history and
law. One of the first in this century to see the enduring relevance
and importance of Charles Peirce, he edited *Chance, Love, and Logic*,
a collection of Peirce's journal articles. His chief contribution to
metaphysics was his advocacy of the "principle of polarity." Although
there has been criticism of this idea as vague or ambiguous, I for
one have found it helpful. One way of putting it is, "If we affirm
one side of an ultimate contrast, such as universal-particular, abstract-
concrete, necessary-contingent, we should affirm the other as applicable to the same situation, though not, of course, to the same aspect
of the situation." Reality everywhere has aspects of particularity, also
of generality; of concreteness, also of abstractness; of contingency,
also of necessity. Peirce, who may have influenced Cohen in this
respect, once defined nominalism as the denial that logical distinctions
have ontological correlates. To assert that reality consists exclusively
of instances of particularity or individuality is nominalism in its most
usual connotation; but for Peirce it is equally nominalistic to suppose
(as Brand Blanshard, at least at one stage in his career, has done)
that what we call individuals are really only bundles of universals.
Cohen's principle may be interpreted as a rejection of nominalism
in Peirce's generalized meaning.

Cohen, an agnostic or atheist, did not apply his principle to
theological questions. In this application it becomes what Whitehead

terms the principle of divine dipolarity or what I call dual transcendence. Thus: God transcends all other realities by being uniquely infinite, independent, absolute, and unsurpassable; but equally, and no less importantly, God transcends others by being in a uniquely excellent sense finite, dependent (receptive of influences from others), relative (intrinsically related to others), and surpassable (though only in the form of self-surpassing). The consistency of this apparently paradoxical double affirmation I have defended at length in various writings. I have always regarded it as in the spirit of Cohen's principle, however little he might have liked this application of it.

Of course there are more or less close precedents for Cohen's principle, including Heraclitus, Fichte, Schelling, Hegel (truth is the unity of contraries). My own form of it is given in my discussion of the logic of ultimate contrasts.[2]

Cohen reacts negatively (as Sheldon does) to the doctrine of panpsychism, which I prefer to call psychicalism. What is the use, he asks, of attributing feelings to our clothes or our furniture? As a student of the history of philosophy, he should know that no psychicalist makes this attribution, if it means supposing that one's shirt or one's chair or table is a subject that feels as an individual. No one that I know of makes such a supposition. Since Leibniz, the founder of psychicalism, the assumption has usually been that ordinary inanimate objects are insentient entities, taken as wholes, in the sense in which a group of sentient creatures does not have its own feelings additional to those of the members of the group. The Greeks suspected and modern physics has established that the human senses fail to distinguish individuals, apart from animals, in nature. A shirt is a vast group of invisibly small entities. To infer the properties, positive or negative, of the single entities from those of the group may be to commit the fallacy of division. "A shirt does not feel" by no rule of formal logic entails, "the molecules in the shirt do not feel." Cohen surely was not ignorant of my reasons for making these points. However, why should one take seriously a criticism that so obviously misstates the issue?

Cohen, with his pupil Ernest Nagel, wrote a textbook of logic that was widely used in its time. Within certain limits he was an able philosopher. His appreciation of Peirce was probably one of the factors that led Paul Weiss to volunteer to help in editing the Peirce papers, a fortunate move for philosophy. Cohen's influence probably aided that publishing project in still other ways.

B. Wilmon H. Sheldon's Classical Theism

In his book *God and Polarity: A Synthesis of Philosophies* Sheldon (1875–1979) gives us a critical, argumentative survey of the philosophies, Occidental and Oriental, influencing the world in the middle of this century.[3] His opinions are generally well informed and always expressed with grace and verve. Abundant and well-chosen quotations (partly accounting for the size of the book) give direct access to some of the positions. The entire discussion is planned—and the strategy has its grandeur—to justify the author's own position, a "synthetic" view in which Thomism is the chief ingredient. The author claims it is the most synthetic. All systems are true so far as they are positive and nonexclusive of one another. Many thinkers, the author concedes (Leibniz for one), have said as much; but always—not completely excepting even the Thomists—they have fallen into exclusions.

How, according to Sheldon, is this unfortunate defection from the program to be avoided? (1) We must take into account not theoretical exclusions alone, but in addition those concerning attitudes and values; (2) we must overcome any exclusiveness typical of the Occident as such or the Orient as such; (3) we must bring to the task a generosity related to Christian love, a renunciation of the desire to dominate. Also expendable is the passion for absolute unity, in place of which we need a principle of polarity that formalizes the synthetic project, a rule of "both-and," of cooperation between contraries as neither wholly independent nor merely dependent in relation to one another, but something of both.

Mere intellect, Sheldon holds, gives insight into possibles, essences, but not existents; through practical reactions only do we learn what things exist. Existential evidence is pragmatic and experimental. But the mystic way is also an experiment and its practical results (happiness and effective, virtuous living) testify to the reality of a supreme spirit. However, the experiment does not show the unreality of the world. Rather, this conclusion would contradict the pragmatic import of the experience. Nor is the "impersonality" of the supreme spirit vouched for. I heartily recommend, to occidental and oriental readers alike, the sections on Hinduism, Buddhism, Taoism, and Confucianism, as well as those on the more characteristically Western doctrines of materialism and naturalism.

Also evaluated are idealism, personalism or pluralistic idealism, Thomism, process philosophy, and irrationalism (including existentialism). The author feels that the true nature of Thomism has been little known to its critics. I at least had scant sense of novelty while reading this enthusiastic chapter of one hundred pages—until I reached the author's own doctrine of possibilities as, in a sense, distinct from both God and the world, but influential upon the creation of the latter via the principle of plenitude, so that *all* possibilities lying within certain limits (fixed by natural law deriving from divine fiat) *tend* in the long run to be realized. Brilliant application is made of this to the current scientific idea of law as order in randomness and to the notion of an evolution of law tending in the long run to exhibit every possible type of law. From all this the author thinks Thomists might learn something!

Has Sheldon really eliminated all exclusions? How can we know that a rejected doctrine is not a positive insight? In some cases it seems clear: Pure monism excludes the positive idea of plurality; pure necessitarianism excludes contingency or real possibility; pure materialism, consciousness; pure intellectualism (some of it in Thomism) excludes emotional and volitional factors. Pure irrationalism excludes intellect. Perhaps it is similarly obvious that atheism, the denial of a supreme, uniquely perfect being, is essentially exclusive. But if, with Thomism, one construes "perfection" as the absolute maximum of value in every sense and aspect, or as "pure actuality," in no sense capable of increase, does one not exclude a great deal? For then there can be no contribution of creaturely living to the divine life and no ideally adequate recipient of our (or God's) creative achievements. Sheldon seems content with the view that we serve ourselves and one another, but not—except verbally—God, in our ascent toward the divine. Collective egoism of creatures is the last word of motivation. This excludes as absurd or sacrilegious the wish (naively present, as Buber notes, in primitive religious sacrifices) to contribute to a good that is more inclusive than the merely private good and more unitary than the "social" good.

In his critique of Hegel, our author seems to duplicate the Hegelian blurring of the distinction between "the absolute requires the relative" (as such, that is, requires that there be *some* relative things or *other*) and "the absolute requires just the sorts of relative things that in fact exist." Pointing to the untenable consequences of the second version, Sheldon overshoots the mark by proclaiming also the untenability of the first. Not only must God (for Sheldon purely absolute) be free to create or not to create this particular world that in fact exists but also God must be free not to create at all. Thus the extreme denial of metaphysical freedom is replaced by an equally extreme denial of any necessity in creation. Is this really a synthesis? Again, rejecting, for good reasons, the monism that posits a necessary whole excluding any contingency in the parts, must we therefore, with Sheldon, accept final dualities neither member of which embraces the other? Logic requires that wholes or inclusive realities should logically entail their parts or included elements; it does not require that the parts should universally entail one another. Indeed, logic forbids this, for it would make all analysis simply false. An all-inclusive reality thus need not be a necessarily existing, mutually implicative system. It need include as actual only what is actual, and unactualized possibilities only as such. If, then, some of these become actual (according to the hypothesis, this must be possible), a new inclusive reality becomes actual. When there is more to include, the "all-inclusive" includes this more. Thus, plurality is not excluded, indeed, the concrete denotation of "the all-inclusive" is itself plural, as just shown. Yet, by the "incremental view of time," which Sheldon expounds, but seeks to limit in application, the latest all-inclusive reality embraces its predecessors. It is not that "everything changes," as Sheldon expresses the process view (fallacy of distribution!), but that, if anything changes, the inclusive reality does so, since it includes both whatever is unchanged and the results of the change. Similarly, contingency is inclusive: the conjunction of a necessary proposition and a contingent proposition is a contingent proposition. If a totality could not be otherwise, neither could any item in it. Sheldon sees that to take the necessary or absolute as inclusive is to condemn the contrasting aspect as "unreal"; he seems not to see that the converse inclusion avoids the difficulty.

The same point applies to the relation between mind and object. "The subject overlaps the object"—this Hegelian saying is a positive element of agreement in modern idealism. Can it be excluded in a really synthetic, all-harmonizing doctrine? If there be experience *and* matter, is the "and," the relation between them, material, or is it constituted by experience? In mind is actualized its relation to things known, not in the things. Were the relation in the things, then our knowing would constitute the things. The very independence or absoluteness of what we know with respect to this knowing—which Sheldon and other realists affirm—means that the relation, the relativity, must be in the knowing. Thus, as the relative is the synthesis of itself with the absolute, so mind is the synthesis of itself with its objects. A synthesis can be synthesized with other synthetic wholes to form ever-new wholes, and minds or experiences can be embraced as data in further experiences (memory). Thus the incremental view of time fuses readily with the basic principles of idealism *and* realism, with panpsychism a corollary. Sheldon misses much of this. He strangely interprets Whitehead's innumerable psychicalistic utterances (he quotes some; I add, "apart from the experiences of subjects there is nothing, nothing, bare nothing," or "I entirely accept the subjectivist bias of modern philosophy") as though they did not say anything like what plainly they do say.

Sheldon insists upon the notion of "merely physical" things. Granting spatial and causal, and in this sense physical, realities, what pragmatic test or need justifies the "merely"? We may need to treat stones as if they had no feelings that we ought to try to spare. We must do much the same, however, with microbes and even insects—or, on occasion, lions; and our justification in these cases is that we lack sufficient understanding to take possible feelings into account, save perhaps in crude fashion, or that the understanding we do have indicates the superior quality of the feelings of higher animals, most of all, human beings. But we are told that it is "contradictory" to attribute certain traits of mind to physical things. Thus in memory the separateness of events in time is somehow suspended, and in thinking of remote objects, spatial separateness is overcome. Does it follow that physical (spatial) reality is simply one thing (with simple location?) and mind simply another (with no location?)? By the pragmatic test of location ("my neighbor is he with whom I intimately react"—Peirce), an experience is where its most immediate causes and effects are; thus in much of the bodily region. Hence it is extended, and we need no dualism of inextended mind and extended matter. If the past is present in memory, so is a physical cause involved in its physical effects, and in so far there is no simple location of the physical. Whitehead's theory of causation as "physical memory" is the deliberate denial of the sort of dualism that Sheldon defends. Yet what pragmatic truth has Whitehead overlooked?

Sheldon confronts the panpsychist with a dilemma: Either all individuals are asserted to have *conscious* feelings, or "feeling" is being used as a mere synonym for process as affected by previous process (the view Sheldon foists upon Whitehead). I reply with another dilemma: Either to feel is the same as to judge *that* one feels thus and thus (and then how are infants and dumb animals to be interpreted?) or there is a distinction. In the latter case we may sensibly speak of at least relatively unconscious feeling, and even if a bare minimum of "consciousness" must go with feeling, how is this minimum to be defined so that the behavior, say, of atoms contradicts the assumption of its presence?

187

Sheldon says some interesting things about polarity in life and nature. He is eloquent and even profound concerning the sex polarity (though not to my taste entirely free from male bias), also concerning "mind and body" (a very different distinction in my view from that of mind and mere matter). On the whole, the book is a noble one. It may please some conservative thinkers only too well and may be unjustly neglected by many others. Current fashions of linguistic analysis and positivistic purity will be against it, though the author's remarks on these fashions are themselves interesting. The book does treat the human problems with which philosophy is ultimately concerned in a large-hearted and large-minded way. Sometimes I feel that Sheldon needs some linguistic analysis to get beyond vague or ambiguous verbal associations; but it seems to be true that those who worry too constantly about the meanings of their terms are likely to end up without the capacity to use meanings for certain (as I believe, with Sheldon) quite genuine purposes. Probably he excludes some positive and nonexclusive insights in current analysis, though perhaps no more than it tends to exclude the worth of classical and recent ontological philosophy. At least the book is fun to read!

C. Second Thoughts After Twenty-Eight Years

Sheldon was a delightful gentleman. He was witty, and I seem never to dislike witty persons. But wit in doing metaphysics is a treacherous resource. It tends to dynamite the argument and enable its possessor to escape effective refutation. This may mean failing to acquire real discipline in thinking. I learned about this in arguing by correspondence with Sheldon. I had done the same with Brightman, who never took refuge in wit or other rhetorical escapes but stuck to the line of argument with grim seriousness. Thus, one could clarify precisely the points of difference. With Sheldon it was otherwise. I soon gave up. As one reads his book critically, one sees a very agile mind leaping deftly this way and that to escape the force of objections. It is clever, but is it serious inquiry? High ideals inspire the book, which was clearly intended to be important. It was said that Sheldon was deeply disappointed by its reception. My review could not have pleased him. Yet I now feel that I slightly overrated the book. It shows a lack of firm logic where logic is needed. The theory of polar opposites is developed at length but in loose terms. The looseness is in a way admitted and claimed as a virtue, being connected with the current tendency in science to give up strict determinism and admit aspects of chance and irreducible probability. But to think in probabilistic terms is not to think loosely. The mathematics of probability is hardly home ground for loose thinkers. Sheldon takes mind and mere matter (strictly insentient) as a typical polarity. But one side of this contrast is a mere negative, unless matter can be shown to have some positive property impossible for mind. Sheldon proposes strict location in space for this. I hold that in whatever sense we need such location (and physics has things to say about this) there can be forms of mind possessing it. Sheldon also argues that to interpret all unit actualities as at least sentient, as I do (Sheldon was one of the first of my older contemporaries to take my views seriously), is to impoverish reality. I say that he impoverishes reality in a more significant and definite sense in limiting the forms of the psychical to those found on the level of living organisms, perhaps even of animal organisms. (Sheldon was a botanist and discovered a species of grass.) Above all, Sheldon talks about his polar contraries in rhetorical, not logical, terms, about their generosity to each other, and the like (p. 677). Noting this aspect of Sheldon's talk about his abstractions led me to wonder if Paul Weiss, who was Sheldon's colleague for many years, may not have been influenced by him in his own tendency to almost personify abstractions and treat them as agents doing things to each other.

Sheldon holds "an asymmetrical view of reality." There is no perfect symmetry in the interdependence of contraries.[4] Verbally this is the process view also. But the asymmetry is opposite in the two doctrines. Sheldon is a neoplatonist; for him, as for Plotinus, absolute, unitary, pure being precedes, surpasses (and renders superfluous and noncontributory) the variegated actuality that we know. For process philosophy the absolute is abstract, and the abstract is included in the concrete.

Sheldon seems not to have derived his view of polarity from Cohen, and certainly he did not improve upon Cohen in clarity in using the term.

Sheldon pays me the compliment of arguing against views of mine in many parts of this book. He holds that we are in no position to judge how God views our sufferings from our own experience of sympathy whereby another's pain becomes in a manner also ours. He is eloquent indeed about our lack of knowledge of what it would be like to experience as God experiences. (Granted the classical theist's notion of absolute timeless perfection, then I hold with Hume's Cleanthes that our ignorance of what this could consistently mean virtually abolishes or renders deeply problematic any difference between theism and atheism.) Sheldon makes ingenious use of various maneuvers, for instance, mention of the theory of reincarnation as possibly meaning that innocent sufferers were not innocent in a previous incarnation. Or God may know what wonderful good results may eventually come from present sufferings. All this would be at most barely acceptable, provided the notion of absolute timeless self-sufficient perfection were an essential, uniquely adequate rendering of the religious idea of a being entirely worthy of unstinted devotion or love. Instead I hold that it is a bad mistranslation of the religious idea. We conceive the timeless only by abstraction, as we conceive the necessary only by abstracting what possible states of reality have in common. In worshiping God we are not worshiping any such abstraction. Religion is not relation to the technical Greek idea of motionless self-sufficiency.

"I love you dearly, but you give me no value I would lack were you nonexistent. The entire world of creatures, all of whom I love, makes no value difference of any kind to me by its actuality." The doctrine that implies this as the divine relation to the world may have seemed to Sheldon to say something, but it says only nonsense to me.

Sheldon speaks of God choosing among possible worlds the world that includes certain free choices of its creatures. The choices are divinely made, yet they are the creatures' free choices. Again, I see only nonsense or contradiction. Yet he also writes as though he accepts the idea of chance. Eternally divinely chosen, yet also a matter of chance!

The nature of the task of philosophy and the nature of the human mind are vividly illustrated in the facts that Sheldon could think he was meeting the challenge some of us have offered to the medieval synthesis and that I can and do think he was not meeting that challenge but only "making the worse appear the better reason."

Part of the trouble is Sheldon's attempt to deal with every philosophical current of his time. In a genial way he seems to give every rival view a fair chance. Human capacity does not easily extend so far. It is a magnificent tour de force, but it was intended to be more.

It seems an interesting example of the power of a gifted teacher that one competent and metaphysically concerned formal logician of our time, Richard M. Martin, who studied at Yale and was a pupil of Sheldon, also defends the "scholastic synthesis" to the extent of accepting the idea of timeless knowledge of all temporal truths, thus "spatializing time," from a Bergsonian, Aristotelian, Peircean perspective. Yet Martin is a student of Peirce's and Whitehead's writings.[5]

In addition he is sympathetic to my philosophy. So ineradicable is the personal element in philosophy that Martin and I (who lack his technical ability in logic) disagree not only about truth's relation to time and eternity, but also about Peirce and Whitehead, neither of whom, as I read texts, has any room in his thinking for the idea of timeless truth about particular contingent, temporal facts. Such facts are everlasting, but not eternal, for these writers. (That I had a certain birth will remain true evermore, but it became true near the end of the last century.) Only truths about eternal realities or aspects of reality are eternally true. Among these eternal truths is the general abstract truth that the class of noneternal truths has always had and always will have members. Eternally, truth has a noneternal aspect as well as an eternal one. The particular instances of the noneternal aspects are everlasting.

Of the many attempts I have read to elaborate and justify medieval or classical theism, Sheldon's comes the closest to making the doctrine credible. If the case can be made he has made it.

Notes

1. For an admirable account of Cohen's career and its importance for his time see *Morris R. Cohen and the Scientific Ideal*, David A. Hollinger (Cambridge, Mass. and London: The MIT Press, 1975). Among Cohen's books, *Reason and Nature: an Essay on the Meaning of Scientific Method* (New York: Harcourt, Brace,and Co., 1931) is important for my discussion. *The Meaning of Human History* (LaSalle: Open Court, 1944. Rev. ed., 1947) gives his view of human affairs.

2. *Creative Synthesis and Philosophic Method* (London: SCM Press and LaSalle: Open Court, 1970; reprinted by The University Press of America, Washington, 1983), chapter 6.

3. Wilmon Henry Sheldon, *God and Polarity: A Synthesis of Philosophies* (New Haven: Yale University Press, c1954, 1970). Also *The Strife of Systems and Productive Duality* (Cambridge: Harvard University Press, 1918); and *Agapology: the Rational Love Philosophy as Guide of Life* (Boston: Christopher Publishing House, 1965).

4. *God and Polarity*, p. 5.

5. R. M. Martin has written many books, including *Belief, Existence, and Meaning* (New York: New York University Press; London: University of London Press, Ltd., 1969) and *Mind, Modality, Meaning and Method* (Albany: State University of New York Press, 1984); also numerous articles and reviews in mathematical and philosophical journals.

CHAPTER 15

Blanshard's Necessitarianism

Among the writers who have learned most from the "Idealists" of the late nineteenth and early twentieth centuries, Brand Blanshard (b. 1892) is outstanding in the range of his concerns, the readability and elegance of his writing, and, with some qualifications, the penetration of his thought. His strength is more in his criticisms of views sharply contrasting with his own than in the basic philosophic doctrines he espouses. Indeed, in these he has had few disciples. He is not (and is well aware of this) an idealist in any very significant sense. True, he holds that nothing is independent of mind, but only in the trivial sense that, according to his doctrine of universally internal relations, nothing is independent of anything. Otherwise, matter is not explained by mind any more than mind is by matter. Hegel's dictum, "in the opposition between subject and object the subject overlaps," is not accepted by Blanshard. He is not a psychicalist in any clear sense.

What to this critic is most impressive in Blanshard is his wisdom, not so much in metaphysics or technical philosophy as in judging beliefs that apply metaphysical ideas to more concrete matters or to human institutions. Examples of such beliefs are the Christian doctrine of Christ the God-Man, or the infallibility of the Pope or of Scripture. On the classical topic of *Faith and Reason* (title of one of his books) he is, within certain limitations, a valuable spokesman for an austere rationalism. Although I am more sympathetic to traditional Christianity in some of its aspects than Blanshard is, I find much of his critique cogent and admirable. "Fundamentalism," whether Catholic or Protestant, has in him a formidable judge.

The basic premises of rationalism, as advocated by this heir (but not representative) of idealism, are three: (1) The will to understand, with its postulate that reality is in principle understandable, is to be

192

affirmed uncompromisingly. The rational intelligibility of the real is an absolute presupposition of thought. The second premise is negative: (2) How far we shall succeed in understanding reality or in realizing any of our human aspirations is a relative matter, subject to no philosophical guarantees. Intelligibility is the only unqualifiedly universal trait of *what is* that Blanshard's rationalism can assure us of. (3) To be intelligible or understandable is definable in terms of the formula: "To understand is to see to be necessary." Reality is a perfect system in the sense that every item in it implicates every other. It is not perfect, so far as we know, in any additional way, for instance in the amount of happiness, as compared to misery, it involves.

Blanshard is well aware that this austere and, as he says, "tragic" metaphysics is not that set forth by his idealistic predecessors. They all, in some way or another, offered their readers more comfort than the mere search for theoretical necessities can provide. One must admire the courageous persistence with which Blanshard has sought to keep to his presuppositions. (Thus his intellectual life constitutes a prolonged experiment.) Belief in intelligibility is sacrosanct because to think is in principle to accept that belief. So at least I understand Blanshard to hold.

Of the three premises I have no quarrel with (1), and I can go partway with (2). But (3) seems to me a gross blunder, a doctrine devoid of genuine evidence, an irrational theory of rationality. Formal logic stands or falls with the contrast between relations of necessity (as in '*P* strictly implies—or entails—*Q*') and nonnecessary relations, as in '*P* and *Q* are independent' or in 'though *P* implies *Q*, yet *Q* does not imply *P*, the necessity holds asymmetrically.' One can, of course, reply that this is only what appears on the very abstract level dealt with in formal logic. But the very contrast between abstract and concrete supports the proposition that to understand is in some cases to see to be contingent. Animality is more abstract than humanity; from the latter the former is deducible, but not vice versa. If we cannot understand this to be so, what can we understand? There were once animals but not human animals; there were once human animals but not you or I. It is a doctrine of most logicians that from the less specific, definite, or concrete the more concrete cannot follow. Concreteness is definiteness (however little we know this definiteness). The less cannot contain the more.

Blanshard, to maintain his program, must dismiss all this as somehow confusion or error. His understanding of understanding should, he holds, prevail. I have heard him say that sound "logic" is to be found only in writers who died some decades ago, not in anything that is today practiced under that label.

In another way I refute the third premise by urging the Peircean, Bergsonian, Whiteheadian view of becoming as essentially a perpetual enrichment of reality by contingent increments of definiteness or concreteness. From the less, a particular more emerges. Not all rabbits were previously in some magician's hat. I agree with John Findlay that there is nothing irrational or unintelligible in this. The rationality of necessity is, as seems obvious from formal logic, only one kind of rationality; and to understand this kind of rationality we must (principle of contrast) see it in relation to that other kind which is the quite intelligible relation between the concrete and the abstract, the former not being contained in the latter or in any strict sense implied by it.

The notion that understanding is seeing to be necessary was the classical principle of "sufficient reason" and of "sufficient" causal or logical conditions. Necessary conditions are those without which something is impossible. Granted all the necessary conditions, the something is possible. But "sufficient condition" meant that with which the something is necessary. Thus 'necessary and sufficient' names a symmetrical relation, necessity in both directions—for instance, past to future and future to past. It is neatly analogous to the logic in which any proposition is equivalent to any other. No formal system actually used by current logicians embodies such a logic. It would be useless. It collapses the distinction between possibility and necessity. I conclude that the Blanshard doctrine is modal nonsense.

Of course, if reality is a system perfect in Blanshard's sense, it can give no support to any traditional religious belief in a cosmic intelligence or eminently beneficent will. Blanshard, like many another, brushes aside the idea of freedom in the creative sense of enriching the definiteness of reality. Only for ignorance is anything indefinite or unsettled, open to "decision," in the sense sharply defined by Whitehead (and defended by Bergson, Peirce, James, and others), whether the deciding is by human, subhuman, or superhuman agents. Blanshard never really enters the religious ground. He ignores or slights the philosophers who do deal with religious matters at their center, which is in the idea of freedom in the sense of creativity.

As one-sided extremists tend to do, Blanshard likes to deal with extremists of a variety opposite to his own. Thus he attacks those who regard reality as consisting of *mutually* independent items none of which is either a necessary or a sufficient reason for any other.

Against Hume, Russell, and many another extreme pluralist, Blanshard makes a case. But it is a case against one extreme, not necessarily for the opposite extreme. And one searches in vain for a clear recognition that 'both necessary and sufficient' and 'neither necessary nor sufficient' are contraries, not contradictories. Both may be, and indeed are, false if taken as universal.

The totality of necessary conditions is indeed sufficient for the possibility, but not the actuality, of the conditioned. Freedom is self-actualizing, granted the enabling conditions.

We can thank Blanshard for his splendid style and his courageous experiment; but the experiment supports a negative conclusion: To understand is not always or necessarily to see to be necessary. Very often indeed it is to see to be contingent. The principle of contrast is truer than Blanshard's axiom. Asymmetrical, not symmetrical, necessity is king.

Apart from the limitations mentioned, Blanshard is a classic philosophical writer, dignified, wise, urbane, and learned. He is admirably candid and never hides behind obscurities. It is a great achievement to be so definitely mistaken as he is when he is mistaken. And in much that he says he is, for all I know, not mistaken at all.

Note

Blanshard's philosophy is largely presented in his *The Nature of Thought* (London: Allen & Unwin, Ltd., 1939), *Reason and Goodness* (Allen & Unwin, 1961), and *Reason and Analysis* (same publisher, 1962).

CHAPTER 16

Brightman's Theory
of the Given and His Idea of God

Edgar Sheffield Brightman (1884–1952) was the principal founder of American Personalism. He was a forceful writer and teacher.

In his last book, *Person and Reality*,[1] published posthumously (1958), Brightman appears to agree with the following three propositions: Reality in general is the same as experience in general; momentary experiences are connected with others by one-way relationships of logical requirement, rather than by mere Humean constant conjunctions; temporal order is the basic order established by these relationships. Apparently, also, he concedes something of the contention that the unity of the present self, which he calls the datum self, with its personal past, is akin in principle to that which connects my present with the past of other persons. But whereas for me this means that both the personal past and the past of others are actually given, this givenness being the same thing as causal conditioning, Brightman denies the givenness in both cases and seems (influenced by Hegel, I recall) to take causal conditioning (or the "rationality" of reality) as a primitive self-explanatory term. The present experiences only the present; however, it can "understand" itself only by accepting an order of causes and effects inconceivably more vast than its own internal content.

From some points of view the differences seem but verbal. For I actually *define* the given as the independent causes of experiences; Brightman apparently admits that experiences have independent causes but does not *call* them "data." What then does he call "data"? They are those I should term *"obvious* data," those whose givenness is easily accessible to conscious detection. Such are qualities of red, sour, painfulness, activities of perceiving and thinking, emotions of

196

love, fear, rage, etc. Concerning these, he accepts Donald Williams's principle of the "innocence of the given." In themselves, it is held, they tell no tales about what is not given, that is, the absent portions of the world-system conditioning the experience. At the same time, Brightman holds that the rational explanation of the given data drives us far beyond them, to their causes, near or remote. The doctrine I uphold is that the innocence of the given is the same as the limitations of human consciousness as such, in the sense in which a baby is vastly less conscious than an adult, though what is given to the baby may be rather similar. Brightman brushes aside this distinctive ("Whiteheadian") meaning of "consciousness"; but then he should give us another term for the same very important distinction. The lower animals and infants have but little introspective power; they have data but can not judge that they have, at least not on a scale comparable to the judgments of human adults. Now either-or: Either the human adult possesses the possible maximum of this power, or not the maximum. If not the maximum, then there are data that even you and I cannot detect introspectively. How then does one prove that the causal conditions which Brightman says are not given are indeed simply not given, whether with or without possibility of conscious detection or noticing? I see no way in which he could prove this.

Early in the book, Brightman does offer an argument for his view, but as it stands, the argument is a simple formal fallacy. He protests that the absent factors (which I suggest mean those not obviously given) cannot be "identical with" "the shining present", the momentary experience or datum self. He appears then to infer, "not included in," from "not identical with." But, of course, identity is but a degenerate or improper case of inclusion. So this reiterated argument is, to be frank, absurd. Who wants to identify "the absent" with present experience as a whole? The given is, some of us hold, a constituent of experience; a constituent, however, need not be and normally is not identical with that of which it is constituent.

No doubt the formal fallacy referred to is not quite what Brightman had in mind. Perhaps he was thinking of this: Granted that the absent is constituent of experience, can we really admit that each experience is a whole of which all causal conditions are parts? Am I inclusive of the totality of my past selves, and your past selves as well? My present self seems to lack any such superiority to all that conditions it. And even God as supreme cause would by this logic become a mere part of me, as I am now! This must be what Brightman had in mind. Does it establish his position? I believe it is the strongest argument available for that purpose. And the issue is subtle. Present experience cannot in an unqualified sense be a whole of which any causal condition you please of that whole is a mere constituent. By that principle a mouse which I influence must be more than I was when I influenced it, must be my superior, absolutely.

In reply, we must refer once more to the difference between conscious and unconscious possession of data. If I were absolutely conscious of all my data, then indeed I should be superior to all the causal conditions of my experience. But in truth my conscious experience includes no causal condition whatever without a more or less drastic loss of distinctness or adequacy. If all data are "innocent," it is because all nondivine experiences are but imperfectly conscious and it is for consciousness that the question of innocence arises. Mere feeling or sensory experience puts no general question like that which Williams and Brightman are answering. But, you may persist, if conscious experience does not embrace its causes, does not—on the Bergson-Whitehead-Hartshorne view we are discussing—unconscious experience embrace them, and are we not still faced with the paradox of an experience surpassing all that influences it? In a certain technical sense it does appear that the view assigns to an effect a total complexity greater than that of any of its causes. However, if value is finally measured by consciousness, then experience so far as merely unconscious is inferior to those of its causes which are conscious.

This defence may seem an evasion. But we can perhaps strengthen it somewhat by remarking that, so far as the human self-conscious individual is concerned, what he cannot bring into consciousness is not really "his" in the full sense, so that, granted that my experiences grasp God, for example, it does not follow that I consciously possess God as constituent of myself. On the other hand, God as the sole fully conscious being will without qualification contain every item of reality.

I am well aware of Brightman's reasons for rejecting this view of God (we once corresponded at length about it); but I see in these reasons only a partial neglect or denial of the passive-active structure of experience as such, or of the distinction between what Whitehead calls the subjective forms and the objective forms of feeling. In each case of feeling another's feeling, the first feeler feels the other's feeling in a different manner from the other and yet feels his very feeling. The doctrine of feeling is precisely the view that not only is this not contradictory, but that its denial is indeed contradictory. For, if we feel, what do we feel? Merely our own feeling itself? This is like a sign that means only itself. A basic epistemological issue is whether or not there is an essential subject-object structure running through immediate experience.

Brightman spoils his discussion of "epistemological monism" by taking it to mean the identity of subject and object. It may for some authors, but for others it means rather that the object, as nonidentical with the subject, is directly given to it and *thereby* made a constituent of its total actuality. The subject includes the object, but for that very reason does not coincide with it. My (or your) feeling always embraces feeling which initially was not mine at all. This prior feeling does not thereby become my feeling of it, it becomes rather an objective affective part-content of my total affective state. I feel *how* the other felt, I do not feel *as* the other felt. I see no contradiction here. I may feel how some of my cells feel, for instance, their pain; but for them this feeling was existence itself, while for me it is but one item of feeling among many. So, if God feels our feeling of trust in a false hypothesis, our feeling is on the far side of the duality, "feeling of feeling," not on the hither side. True, the first or divine feeling includes the second but surpasses it as the inclusive surpasses the included. God feels how we trust the hypothesis but does not trust it.

Peirce's definition of belief fits neatly here: Belief is willingness to act upon; God is not willing to act upon our belief, though feeling the full quality of our trust in it. God also feels many other things; and the total divine reaction to the world is negative with respect to the hypothesis. We do something like this in remembering vividly how we formerly felt trust in something that now we distrust. Ability to feel objectively and vividly the quality of the former trust does not at all mean that we now trust the object of the former trust. For we now have additional feelings *about* the former feeling, and its object or context, that we previously did not have. The whole question is whether a subject can become direct object to another subject. Some of us answer this by another question, how can a subject composed basically of feelings have an object otherwise than by a social structure of immediate feeling whereby the other subject is one's own directly enjoyed object?

There are many reasons why this social structure has been missed by most philosophers. It is the stone rejected of the builders, the almost secret bond of intuitive love that holds the universe together. I cannot imagine any other bond that can do this. 'Intentionality' is a name for the problem, not a solution.

What does it mean to say, as Brightman does, that, though the causes of the given are entirely hidden behind the given, yet their being is included in that of the given so far as we understand it? How does this differ from my contention that all causes of experience are data, though data in large part resistant to human introspection? The more conscious we are, the more we grasp experiences as effects of certain causes. At the ideal limit what could this mean if not that the causes, too, would be consciously accessible as data? How else could the supreme consciousness be aware of the causes of its experiences than by having them as fully inspectable data? Must infallible knowledge infer worldly causes by inspecting divine effects in themselves totally "innocent" of their causes?

Let us put the matter in terms of internal relationships. Does Brightman hold with the Humeans that all relations of immediate experience to past, future, or contemporary events are external? This is the clear implication of the "innocence of the given." But then what is the basis of trust in causality or in the inference to a larger world? Does Brightman hold that the relations of experience to previous events are constitutive or intrinsic? Then he is on my side. For the more conscious we become of what an experience is, the more its components, including relational components, will be not only data but consciously introspectable data. So I wonder if there is any real difference between us except that I take an unequivocal stand concerning internal relations. Of course, I equally posit external relations; for things experienced by a given subject are entirely independent of being experienced by it. Internality runs backward from subjects to objects, not forward from objects to subjects.

Some of my main objections to the *denial* of the thesis that causes are always given are as follows. First, it makes causality an entirely independent principle, an arbitrary conjunction that remains inaccessible to direct, and hence, I should think, indirect, awareness. Second, it makes love a derivative principle, whereas my most basic intuition about the meaning of life is that love or feeling-of-feeling is the primary principle, explanatory of everything, including givenness. Third, relations between events must be in some events, and thus be internal; but to say that relation to X is in Y, but X is not, is I hold meaningless or contradictory; moreover, if relations to causal conditions are in experiences (and where else?), then to the degree to which we can be directly aware of what an experience is we must be directly aware of its components, including intrinsic relations and their terms.

I should like to comment upon Brightman's notion of the datum self or shining present. I find this a somewhat ambiguous idea. In my view, the given self is not identical with the self to which it is given. The subject-object duality is never simply collapsed. If the shining present is the given self, then there is another self *for* which it is given. This I take to be the subsequent self. The datum self is then the immediately past self. It is a case of what Brightman calls "the absent"; but it is also present, not, however, in the sense of being the present subject, rather in that of being the present object. Not only is it false that the past is never datum; it is also false that the present is ever presently a datum. The subject-object structure is basically the present-past structure. All direct awareness is "memory"; but memory has two forms, personal and impersonal. Take the first experience by an unborn infant; at first it can remember no predecessor of its own kind; it has no personal memory. Does this mean it is a mere present with no feeling whatever of past (or future)? I suggest that this is a monstrous assumption. More reasonable is the view that in the first experience in an individual's career the individual feels the immediately past state of its own organic components, cells or the like. Thus it has what we might call impersonal memory. Perception in its entirety may be viewed as simply the impersonal form of "memory" or direct sense of the past. This effects an enormous simplification of all our concepts of experience, a simplification whose grandeur suggests genius. And the source of the generalization was the genius of Whitehead, partly anticipated by that of Bergson and Peirce.

If memory is direct sense of the past, then the belief in the pure innocence of the given is mistaken. Note that memory itself is remembered. Immediate retrospection gives us ourselves as just having, in another act of memory, retrospected still earlier experience. So the datum is here past, and the datum is here also an act of experiencing whose own datum was still farther past, and so on indefinitely. Since perception is impersonal memory, and since the nonhuman feelings which are given are also experiences with data and causes, hence are themselves mnemonic in structure, all experience is in principle memory of memory of memory, and so on. That this does not appear in an obvious way to introspection (really retrospection) is the very thing that Whitehead sought to explain by his doctrine of "transmutation." The obviously given in sense perception is a universal, abstracted from the more concrete datum; consciousness is largely limited to the result of this abstraction, for reasons which psychology can, I think without great difficulty, explain. Thus is produced the illusion of the innocence of the given. To recognize it as an illusion is to be out of the solipsistic prison in which Brightman and so many others gladly put themselves, before proposing some ingenious device for sawing through the bars of the prison. There is no present self-contained event, given as such. Givenness is itself a causal and temporal arrow pointing backward and outward in space-time, or better, time-space. As Milič Čapek keeps telling us, time, or as Buddhists say, "dependent origination," is the key to the cosmic structure. Givenness is an actual grasp of actual past events whose being was independent of the present event.

I have been critical of Brightman's theory of experience. I wish now to express my admiration for him in another connection. I think Brightman's defence of what he called the "temporalistic" view of God was a valuable and well-reasoned contribution. Here he was one of the pioneers and a courageous and clear-headed one. I am indignant when he is referred to as a believer in a "finite God," even though he used this expression. He also said repeatedly that he believed in a finite-*infinite* God, and that is not only different, it is infinitely different, from believing in a finite God *tout court*. It should also be said that he believed, not in a temporal God but in an eternal-temporal God, and here, too, the difference is infinite. (It is, of course, the same difference.) Brightman's book *The Problem of God* is his most original one and his essay "The Temporalistic View of God" is one of the better essays in American philosophy.[2]

The finite aspect of God, about which Brightman speaks, not altogether clearly, as "The Given," is, I suggest, the same as the truth that certain things, but not all possible things, are *given* to God. All possible things are indeed given to God as possibilities, and the divine infinity is in this: Whatever possibility were to be actualized, it would be fully and consciously represented in the data of the divine experience, so that to say, such and such is possible, is to say, God could know it as actual. But God does know as actual only what is actual.

Brightman and I disagree as to how each actuality is represented in the divine experience. I say, by inclusion among its data, he says, by inclusion in the rational or causal implications of the data. I find this at best a distinction without a real difference. But the relation to finitude is essentially the same: To know that *this* world is actual and *that* is not is to fail to know what might otherwise have been known and is to be finite in a clear sense.

Brightman's view has the, to me, objectionable feature of making God not simply finite but fragmentary, a part of the total reality consisting of God and the created individuals. However, this is largely verbal, since every item in the totality has to be somehow represented in the divine knowledge. And in any case, the clear and bold insistence that even divine experience or knowledge, will, or love must recognize a difference between worlds experienced, known, willed, or loved as actual, and those dealt with only as possibilities, so that even the divine reality must be finite in a definite sense, was a landmark in the history of religious thought. I suspect Brightman will be honored for this long after the details of his epistemology are largely forgotten. I certainly think he ought to be honored for it. I honor him also for refusing to accept dualistic theories of mind and mere matter, theories which the advance of science will, I am persuaded, cause to seem less and less attractive.

Brightman comes close to solving Plato's problem: What can "God is good" mean if "good" is defined as divinely commanded? A finite-infinite or temporal-eternal deity has volitions that are not eternal and hence (Aristotle, Peirce) are contingent. Our obedience to divine commands (if we know them) because they are divinely commanded is good somewhat as, in a well-governed state, it is good to be law-abiding. Traffic rules, for instance, are partly arbitrary (drive to the right—or to the left) but it is well that they be obeyed. However, the eternal principle of good is God's eternal essence and is in no sense arbitrary or contingent. It is what God could not choose not to will and what we can fail to approve only by failing to understand it or ourselves. It is the beauty of holiness, of incorruptible all-embracing love.

Brightman includes in what God eternally is and knows the principles of rationality (logic, mathematics) and calls it all the Given. What this has to do with given in the sense in which it occurs in perceptions of concrete actualities is inadequately clarified.

Like many another, Brightman seems to imply, without quite stating, a doctrine of dual transcendence. He allows the impression to haunt his discussion of the divine finitude and temporality that the traditional affirmation of the sheer, exclusive infinity or eternity of God was excessive praise, that God falls short of a too absolute ideal. He does not really mean this. But he gives his classical opponents a little too much assistance in believing what they are by habit desirous of believing. Berdyaev takes the right tack here: the sheer immobility of the medieval deity was a "deficiency," objectionable precisely as such. As Plato seems to have known, self-change is essential to soul on all levels, including the highest, that of the World Soul; and so is changeability by others, as is deducible from the truism of Aristotle, accepted by the scholastics in all applications except that to deity: to know something is to be influenced by it. On its own showing, medieval Aristotelianism, which broke with the master at this point without refuting his argument, was inconsistent in attributing omniscience to a wholly independent deity. Brightman was only returning to classical insights after a long detour.

Notes

1. *Person and Reality*, ed. Peter Bertocci, with J. E. Newhall and R. S. Brightman (New York: Ronald Press, 1958); *The Problem of God* (Nashville and New York: Abingdon Press, 1930); *Philosophy of Religion* (Englewood Cliffs, N.J.: Prentice-Hall, 1940, 1958).
2. *Jour. Rel.*, 12 (1932), 545–555.

CHAPTER 17

Pepper and McKeon
on Philosophical Systems

Stephen C. Pepper (1891–1972), in *World Hypotheses*, tried to classify systems under four heads according to their root metaphors.[1] This has two weaknesses. (1) It takes the nonanalytic, organic view of systems: Take them or leave them as wholes. Instead, we should classify views on specific problems, not lump all problems together, assuming a godlike clarity in the individual philosophers as to the degree of consistency and coherence their systems represented. In every culture there are beliefs that are almost obligatory. These beliefs have diverse historical sources and may not be wholly consistent. Great philosophers do their best to avoid inconsistency and achieve clarity. Being human, they partly fail. We should judge not so much their total systems as their views on various issues.

(2) A metaphor, root or not, is a rhetorical device and not the final measure of a system's significance. "The world as a machine," for instance, defines "mechanism" only if we know what is meant by machine. The quantum mechanical view of "mechanism" is basically different from that of classical mechanics, and neither one is that of ordinary common sense. Whitehead uses several basic metaphors, thus: "organism," "cell," "prehension," or "house its actual (past) world." None of these metaphors by itself identifies what is most significant in his philosophy. Whitehead is too much a mathematician and physicist for that. He is interested above all in the logical patterns exhibited in reality: What depends upon what, what is independent of what; are there necessary and sufficient conditions, or only necessary conditions, for what happens? These are literal, not metaphorical questions. Whitehead is also interested in how abstractions are to be accounted for in terms of concrete experience.

As what is a machine actually experienced? Or an organism? Or "form"? Or "matter"? All these terms require phenomenological grounding. The only ultimate analogy or metaphor is human experiencing as for us the primary sample of concrete actuality. Pepper comes to grips with that question only in one of his four types, oddly called "contextualism," and this odd labeling indicates some confusion, it seems to me. It is a metaphorical description of what can be said more literally. And Pepper dismisses "society" as a poor root metaphor, although it is the one that concrete experience most vividly and emphatically supports. We know social relations if we know anything. The question is, how far can social order be generalized beyond the merely human-to-human case? The context that we cannot deny is the social context.

Pepper had a clear and seemingly unresisted antitheistic bias. For him, theological ideas are not even challenging.

Both Pepper and Richard P. McKeon (b. 1900), in early phases of their work, tried to put all philosophies into a classification of types, and they contended that no one of the types is simply right or simply wrong, since none can definitively refute the others; and they seemed to think that any attempt to find a higher synthesis combining the truths in them all without their exaggerations or omissions is misguided.[2] Pepper labels and depreciates as eclecticism any such attempt.

Another feature the two writers have in common is this: Of the types recognized, they prefer one and, as they characterize the others, they do well to prefer that one, for it alone is free from rather obvious absurdity. Any sensible person would do well to start with the preferred type and try to remove its excesses or transcend its limitations. But this would, by these authors as I read them, be judged eclecticism in the bad sense or a weak compromise. Thus the scheme is not entirely neutral or merely historical.

What McKeon and Pepper prefer is a cautious view of the human situation and of philosophy as concerned with that situation and its practical, social, and political problems. They are instrumentalists or operationalists, strongly influenced by Dewey or Bridgman—but hardly by Peirce. It may be wise for many to restrict themselves to the problems that Pepper and McKeon have in mind. But the religious problems are scarcely reached in this way, nor is there much contact with the problems of natural science. And the scorn of eclecticism is a counsel of despair. It forbids us to look for a way to transcend or resolve the customary oppositions and violent disagreements. The great philosophers (and in this we, or some of us, should imitate them) have looked for such a way. That in this attempt success can be only partial does not make metaphysics radically different from most human endeavors.

I agree with McKeon, as against Pepper, in looking to logical rather than metaphorical aspects of systems as essential. Thus McKeon contrasts views that take the inclusive whole of reality (Parmenides or Plato) as the primary object of inquiry, with those that take the least parts (atomism) as the object. Then, contrasting with both the others, there is the middle-ground view of the human being, looking perhaps toward an inclusive whole but unable, it may well be, to reach it, and also looking toward smaller and smaller parts but unable to know the smallest. Dismissing these probably insoluble problems, we concentrate on that middle region in which, for better or worse, we have to live. And Pepper's contextualism is similar. The world is not known to be simply a machine or an organism, and what we most need to know about is the context of our human experiences.

My view is that certain extreme organicisms or holisms, for logical reasons, could not possibly be true, and certain extreme pluralisms or mechanisms, also for logical reasons, can only be exaggerations. Similarly with formism or essentialism or the contrasting pure existentialism. I am committed to the search for a higher synthesis of all such extremes. All my mature life I have sought it. I think we can, approximately at least, arrive at it, or make progress toward it. But I agree that we must start where we are, with ourselves as neither inclusive wholes nor least parts, neither mere machines (as these are already defined) nor mere organisms, but experiencing human animals, and inquire what indications there are in this human reality, as given, concerning the larger environment and the micro-constituents of ourselves and other manifest things.

It is logical questions that we need to put. What is the logic of causality? Of the relations of experience to its data? Of things-as-given to things-as-known-in-science? What is the logic of the religious idea of God? Is God to be defined as simply cause, not effect; simply actual, not potential? Does being include becoming, or becoming, being; which is the more concrete and inclusive idea? What is the relation between strict and genetic (or personal) "identity? " What kind of "whole" could reality be: a whole complete and fixed once for all, or one added to in each moment? Are past events still somehow real? If not, is history about nonentities? Are future events real? If so, in what sense are they future? And how can future events be open to further decision if "what will be will be? " These are my kind of questions. Any scheme that seems to forbid asking them is unacceptable. And I am not asking: "How do we answer such questions if we are Platonists or idealists, and how if we are instrumentalists? " I want to know, if possible, or make an intelligent guess, before I die, how we are to answer them as reflective human beings who know the historical answers. And how carefully did the great philosophers arrive at their answers? On some of the questions I see Dewey as careful, on some, Plato, on some Leibniz, on some, Bergson or Whitehead. On no question, so far as I can see, has every philosopher been careful, or in a position to see the issue clearly.

Both Pepper and McKeon have eventually experiemented with other ways than those mentioned above of contrasting systems and understanding their evolution and rivalry.

One of the ways in which philosophers differ is in the degree of complexity with which they are comfortable. Russell's tolerance for complex ideas was less than Whitehead's, who considered Russell "simple-minded." Russell considered Whitehead "muddle-headed." Paul Weiss has a high tolerance for complexity, and I tend to find him a little muddle-headed. Pepper I find too simple, although admirable in his favorite specialty: aesthetics. With McKeon, who is certainly not simple-minded, I confess I am somewhat at a loss. His degree and kind of complexity is for me so little manageable that I cannot even call it muddle-headed. For how am I to know that the trouble is not with my simple-mindedness? Certainly there is vast learning in this complexity. Harry A. Wolfson (who could write very simply) was learned in the history of Western philosophy down to Spinoza and (he said) fairly competent down to Kant, but not for developments since. But McKeon's grasp seems to cover the two and one-half millennia and not to be entirely limited to the West. His sentences, paragraphs, and essays have some reason for their intricacy. In talking to McKeon about the history of ideas I can enjoy his knowledge. But in reading him I have more trouble.

Long ago in Chicago a student of mine and of McKeon's (he later became a distinguished psychiatrist) wrote an essay for a campus student periodical on what he learned in McKeon's classes. The point, he said, is not to analyze reality, but to "analyze analysis." Thus, in the two short books, *Renaissance and Method in Philosophy,* and *Freedom and History: The Semantics of Philosophical Controversies and Ideological Conflicts,* what one finds is philosophizing about philosophizing, not about God, nature, or even our animal species, although the last comes closest to what is going on. I have never learned anything about nonhuman nature or God from hearing or reading McKeon, but I have, I hope, learned a fair amount about how philosophers (for example Plato and Aristotle) have differed, about the complexity of intellectual disputes, the variety of philosophical methods, the impossibility of an absolutely and uniquely right method, and the tendency of philosophical fashions to follow one another in a somewhat cyclical or spiral fashion, without their being any unambiguous progress away from error and toward truth. "When someone says, 'There is one truth and I have it,' I walk out," he said once after doing just that at a meeting between some American and Soviet philosophers.

Perhaps posterity will produce another historical scholar able to do justice to the subtleties and vast scope of the concerns with which McKeon deals. There may be such a scholar somewhere now, although I do not know his or her name. And I am too dedicated to philosophizing about something other than philosophizing to try to do what seems needed.

One contention of McKeon's I do understand and see the point of. In the end, this instrumentalist holds, philosophical issues are not merely intellectual puzzles, and a philosophy is called upon to illuminate human problems of freedom and its absence, of life and death. In our time, he adds, the outstanding problem is that of war and peace. The worst thing we can do with philosophical disagreements is to use them to lessen the prospects for peace. We must cooperate for peace with our philosophical opponents as well as with our philosophical friends. Philosophical agreement is not a precondition for peace. If it were, our situation would be hopeless, considering what avoiding war has come to mean for the survival of our species and its cultures. I hope McKeon's efforts in international affairs have contributed to the end here envisaged. Which of us can be boastful about his part in this immeasurably important matter?

What McKeon does (apart from his contributions to international institutions) might, I should think, be called metaphilosophy. It is highly historical in a sense—or is it metahistorical? My late lamented friend Julius Weinberg, also a specialist in medieval philosophy, once said, "As for metaphilosophy, we should leave that to God." Or should he have said, "We should leave that to McKeon"? If *he* is not doing it, I do not know who is. Or should one rather say that he is indeed philosophizing, not simply about philosophizing but about our basic human problems so far as these are in part produced and, one hopes, helpfully influenced by the divergent ways of philosophizing? Here the influence of Dewey is surely at work. As McKeon puts it, "Philosophies are transformed in action to forces in competition with other forces determining behavior." There seems to be a moral suggested here, but it evidently does not lend itself to any simple summary. That the matter is important is clear enough. The four qualifications "dialectical," "logistic," "semantic," and "problematic" or "operational" by which philosophical methods are characterized and contrasted, with apparently some provision for a certain amount of eclecticism (legitimate?), may prove illuminating if they are carefully studied. I suspect that they are somewhat arbitrary and if applied too confidently will bar the path of inquiry. But with so subtle a writer the question remains moot. I presume that I am a dialectician; but I make definite use of some principles of formal logic and defend both internal and external relations. I also accept a certain form of pragmatism; and I welcome semantic analysis. Posterity will classify my work, and McKeon's also, assuming that both are remembered.

Notes

1. Pepper's metaphysical books (really empirical cosmologies by my standards) are: *World Hypotheses: A Study in Evidence* (Berkeley: University of California Press, 1942; reprinted in 1970); *Concept and Quality: A World Hypothesis* (LaSalle, Il.: Open Court, 1967).

2. Good brief accounts of Pepper and McKeon are given in W. L. Reese's admirable *Dictionary of Philosophy and Religion* (Atlantic Highlands, N.J.: Humanities Press, 1980; Hassocks, Sussex: Harvester Press). McKeon is perhaps best known for his scholarly works on Aristotle and philosophers of the Middle Ages. He gives his own ideas about philosophy in general in: *Renaissance and Method in Philosophy* (New York: Columbia University Press, no date given); *Freedom and History: The Semantics of Philosophical Controversy and Ideological Conflicts* (New York: Noonday Pres, 1952); *Thought, Action and Passion* (Chicago: The University of Chicago Press, 1954).

CHAPTER 18

Montague's Animistic Materialism and Promethean Religion

William Pepperell Montague (1873–1953) was a brilliant, enthusiastic thinker of comprehensive interests.[1] Before G. E. Moore's famous 1903 article, "The Refutation of Idealism," Montague had made much the same point in his "Royce's Refutation of Realism."[2] True, Peirce had made it still earlier. Here were American anticipations of an important intellectual event in the Old World.

Montague said that as a student he had for Peirce "a kind of worship." He found Peirce, who criticized some of his papers, "in intellect cold and clear, but in metaphysical imagination capricious, scintillating, and unbridled." From Santayana Montague derived an extreme form of Platonism that takes rather too little into account Plato's more mature dialogues. From James and Peirce he learned to distrust classical determinism, Royce's absolutism, and any usual form of materialism or dualism. From Royce he learned not to believe as Royce did, but to appreciate the great philosophers of the past. All this is delightfully told in his essay, "An Animistic Materialist."[3]

Montague adopted Peirce's realism and his idea of an initial chaos gradually developing into an approximately but not absolutely orderly cosmos (a tychistic element remaining still); he accepted Bergson's distinction between merely physical time and psychical time (in which the past is incorporated into the present) and tried to derive from physics, with its equation of mass with energy, support for his "animistic" view that the inner nature of matter everywhere is psychical, as in our brains we experience it to be. Leibniz enters into his thought here, along with Fechner, and various others.[4] The admission of an aspect of randomness or chance in quantum theory he saw as suggestive of a "spontaneity" (a favorite word of Peirce's),

211

a minimal kind of freedom even in inanimate matter.[5] If this was "materialism" it was certainly of a refreshingly novel kind.

Probably without knowing it, Montague acted as though he were determined to actualize the program sketched by Peirce as follows: "To be idealists we must be materialists without flinching." Consider the conclusion of Montague's Howison Lecture.

When minds themselves are shown to be purely physical, then the physical itself is shown to be purely psychical. Materialism, if sufficiently radical, will lead us to a new type of idealism in which matter is not denied but transfigured. For we must remember that there is a mighty energy that creates the expanding hypersphere of our four-dimensional universe. As the systems of energy that pervade our brains are our very souls, so, too, that cosmic energy may be *in itself* a soul, akin to our own, and in touch with our own.[6]

Accepting from Bergson the idea (Peirce had it also) of becoming as cumulative, or as growth without loss, Montague applied it to nature as interpreted in quantum physics (for example, by Schrödinger) and to deity as worshiped in a "promethean" religion.[7] The wave aspect of matter was its aspect of potentiality, or determinable indeterminateness, and also its aspect of mind. At least in a minimal sense creative freedom was pervasive, human freedom being a high level of this. Deity is the eminent level. Divine power is finite, but divine goodness and (he almost seems to say) knowledge is not.[8] In this combination he resembled E. S. Brightman.

I imagine that one could almost have convinced Montague that, understanding by 'power' capacity to influence and inspire the nevertheless partly self-determined activity of others, one can regard God's power as unsurpassable by any conceivable being and thus as infinite in the same sense as divine goodness or knowledge. To know something is to be influenced by it; hence no knowledge can be wholly independent or in every sense infinite. But this does not, so far as anyone has shown, entail that there must be error or ignorance in the highest conceivable form of knowing. Error is not definable as, or implied by, openness to being influenced by the thing known, nor is ignorance so definable. Indeed error and ignorance might almost be defined as the state of not being precisely and adequately influenced in one's awareness by what exists. Kant's contrary view— inherited, as I have argued elsewhere, from medieval theology—is illogical.

212

Montague sees that, because of the Leibnizian principle of incompossibility, there can be no knowledge that knows as actual all that could be actual.[9] Thus in richness of content no knowledge whatever can be "absolutely infinite," in spite of Spinoza's belief to the contrary. The function of the creatures is precisely to contribute to the endless growth, permitting no final maximum, in the aesthetic richness, the concrete value, of the world as enjoyed by God.[10] If anyone in this country anticipated Whitehead's vision on this point, it was Montague. In Europe it was Fechner. Varisco seems to imply the view, but his account is less elaborately formulated.

That Montague received no great attention for this achievement is not surprising, considering what happened to Fechner and, earlier, to the Socinian theologians. One's best contemporaries are still human and partly blind to what is before them.

Montague was with Leibniz, Edwards, Samuel Johnson, and Royce in avoiding the false position of a theism that accepts the idea of mere insentient matter together with the idea of God as supreme spirit. Sooner or later (and it is now fairly late) this kind of dualism must go if atheism is to go. Supreme spirit creates lesser spirits, not bits of what Whitehead dismissed as "vacuous actuality," empty of life, sentience, value, anything intelligible to mind, "the sole self-intelligible thing" (Peirce).

Montague was less successful than Brightman in establishing a school. Not all the reasons for this had anything to do with the relative merits of the thinking of the two men. Montague was more iconoclastic in his philosophy of religion. He called omnipotence "an immoral doctrine." He was more enthusiastic about Bergson than was Brightman. Yet, very unlike Bergson, Montague was an extreme platonist in his doctrine of eternal forms or possibilities.[11] He was, I am told, aghast when on an oral examination a certain student (who has become one of the most learned historians of philosophy this country has had) said that the "platonic theory of ideas" was first formulated in Aristotle's *Metaphysics*. This same student, R. P. McKeon, has said Montague had one of the finest capacities for metaphysical speculation of anyone in the country. Montague's *Great Visions of Philosophy* is a fascinating journey through the history of philosophy.

Like James and Brightman, Montague overestimates the scope of the empirical method. Yet he is not certain that the ontological argument is a mere fallacy.[12] Were it so, of course the question of God's existence and defining characteristics would be an empirical matter entirely. But then, as Peirce clearly saw, the term 'God' stands for a "fetish," not the God of the high religions. Theism is a piece of metaphysics, and in metaphysics, as Peirce wrote in his early twenties and never retracted, error is absurdity, not misstatement of observational facts. Whitehead is not very explicit on this issue, but I interpret him as taking this side of the controversy.

Montague, in a somewhat Jamesian vein, speculates that the origin of the conscious God aware of the world is in a primordial principle of growth and diversification (reminiscent of Herbert Spencer's Unknowable) that gradually becomes the conscious, loving God of high religion.[13] One is also reminded here of S. Alexander, who influenced Whitehead. But Whitehead regarded God as primordially conscious— when one takes into account that God primordially has a "consequent" aspect that is conscious. Whitehead's God never was without a world and is "with all worlds, not before all worlds." Process theology and more definitely still, neoclassical theism recognize classical theism as close to the truth about one aspect of deity. When Montague writes that the will of God is "purely good," but that it is "one force among others," he is, I believe, not fully succeeding in clarifying his intuition of the unacceptability of classical theism. God is the being strictly unsurpassable by conceivable others— unsurpassable whether in goodness or in power. But the only intelligible meaning of power is capacity to influence others who also have some power. So there are other powers and not by accident, but necessarily. Each other such power is contingent, but that there are some besides God is an eternal necessity. A mere empiricist could not say this.

Montague toys with vague ideas of immortal posthumous careers for human individuals, perhaps for other animals.[14] Again, this is, or is not, an empirical question. I think it is not. And one feels that Montague was preoccupied with the possibility of a posthumous relation to God as a value for us rather than as a value for God. He did not arrive at an adequate vision of the light it casts upon life to regard all of it as contributory to the all-embracing life, as he describes the divine reality. Finally, we are for God, not God for us. So I interpret loving God with all one's being.

Montague's overextended empiricism or, the same thing, his over-extended contingentism (to coin a word) appears in his treatment of the ontological argument for God's existence. Montague, in this matter, was too much like nearly every American philosopher before I, first, and then Norman Malcolm (independently and in some respects with more rhetorical adroitness) pointed out the two forms or stages in which Anselm presented his argument and the possibility of taking the second form as by itself far stronger than the other by itself. The point is not that existing is better than not existing and therefore the unsurpassable being must exist; the point is rather that a being that cannot be conceived not to exist but can be conceived to exist is better than a being that can be conceived not to exist and also can be conceived to exist. In short, a necessarily existing being is better than one that, whether or not it exists, exists or fails to exist contingently.

Montague is well aware that contingency involves incompatibility among possibles. I seem to recall his saying somewhere that if it could be shown that the divine existence is compatible with any conceivable other existence, this would mean that the divine existence was noncontingent. But, he says, this has not been shown. I have filled many pages with efforts to show precisely that. God's power to coexist with others is unsurpassable, infallible, unqualified. Contingency is an aspect of incompatibility with other positive possibilities. Each of us exists by occupying space and performing roles that, because we occupy or perform them, others cannot. Contingent existence is competitive. Divine existence is, by both classical and neoclassical theism, conceived as noncompetitive. Ergo.

What still remains to be shown, and Anselm did not show it, is the question, "Can God, as defined in some available way, be conceived to exist? " If not, then the absurdity of atheism is matched by the absurdity of theism, and the positivists, Carnap, for example, are right, the idea of God fails to make sense. As there are mathematical statements that are either necessarily true or necessarily false but could not be contingently true or false, so there are existential statements about God (also about nondivine reality as such) that are in the same class. Anselm did not refute atheism, but he did refute unqualified empiricism, whether it takes a theistic or a nontheistic form. Carnap emphatically rejected the label "atheism" for his doctrine. He overlooked the possibility (suggested by Charlesworth) of calling his positivism "a priori atheism," but he was right in denying that he was an (empirical) atheist.

That multitudes of scholars have failed to see what I have just briefly outlined is somewhat surprising. Still Leibniz saw it, as did Ralph Cudworth. Karl Barth in his book on Anselm seems to see it. Descartes in one passage virtually states it. But Kant refutes only Anselm's first argument and has misled a host of philosophers since. Nor does he really refute Descartes as (in the *Replies*) that writer responded to Gassendi, who anticipated Kant's very objection (to the first and weak ontological argument). Leibniz with customary neatness

215

and clarity had it right. "If God is possible, then God exists (without possibility of not existing)." But is God possible? Carnap's question is the prior one. Arguments other than the ontological are required to answer it. Leibniz tried to furnish such another argument. Kant rightly denied that he had succeeded. And this was the most valid point in Kant's famous refutation of the Anselmian reasoning.

In *Great Visions of Philosophy*, his Carus Lectures, Montague purports to explore historical philosophical systems as showing what is possible, leaving to observational science the determination of what is actual.[15] What neither philosophy nor science does, according to this scheme, is to consider what all possible states of reality have in common, or (the same) what exists necessarily. Moreover, Montague himself seems repeatedly to suggest that the great systems describe impossible rather than genuinely possible worlds. They do not entirely succeed in showing even what reality might conceivably be.

Generalizing Montague's idea of the function of philosophy to take necessity and impossibility, as well as possibility, into account, we may say that philosophy (as metaphysics) at least tries to make true modal statements, to tell us what conceivably could (or could not), and, out of what could, what must, exist. As I have argued elsewhere, an abstract property exists if it is somehow actualized in particular instances. Just how or in what instances it is actualized I call actuality. It follows that mere existence is less specific than actuality. The dichotomy essence-existence, or essence-actuality, is radically inadequate. This is one more instance of the limitations of merely dichotomous thinking. Trichotomies are incomparably more adequate, as Peirce, Hegel, and others have more or less clearly seen.

What Montague (and nearly all his contemporaries) overlooked was that, although no particular or concrete actuality is necessary, certain extremely general abstractions must be actualized somehow, in some suitable concrete form or state. The abstraction *deity* (if it makes sense) is one such abstraction, *nondivine actuality* is another. The idea God-World sums up the content of metaphysics. As necessary, it is infinitely abstract; God-as-knowing-Montague is a contingent actuality that might not have been. Here there is freedom, creativity, in both Creator and creature. Empiricists who overgeneralize contingency are in error, not because it is certain that deity exists but because the logically viable alternative to the divine existence is the divine impossibility. Either way a very important question is not adjudicable empirically, but only by conceptual analysis, or by faith, the faith that we know what we mean by 'God.'

216

I am not absolutely certain about the existence of God, but I am certain that the truth about that existence is noncontingent. No observation could logically count against it. For the believer any observation counts for it. (Any effect fully understood must reveal its causal conditions, but conditions never reveal their precise consequences.) The creatures exhibit the Creator, if either idea makes sense. The Creator's existence, however, does not entail the particular creatures, for the creatures must finally determine themselves. That the Creator exists is not by choice or chance, but by eternal necessity, unless some eternal a priori impossibility prevents it. If Montague had only partial grasp of these propositions, it was at a time when no one had spelled out the whole story. It must be said, however, that Whitehead (well before Montague's last two books) had come closer to doing so than Montague seemed to realize. In his references to Whitehead he simply ignored that writer's form of theism and showed little comprehension of his metaphysics as a whole. This is a form of cultural lag that would scarcely occur in a science.

Two final thoughts about this wonderfully imaginative and daring thinker concern his view of the relation of genetic identity to the sense of the personal past, and the relation of God as supreme consciousness to the universe of nondivine creatures.

The most important occurrence in his life, Montague wrote, was a momentary experience in which he intuited the "indefinitely rich system of memories" in present experience whereby "a sequence of successive moments . . . could . . . be felt as a solid chunk of duration extending back and down into the past." [16] This seems to me to agree nicely with Whitehead's doctrine of the immortality of the past as (mostly subconsciously) prehended in present experience (most fully only in God). Montague connects the insight with physics and physiology as follows:

> "What, from the standpoint of the physicist is mere potentiality of future motion, is in itself the actuality of feeling and sensation. . . . Their traces . . . constitute the memory system of the individual . . . and modify the responses to later stimuli. . . . The potentiality of external motion is the actuality of internal experience." [17]

The similarity of all this to Whitehead seems considerable.

Like D. C. McIntosh but unlike Whitehead, Montague, in his theology, uses the Platonic analogy of the World Soul. The cosmos is God's body, a purely "internal environment" for the divine spirit. [18]

217

It is easy to object to the analogy, just as it is easy to object to the analogy of God to a king, father, friend, or other kind of human person. But the sheer rejection of such analogies reduces deity to an empty cipher of no religious, ethical, or other positive value. Peirce said that all human thinking is anthropomorphic. In some sense this is tautological. I add that in my short experience of McIntosh—to whom Montague refers as one of the "unofficial realists"—he impressed me as one of two or three theologians I have known who could be considered saintly, or who clearly embodied the love they talked or wrote about. Another was the logician-theologian Heinrich Scholz, who similarly impressed Karl Barth.

I knew Montague only slightly; but his writings show a person of rare qualities whose reach exceeded his grasp, so that probably what is of most value in his "philosophical experiments" has (or will) come to fruition in more satisfactory form in others whose technical competence in the exact sciences and ability to organize their speculations exceeds his. But it is hard to be sure, considering the range of his ideas. In any case his intellectual career is colorful and his candor and eloquence engaging. It was he himself who confessed to the "taint of the circle-squarer" as he attempted to explain his theory that psychical actuality is the internal aspect of physical potentiality, or his rejection of the Einsteinian relativity of simultaneity.

Notes

1. William Pepperell Montague's books are: The Ways of Knowing (London: Allen & Unwin; New York: The Macmillan Co., 1925, 1953) Belief Unbound (Salem, N.H.: Ayer Co., 1930) The Ways of Things (New York: Prentice-Hall, Inc., 1940) Great Visions of Philosophy (LaSalle, Il.: Open Court Publishing Co., 1950) Hereafter Great Visions.
2. Philosophical Rev. (Mar. 1901.)
3. The Ways of Things, pp. 648–675. Hereafter WT.
4. WT., pp. 293, 654.
5. P. 293.
6. Pp. 406–407.
7. Pp. 293, 414–417, 517, 525, 527.
8. Pp. 122–123, 274.
9. Pp. 267, 275; Great Visions, pp. 278–360.
10. Pp. 534, 538.
11. Pp. 275–280, 652.
12. Great Visions, pp. 224–230, 235, 254, 343; WT, 536. For Montague's empiricism see WT, pp. 276–341.
13. Great Visions, pp. 533–539.
14. Pp. 540–549.

15. Prologue to *Great Visions.*
16. WT., 668.
17. 669–670.
18. 122–123, 664.

CHAPTER 19

Weiss's Phenomenology of Religion

Paul Weiss (born 1901) is a highly gifted and versatile writer and teacher; he is also the founder of both an important society, The Metaphysical Society of America, and an important journal, *The Review of Metaphysics*, of which he was for many years the sole editor. He is original; indeed, he has a way of doing philosophy that is different enough from the ways of most of the rest of us to present a problem. This could mean constructive originality of a prophetic kind from which our descendants would learn much. But it could mean instead a somewhat sterile eccentricity from which only Weiss's own pupils and a scattering of readers from the lay public are likely to derive much profit. Or it could mean something partway between these extremes. One thing seems clear, and I expect that Weiss would agree with me in this: *Either* certain simplifications or conceptual integrations that some of us have learned from "process philosophers" or in part from metaphysical idealists are unjustified *or* the remarkable complexities and, for my intellectual taste, inelegancies and obscurities of his system are needless. But I leave adjudication of this issue to others. As one indebted to Weiss for his invaluable help in editing the writings of Peirce, and as one who has admired and enjoyed his combination of wit, wisdom, humor, ingenuity, and good will for more than fifty-five years, I find my near inability to read his recent works embarrassing. Yet Weiss deals with subjects that are important to me, we share some common convictions, he has learned from many of the same philosophers (Peirce, Whitehead, Dewey, and many others). And he has a carefully polished style. Even so the not entirely eliminable personal aspect of philosophizing manifests itself.

I shall, for the most part, limit my discussion of Weiss to the expression of his thought in what for me is one of the most readable of his books, *The God We Seek*.[1] The publisher's suggestion that this may be the most important of Weiss's works expresses what I am inclined to feel. To some extent this is a subjective judgment. For in *Modes of Being*, more recent metaphysical or epistemological works, and even in Weiss's works on aesthetics, he is dealing with problems to my solution of which I am perhaps all too much attached. When Bruckner was asked what he thought of Brahms's music, he replied, "All respect! However, I prefer my own thing."

What Weiss aims to do in *The God We Seek* is to give a sort of phenomenology, to use his own word, of man's religious life. It is a philosophical anthropology more than a philosophical theology. I suppose I have, here and there, offered fragments of such a study, but in this book the focus is throughout on man's search for God as this search is found in the various religions. The primary emphasis is on the rivalry of religions, or of religion with philosophy, rather than the rivalry of philosophies. Comparative religion, not comparative philosophy, is the main approach. Still, Weiss is very much the philosopher in this book. He is philosophical in an existential way, with emphasis on relevant experiences of a profound sort. His own systematic metaphysics is kept in the background. True, he speaks rather constantly of "substances" or "beings"; but then every philosophy must have a translation for this term. Even the Buddhists have it, and certainly Whiteheadians and Peirceans do. But on the whole the discussion is philosophically nontechnical or neutral, and this has its advantages. The discussion of religious language is penetrating and judicious.

The heart of the book is an original version of the idea that we know God by encounter, by religious experience. We know God as the universal Other by whom all ordinary otherness is made possible. We find ourselves in contrast to and dependent upon all sorts of things that, collectively, may be called "the world." Collectively, these things are indifferent to our needs or wishes. Moreover, they are so various and inconstant that, so long as our interest is solely in them, we lack integrity and do not know who or what we ourselves are. To find ourselves, and to avoid endless frustration and confusion, we must at times detach ourselves, turn away from the world. Weiss is vividly aware how much of Oriental religiosity has consisted precisely in this turning from the world; but he knows also that it is an element in all religion. On the other hand, he urges eloquently that the point of turning from the world lies not in definitive escape from relatedness to it, but in discovery of better modes of relationship than are possible for those who think only of the world and them-

221

selves as in it. In detachment we should find the One by attachment to whom we achieve the right way of attaching ourselves to the world. Attachment to God is attachment to that in which (Weiss's deity sometimes seems in no sense personal) or the one in whom, all things are unified and ennobled. Only in God is there any permanence, or any just assessment, of value. Thus our otherness to God is the abiding meaning and measure of all otherness. I am not using precisely Weiss's language. But something like this seems to be his meaning. I feel much depth and genuineness in his way of putting things; although I am also frequently a bit puzzled by it.

It is encouraging to find a contemporary writer who, with so little that is merely provincial or sectarian, with such a broad grasp of contemporary knowledge, can deal so vividly with the essential religious situation. Sometimes I wish he had used different words. For example, in a few places he says "eternal" where I think "everlasting" would be less misleading. And I wonder that he seems to use "omnipotent" without misgivings, while at the same time denying that God creates the world, "interferes with its course," or causes the evils we experience. But his insistence that God is genuinely relative to us, involved with us, and is no "unmoved mover" or "emptiness possessing no features," and that He takes the world into Himself in such a way as to maximize its values and immortalize its achievements—these are insights that religious men and philosophers, from Socinus to Whitehead, have been trying to express and communicate for some centuries now. Weiss's strong defence of them is most welcome.

A central insight which Weiss has had almost throughout his writing career is that the ultimate task of thinking animals such as we are is to make their actions serve a universal good, and that this is possible only through the cooperation of God. So far as I recall, Weiss has never taken seriously the idea that future personal advantage can be the principle of rational action. The good to which we ultimately respond is the general good, not our good. This seems to me to be the only honest explication of the injunction, Christian as well as Judaic, "Love thy neighbor as thyself." I take this ideal to contradict the idea that altruism must be derived from enlightened self-interest. If we love others for their usefulness to ourselves, then we should equally love ourselves for our usefulness to others. It is the good, wherever it is or can be, that concerns us as truly rational or truly religious.

Weiss seems to agree with me, as with Kant, that reason evaluates ends, not means only. Mere feeling attaches us to our own advantage, at least for the very near future, even as it also often attaches us to the good of others, at least for the near future. This can be seen in subhuman animals and in children. But feeling alone does not consistently aim at future good for anyone, self or another. It is capricious, shortsighted, inconsistent. The function of reason is to universalize regard for good, no matter whose, and no matter how remote in time, so far as our actions can contribute to it. But in abstraction from God, and in view of the mortality of all others than God, in view also of the uncertainties of life, what definite idea can there be of future good as enhanceable by our choices? We help our children, but they will eventually turn into dust, as the Bible has it. And who can tell what may happen to the human species, with or without our help? Besides, all actual good is enjoyed good (I am not sure that Weiss has said this), and who can enjoy the "good of all" in all the future? Without God there is no definite universal good to which all may contribute. Each of us possesses only his or her own good: less than that, only his or her own good at the given moment. Where and whose is the good of all throughout their careers? It is in God that the many goods are united and made permanent. Only in God and his appreciation does it all add up to anything.

The foregoing is perhaps more my way of putting it than Weiss's. But I hope it is consistent with his. He stresses the need to admit not only God but an objective ideal valid for God as well as all others. Indeed, God acts in the light of an ideal and therefore depends upon that ideal. If one recalls the Socratic argument against the notion that something can be right merely because God commands it, one sees how Weiss can take this position. If something is right only because divinely commanded, it becomes meaningless to say that God commands rightly. My own position is that one must distinguish between contingent and necessary aspects of divine action. "God is good" means that He-She (sex being irrelevant here) cannot choose between better and worse but only between actions all unsurpassably good. Weiss admits the idea that God exists necessarily, but I take him to imply, if not say, that God has contingent as well as necessary aspects. The necessity is that God must always act unsurpassably well. However, (as I believe Weiss also holds) it is a false notion of the function of the ideal to suppose that it can specify concrete acts. Hence, however God responds to the world, God could have responded otherwise, though not better. There is never only one possible perfect solution to the problems that the world poses for God.

It may still be asked about the ideal implied by such terms as "unsurpassably well." Is this not independent of God? Now I deny that independence between two terms has a clear meaning where both terms are necessary. For Weiss, as for me, it is no accident either that there is an ultimate ideal or that God exists. Hence we must say that God and the ideal are interdependent, or reject the question. Weiss takes the first course, as I understand him. And I agree: God, so far as necessary, and the necessary or eternal ideal are interdependent. And both these factors are independent of any contingent aspects, whether of God or of the world. (They could and would have existed, had the contingent things all been otherwise.)

However, there is one more step, that I take, but that Weiss, it seems, does not. I insist that subjects include objects in principle and that divine subjects include objects both in principle and without qualification. This is what "omniscience" or divine "infallibility" means to me. Hence we do not need to say, "Beside God there is the eternal ideal." God, as eternally having this ideal, includes it. Thus to say, "God and the ideal" is to say no more than "God." It is like saying, the man and his character. One has merely explicated the first term, not added to its denotation. On the other hand, there is addition if we speak of God as He-She eternally, necessarily is and God as having us and our world. For God as related to us is more than God merely as Him-Her-self. Weiss is not very explicit at this point. He is, it seems to me, committed to the doctrine that God as merely God is the same as God having some world or other, no matter what. For he seems to agree with those of us who contend that God does not confront a choice between world and no world, but only between various possible world states so far as these depend upon divine freedom rather than upon the freedom of the creatures partly determining their own fate.

Weiss's denial of "creation" seems to me partly verbal, if he admits that God universally influences the creatures and yet these have a measure of freedom. They are thus in their humbler way creators. But God, as unsurpassably creative and influential, is *the* creator in the only sense admissible in a philosophy that makes creative freedom a universal category, as Weiss seems to do. Or does he? I personally take the laws of nature as the chief identifiable aspects of God's creative action. So far as the laws are contingent, they imply divine creativity. I also agree with Aristotle that nothing eternal is contingent, hence no law is eternal unless it is without possible alternative.

The issues just discussed are rather technical and almost verbal. I feel that Weiss's religion is rather close to mine. Another subtle

224

technical issue concerns his use of "substance." I have said that we must all have some such term. However, I think there is a price to be paid for taking this term as altogether ultimate, in comparison with such terms as event, state, happening, occasion, momentary actuality. One price is that it makes difficulties in microphysics, since electrons seem not to be substances. Another is that it tends to encourage self-interest theories in ethics and psychology. Still another is that it tends to create confusion in discussions of death and immortality. Death is the destruction, the ceasing to be, of an individual substance. Is it the destruction of the series of states constituting the individual's life? Is the past destroyed by the becoming of the present? This, not death, is the ultimate problem of impermanence, and Weiss seems to see this. But substance philosophies have, with almost unanimous consistency, confused the issue.

They have also confused such technical philosophical questions as the subject-object relation or Hume's question of causal connections. Thus, in memory the object is a previous subject, although actualizing the same substance. Present experience is aware of past experience. This is not X aware of X, but X aware of V or W. Moreover, in some respects it is the paradigmatic case of awareness, of the subject-object relation. No substance philosophy that I know of has been clear on this matter.

Let us relate the question to the ethical issue about altruism. For substance philosophies there are two types of concern that differ absolutely, self interested in self and self interested in another, or X interested in X, X interested in Y. From this we get the assumption that self-interest needs no rational grounding since it is an identity relation, hence inevitable; while interest in another sets a problem. It follows that we cannot literally love another as we love ourselves, and not only can we not do this completely, we cannot do it at all. For genetic identity is being taken as absolute, and nonidentity as equally absolute. For an event-philosophy these difficulties disappear. The present self loves other momentary selves, some past and actual, some future and potential. Whether these other actualities belong to the same intimately related sequence that we have in mind in regarding them as constituting the career of one substance (or what Whitehead calls one society, or socially ordered series) is a secondary, though for some purposes important, matter. In either case we have multiplicity, not mere unity or identity. I am not merely identical with myself, nor merely nonidentical with other persons. For sixty-five years I have disbelieved in the radical difference between self-interest and altruism that substance philosophies seem to imply, though it took Whitehead to make altogether clear to me the role of the substance concept in the matter. If Weiss has escaped the errors about motivation that I have in mind, he is almost the only substance philosopher who has (one other I know of is A. O. Lovejoy in his book, *Reflections on Human Nature*). Moreover, I hold, Weiss has done this in spite of, not because of, his acceptance of the ultimacy of substance. On this issue I side with the Buddhists, or with the more adequate actual-entity concept of Whitehead. I do this although I am well aware that it is Weiss's usage and not mine that most people are able or willing to adopt. For twenty centuries Buddhists have failed to convince non-Buddhists by their analysis of substance into momentary actualities. Nevertheless, I see no option but to declare, whenever the question arises, that they have been right all this time.

No summary can do even slight justice to this book. To select special topics for mention seems almost wholly arbitrary. Certainly the treatment of prayer (pp. 221–223) is among the best ever written. Prayer is "a plea to be properly related to, to have an excellent form of togetherness with, God." It "is answered in the sense that it embodies God, and through this embodiment directs and guides men." Both God and man are "transformed in the prayer itself." "Though God is always immanent, prayer makes Him be as intimate as it is possible for men to have Him be."

A second point I wish to mention is Weiss's insistence that the unity of God must be understood in relation to our own self-unity, and that this is irreducibly emotional, irreducibly concerned with values. Moreover, the divine unity must contain all "the felt values of the things we experience within and without us." It must be spiritual, "something like us," but yet "everywhere if it is anywhere," and such that anything whatever must be related to it merely by existing. We are concerned with God because he alone is adequately concerned with all things. Thus, though Weiss does not quite say this, the idea of God is analogical and therefore has two aspects: the aspect of similarity (God and human beings have feelings, "privacy," concerns, spirituality), yet with an immeasurable difference between deity and any other form of spirituality. As Hume was one of the first to see clearly, the great question has always been, Can the similarity and the difference that any analogy implies be mutually consistent where the difference has the magnitude it must have in this theological use? It is easy to say that God is wholly devoid of relativity, finitude, growth, dependence, that "he, she, or it" "has no body, parts, or passions," and so on and so on through all the changes of the *via negativa*. It is anything but easy to show how the psychical terms applied to God, for example, knowledge, will, and purpose, have any trace of meaning left if the absolute negations referred to are left unqualified. There seems to be some agreement between Weiss and me that this is impossible. And even Barth has, so far as I can make out, come to this conclusion. (Thus he says there is a kind of holy change in God.)

I have been trying for many years to work out the qualifications without which the negative theology is simply, as Hume's Cleanthes said, a form of atheism. The needed principle seems to be that of "dual transcendence." God is both dependent and independent, finite and infinite, changing and changeless; but (a) the contrasting terms apply to God in diverse respects, and thus there is no formal contradiction; and (b) the dependence, finitude, or change in God is of a uniquely excellent kind compatible with the requirement that God, though self-surpassable, is beyond all possible rivalry by another. Thus divine change is wholly in the form of increase in value and includes all lesser changes as contributions. As to precisely where Weiss and I differ in such questions I have never been very clear, but we seem to be not hopelessly far apart.

Weiss in this book has one reference to me, on the matter of my panpsychism. He does not see "why thinking or acting are less legitimate ways than feeling to get to . . . reality." However, if the felt unity of experience is the basis of the very idea of unity, as Weiss seems to suggest, then the general concept of concrete singular reality can only be the most generalized concept of this unity. Mere thinking gives us the abstract and not the concrete; action alone, abstracting from feeling, will not remedy this abstractness. Aesthetic appreciation, broadly construed, is the most concrete form of awareness, taking structure as well as quality, both as felt values, into account. The scientist and the engineer tend to think only in terms of structure. But qualities must also be everywhere. As Peirce held, in his theory of Firstness as feeling quality, no ultimate distinction can be made between the simple or nonstructural aspects of reality and qualities of feeling, since the only way to know such a quality is to feel it (mere thinking cannot generate a single one). Thus the world of possible (knowable) qualities is duplicated by the world of possible feelings. Whitehead has a similar view. Weiss and I, both having studied Whitehead and Peirce, have always somehow disagreed on this. It is true that I had the conviction before I knew any of the three philosophers just mentioned.

In spite of such technical differences, I deeply admire this book. It teems with wisdom and understanding of the human condition. It is profound where so many today are shallow; it expresses a marvelously enlightened, shrewd, and yet truly good human spirit, admirably aware of the dignity and the limitations of man.

In his more purely metaphysical works, such as *The Modes of Being*, I am troubled by Weiss's reification of abstractions (called Finalities) and the use of vague metaphors about the relations of these abstractions to one another and to concrete actualities. Two of my basic ideals of intellectual method are violated in his procedure: the ideal of paying careful attention to degrees of abstraction, avoiding "the fallacy of misplaced concreteness," and the ideal of optimizing conceptual clarity by judicious use of logico-mathematical models (like that of the asymmetry of logical entailment).

Notes

1. Many of Weiss's books have been published by Southern Illinois Press (Carbondale). These include: *The God We Seek*, 1964; *Modes of Being*, 2 vols., 1958; *Beyond All Appearances*, 1974; *First Considerations: An Examination of Philosophical Evidences*, 1977; *Privacy*, 1983.

The first and last of these books seem to have some similarity in being contributions to philosophical anthropology rather than to metaphysics or epistemology. If what Weiss means by privacy is about what I mean by feeling, including on the higher levels "intellectual feelings" (Whitehead), that is, thoughts, I perhaps understand him. Otherwise I may not. This is a similar issue to that discussed in chapter 21 of the present book.

The Making of Men (1967), dedicated, I am pleased to say, to me, I consider a fine treatise on the philosophy of education. The title is a superb expression of what education, in the broadest sense, truly is. I am enough of a feminist to have preferred "the making of persons," but otherwise I have no cavil about this book.

Weiss is writing a book on politics. From this I have hope of learning much. The subject is baffling and Weiss is a shrewd observer of human affairs.

CHAPTER 20

Adler's Neo-Aristotelianism

Like Paul Weiss and in some ways much more so, Mortimer Adler (b. 1902) has stood somewhat apart from the main stream in philosophy. Deriving his support for many years from Robert Maynard Hutchins, not from colleagues and chairmen of departments of philosophy, Adler has charted his own course to an unusual extent and has appealed to a broad public. He is more readily dealt with than Weiss because of his lucid style and relatively simple point of view. Moreover, he is essentially in the Aristotelian tradition.

In this chapter I shall be able to do only scant justice to all that this man has accomplished. For instance, I do not own and have scarcely used *Great Books of the Western World* or *The Great Ideas* (the *Syntopicon*).[1] When the plan of the latter was announced and my opinion asked, I replied, half-jokingly: "It seems to me an excellent instrument for the perpetuation of ancient errors." What I meant, so far as I really meant what I said, was that by going through all the centuries for the opinions of men of genius, omitting those still living, one is likely to give to ways of thinking that have been made more or less irrelevant by intellectual progress greater prominence than they deserve. There was also the objection that in all this work only the Occident, not the Orient, was represented. Nevertheless, these are great achievements.

As director of the Institute for Philosophical Study, Adler has used substantial sums of money for a research team to investigate philosophical issues. The first of the resulting books, and the only one that I have studied with care, is *The Idea of Freedom*, Volume I.

I find this an excellent introduction to the entire history of thought about this topic. Three basic procedures are distinguished and various versions of each set forth: (1) One may seek to provide for freedom by taking human volition to be an exception to the general principle

229

of causal determinism otherwise obtaining in nature. (2) One may insist that strict determinism is universally valid, even in application to human behavior but argue that this does not contradict freedom in the significant sense of unconstrained voluntary action. (3) One may hold that unqualified classical determinism, as in Laplace, is nowhere literally true and that human freedom is merely a high-level, intensive case of the general principle that causal regularity is never absolute, in application to individual or singular and concrete events or actions, but is always only approximate (or statistical). I am cited, rightly, as holding this third view, along with Whitehead, Peirce, and others.

I do not know how to estimate whether the money spent in producing this work (and several others like it—on Justice, Happiness, and Love) was well spent or not. Most books, including most great books, result from more modest outlays. But surely the method of teamwork in research needed to be tried in philosophy; and for all I know the results justify the elaborate means taken to produce them.

In *The Conditions of Philosophy* Adler shows his extraordinary breadth of knowledge of the subject, both in its (Western) history and its present state. He rightly defends the view that philosophy is concerned with more than language; it appeals to the quite general data of experience, those not requiring special apparatus or a special locus in the world to make them accessible. This was also Charles Peirce's view.

In this book, which, like all his works, is admirable for its neat and vigorous style, Adler defends a "commonsense" realism of individual "substances" and ingeniously tries to dispose of the physicists' rejection of substance at the particle level by quoting Heisenberg on the merely potential status of particles. Whatever the success of this tactic, the concept—before Whitehead, radically avoided only by Buddhists—of substances as the final units or singulars of nature seems at best needless in natural science and worse than needless in philosophy. So far from events being mere adjectives of substances, the idea of substance is merely a (very important) way of expressing the natures and relationships of events. (The argument for the primacy, in scientific and philosophic contexts, of the event language is set forth in my book *Creative Synthesis and Philosophic Method.*)

The acceptance of substance as the ultimate unit of reality, in Adler's case, as in the history of philosophy in general, brings with it a theory of enlightened self-interest as the basis of moral obligation. Of all those who have taken this path in ethics, from Plato (in some passages) and Aristotle to Thomas Aquinas and later philosophers,

Adler (in *The Time of our Lives: The Ethics of Common Sense*) is perhaps the most nearly satisfying. Michael Scriven is also good. Each man desires and should seek "a good life for himself," and his obligation to be just to others springs from the fact that a just society is necessary to his own achievement of such a life. Adler admits, however, that religious beliefs or divine grace may qualify this reduction of altruism to a form of self-interest; and also that love (which cannot be obligated, secularly speaking) may to some extent lead a person to act directly for the sake of another.

By a good life Adler means one in which, in due proportions, all real or natural, rather than merely fancied, needs or desires are fulfilled. A basic need is to grow mentally and spiritually, to learn, and to cultivate one's capacities as a person. Moreover, a good life is one that is good as a whole; it is no mere succession of "good times" or pleasures, although pleasure belongs in it. Much wisdom is embodied in this description of the good life. Enlightened self-interest cannot easily be better characterized. But there is a curious paradox. No life, says Adler, is definitively good until it reaches its end. Until then, the life is not good or happy, it is only becoming so. It is admitted that at no time will one possess the goodness of one's life as a whole; for, when the job is finished, one is no longer there to enjoy it. The picture is complete and well painted—for whom?

In contrast, the nonsubstance philosopher will say that each moment of life is, first of all, its own end, good in itself in some degree; second, it is a contribution to the future of life—whose life? All life that is in a position to receive the contribution. This includes one's own personal future and human posterity, obviously; beyond that the question becomes religious. Belief in God can, and I think should, be taken to mean that the definitive contribution is to the divine life. If one's entire life should be a beautiful whole, this is finally because of the value of this whole for the One who alone will survey it in its concrete details. However this may be, to value oneself simply as oneself, and not as an example of humanity, is to value subrationally. Therefore, we need no further reason for valuing others than for valuing self. Love is not identity, A = A, but rather unity in contrast; and this can be our relation not only to ourselves as at other times, but to other persons. Adler does admit that we may "identify ourselves" with another. But the rational way to do this is to universalize the principle. And then self-love is merely a special form of altruism. Always there is more than mere identity, and only momentary selves are simply nonidentical, I now and you now. In

231

a little time our future selves will inherit from each other's past selves, and there will be partial identity.

Adler may be partly right in contending that those who reject enlightened self-interest as the basic motive are likely to be meddlesome do-gooders or mere sentimentalists. But this only shows that the truth can be misused. Obviously, we cannot equally influence and intelligently benefit all individuals; primary obligations are to those we can most effectively influence and whose needs we can most adequately grasp. Equally obviously, one's own career is normally the one a person is in the best position to influence intelligently for good. I see no priority of self-interest beyond this. It is our animality, not our rationality, that makes it difficult to see the lives of others as of direct concern to us, so far as we can knowingly influence them. If I am mistaken in all this, then Adler's theory of morals is, for all I know, as good as any. As he suggests, it is Aristotle brought up to date and improved.

One final objection: Is it not a "natural need" of a thinking animal to see a meaning to life transcending death, a goal that, when attained, does not vanish into a soon-to-be-forgotten limbo? Also, a goal that is as universal as reason itself?

A number of technical questions about ethics and meta-ethics, about relativity and absoluteness in ethics, are excellently handled in this work. Adler shows, I think, that much that is thought to be new in current controversy is old and that some fashionable views were refuted long ago.

In *The Difference of Man and the Difference It Makes* (a fine title!) Adler tackles the question of human equality as a politico-social ideal. He thinks that if the difference between man and the lower animals is taken as merely one of degree, then the value of the distinction, for moral and political purposes, is lost. But is it? The distinctive power of man is, of course, the symbolic power—the ability to form concepts and thereby to achieve a certain freedom from instinct in making choices. Other animals, Adler argues, have no such power. But this suggests endless and politically irrelevant controversy. Quite recently two chimpanzees have been doing what looks wonderfully like learning a primitive sort of visual language in which appear symbols that seem to function both as words and, in combination, as sentences. However, this probably only shows, at most, that the higher apes may reach the level of very young children in concept formation. They would still be far below the level at which they could function politically as citizens or officeholders. In this book, as in a provocative speech Adler gave long ago criticizing the theory of the evolutionary origin of man, he seems to forget that human infants are only potentially "human," if that means concept-forming creatures. (We now know that the brain cells are far from fully developed and like those of subhuman animals during the first weeks of our lives.) The gap that some have held can only be bridged by supernatural means is actually crossed after birth by each of us! In an infant there is no more than the potentiality of rational thinking. And, after all, the potentiality for prehuman apelike creatures eventually to evolve into human beings is as valid an application of this term. The time gap is greater, but what of it? Words like 'soul,' 'substance,' and the like add no iota to the solution of such problems. But by neglecting Oriental (Buddhist) thought, and that of Whitehead, Adler has limited his insight at this point.

My distinguished contemporary can hardly deny that the difference between politically disfranchised children and politically eligible youths or adults is made more than one of degree only by arbitrary convention. Must not the same be said of Adler's other distinction between those excluded from voting or office-holding because of "pathological deficiency" to the extent that they must be hospitalized?

Having said so much, I must add that I deeply share Adler's concern that the universal rights of human beings, the only political animals on earth, should be given institutional recognition. But in order to stop mistreating fellow human beings we need not waste energy on irrelevant quibbles. A sufficiently great difference of degree can, for some purposes, make all the difference. Any reasonably adult, not drastically subnormal, human being, able to employ language and other symbols sufficiently to express preferences on issues and candidates, has the capacity to function politically, and it should be our ideal that he or she should have some opportunity so to function. Capacities are to be used. Those have rights in the strong sense (all animals do in a weaker sense) for whom there is such a thing as the concept of right. It is a very subnormal adult of whom this is not true.

Adler discusses, without reaching a final conclusion, the question, "Might not robots reach such a peak of development that we should have to conclude that they have concepts and hence political rights?" In this interesting discussion what I miss is the following. All value, other than instrumental, consists in experience, which always has an emotional aspect or feeling-tone, whether or not there is much problem solving going on. Machines can solve but do not have problems. The problems they solve are ours, not theirs. In short, to think in the full sense is to care about answers to questions, not just

233

to produce answers. We know that other animals have feelings because (a) we have them, and (b) not only their behavior but also their internal bodily structures resemble ours, including structures that influence emotions and sensations, rather than merely determining actions or solving problems. Most philosophical traditions throw little light on the mind-body relation so far as emotional and value aspects are concerned. No robot now planned or foreseeable is likely to have an emotional life of its own. However complex the tasks it performs, it will be but an instrument, with no political rights at all.

An example of the price that Adler pays for his scorn of degree versions of the animal-human distinction is that it forces him to reject the third, and I believe correct, view of freedom mentioned above, that to be a creature is to have at least some slight freedom. Since he also rejects the second view, that favorite sophism of intellectuals, the notion that a thinking animal could fit its thinking and action into absolute and precisely predetermined causal patterns, he is left with the first or dualistic view that man is a sheer exception to the order of nature. In this, he is defying the basic intuitions of scientists generally. And why does he reject the other nondualistic solution—the view that all individuality, even of a cell or an atom, implies at least some trivial escape from any absolute routine? He rejects this because, if the atom is free in this sense, then the difference between man and atom, or man and ape, is one of degree; and he wants a difference of kind. But what has this to do with politics or morals? The freedom of an atom obviously is not moral or political freedom, according to any philosophy. And neither is the freedom of an ape. So the absolute difference asserted between man and the other animals is superfluous for the purpose Adler wants it to serve. But the intellectual repugnance many of us feel for dualism is needlessly brought into play by Adler's tactic. He has gained nothing essential for ethics or political philosophy but has lost something for cosmology.

I have been quarreling with my fellow philosopher in a manner that, I hope, shows that I consider him one of the ablest writers alive in our subject, one of those most worth taking seriously. Moreover, when it comes to Adler's *The Common Sense of Politics*, my attitude becomes one of wholehearted admiration and deep agreement. Here Adler shows where his greatest talent or genius lies. Above all, he is a political philosopher. Here I look up to him; he teaches me more than I could teach him. Any defects in the rest of his thinking seem to become insignificant in this part of it. He knows what the best students of the subject have written; he knows the most relevant aspects of the contemporary situation; he employs most happily his ability to formulate issues sharply, to marshal pertinent arguments bearing upon possible solutions, to avoid undue elaboration of secondary matters while being sufficiently explicit on the main lines of his doctrine, to be lucid and forceful while avoiding bigotry or mere rhetoric.

This book speaks to our basic needs in our perilous situation. We need to see a star to which we can hitch our wagons, to echo Emerson. Adler sees that star and will, I hope, help many others to see it.

After explaining the nature of political philosophy and its relations to ethics, Adler examines and refutes the currently somewhat popular anarchistic idea that ideally we should have no government at all. He then sets forth three great "revolutions" or fundamental advances in political thought, none anything like fully realized in practice and thus all still continuing movements. The first, or Greek revolution, is the idea of political equality, or democracy, although only for the few, an elite; the second, or American revolution, is the idea of democracy for the many or for all; the third, or Russian revolution, is the idea of economic democracy for all. It seems to me that in this simple three-step version Adler has hit on something superbly right. He argues that without a substantial measure of economic equality genuine political equality cannot be achieved. Kant said as much, but without seeing as clearly as Adler that this poses a perennial problem.

The idea that sums up the three revolutions, an ideal nowhere actually embodied in any country, is that of the classless, socialist democratic republic. But, and this seems to call for a fourth revolution, in order to realize the ideal, we need genuine world peace, which (he thinks) means world government. That this is immensely difficult Adler concedes. (See also his *How to Think about War and Peace*.) His point is that it is inherent in our professed ideals, ideals that we cannot give up. Moreover, the technological feasibility of world government did not exist before this century, for the same reason that world wars did not exist. Thus, it is too soon to say what can or cannot be done. Also, the nature of the two world wars shows that war itself is becoming more and more destructive of democracy. There is then only one path that can in the long run lead toward a better world, the path at the end of which is a democratic socialist world republic formed from smaller republics of the same kind.[2]

"Socialism" as an ideal does not for Adler mean state capitalism (as in Russia), but "universal capitalism," in contrast to "mixed economies," and in sharper contrast to the oligarchic capitalism we now have in some countries. The mixed economy tends toward state capitalism, which can never be classless, even if it succeeds in providing a decent minimum of economic resources for everyone. One wishes that Adler had given an additional lecture or chapter on possible ways to work out the concept of universal capitalism. Here a team of economic theorists might be helpful. Adler mentions still another form of socialism, the cooperative or syndicalist form. He allows for the possibility that neither this nor universal capitalism is feasible, in which case we must do the best we can with mixed capitalism.

If the foregoing is not in outline what we should try to find our way toward, I have no idea what is. Obviously something is wrong when one must be at least a millionaire to run for office, while large segments of the population are economically insecure or miserably destitute. Moreover, so long as we fail to see that Russian or Chinese idealism tends to be strong just where ours is weak, we shall not have the right attitude to achieve peace with our two most populous national rivals. The mere capitalism-socialism dichotomy leads nowhere but to conflict and misunderstanding. All industry is capitalistic, but ours is obviously and rather grossly oligarchic. That is what we need to reflect upon if we are to bring home to ourselves the truth that we are not simply "the good guys" and the others, "the bad guys." We are all somewhat bad and somewhat good. The point is not merely to preserve our good from the others' bad, but to preserve the good wherever it is found from the bad wherever it is found. And some of the bad is here.

Apart from the question of war, the political problems that Adler deals with were also considered, nearly four decades earlier, by W.P. Montague in his address to the Eighth International Congress of Philosophy, in Prague, 1934, "Democracy at the Crossroads." [3] He has a somewhat different solution from Adler's of the socialism-capitalism dilemma in his "economic dualism". It might be called a special form of the mixed economy, for unemployment benefits substituting communistic style communes, enrollment in which is voluntary. Work in such a commune would not be paid in money but in goods produced by the communes. They would be non-capitalistic islands "insulated" from the money economy of capitalism. Communes would also exchange goods with other such islands. How possible this is I leave to others. Like so much of Montague's thought it is imaginative and shows a deep sympathy with human needs.

Nothing is easier than to accuse Adler's book of oversimplification. All human thinking simplifies or it loses itself in indecisive and unhelpful qualifications and nebulosities. As Whitehead put it, we should seek simplicity—and mistrust it. But first we must have the simplicity, or we have nothing. Now it seems to me a superb achievement that Adler really has succeeded in presenting, with wonderful lucidity and economy, a plausible view of the ultimate ideals by which political thought should henceforth be guided and the most essential considerations supporting their validity. It is arguable that they are less completely and literally "feasible" and more "utopian" than he admits. However, he is right to stress, in time of ever-changing knowledge and ever-new technological resources, the difficulty of knowing what the limits of human action may be. And even if he is mistaken in thinking that institutional political progress could reach an absolute goal, he is right in making the point that in any case individuals would always have something to strive for in teaching and learning from one another, in friendship and love, since the absolute goal of our existence is more than political or institutional but is the good life for every individual.

Adler makes a careful distinction between a philosophical theism and a concrete religious faith, such as that of traditional Christianity. I too make such a distinction, but not as Adler does. For him the existence of God as omnipotent and omniscient is rationally justifiable; however, that the all-knowing, all-powerful Being is benevolent or loving requires a faith transcending mere reason and more than philosophy as such can advocate. I hold, on the contrary, that traditional philosophical concepts of omniscience and omnipotence are defective and that the ancient saying, "God is love" is more unambiguously supported by reason than those concepts, which indeed in their usual form are contrary to reason. Sympathy ("feeling of feeling") is for me, as for Whitehead, the universal principle of the concrete subject-object relation. Without use of the idea of sympathy, God is inconceivable in this philosophy. Moreover, all that we know about hate and indifference to others supports the view that these are weaknesses or distortions of consciousness, intelligible in localized beings open to destruction, competitive for scarce resources, partly ignorant and self-deluded, and such that they are incapable of fully knowing the harm they do to others, and also, and above all, incapable of fully knowing and sharing in the good they do to others. But a cosmic, indestructible, all-embracing consciousness would only torture itself by inflicting suffering on others and would lose potential values for itself by willfully depriving them of joys. The idea of a malevolent or indifferent deity is for me a nonidea. I make nothing of it. The Greek idea that "virtue is knowledge" is false only because of the human being's weakness and lack of comprehensiveness in its awareness, and its necessary partial reliance on unconscious or indistinctly conscious operations and mere blind habits. I hold that the truly religious idea of deity as the perfection of love (rather than of some more abstract attribute of mere knowledge or sheer power) makes better philosophical sense than classical theology ever did.

I agree with Adler that religious scriptures and traditions involve many elements that are scarcely susceptible of cogent support by secular reason, much less so than belief in the eternal (though not immutable) divine Love. This latter idea was viewed with suspicion by some philosophers who attempted to combine it with notions of all-determining power or of an in every sense unsurpassable Reality incapable of growth or increase of any kind and not open to influence by others. The arguments against divine love were always based on assumptions that begged the question from the outset. It is unqualified omnipotence and omniscience (in the timeless immutable sense) that are least able to justify themselves philosophically and religiously, not the intuition of an all-loving being. For me the heavier burden of proof is on assumptions incompatible with *Deus est caritas*, not on that saying itself. The Greek shrinking from becoming and creativity in favor of mere being is an uncritically accepted handicap of classical theology in the West. In India a somewhat different prejudice, a sense of mystical identity, produced somewhat similar results. Several centuries ago, in India Sri Jiva Goswami, founder of the Bengali School of Hinduism, and Faustus Socinus in Italy and Poland independently managed to escape from the worship of being (ontolatry) or bias against becoming of their respective traditions.

Mortimer Adler is a notable case of conservatism in philosophy. He declares that Aristotle, Thomas Aquinas as commentator on Aristotle, and Maritain as heir of the other two, have taught him what he knows in metaphysics. To me it is wildly implausible that these three ae essentially right and Spinoza, Leibniz, Hume, Kant, Hegel, Peirce, Bergson, Whitehead, Wittgenstein, and the Buddhists have nothing important to teach that Adler's favorites did not know. Every great philosopher teaches me something, including Aristotle and Thomas. But none teaches me everything. Moreover, while in a certain formal sense I agree with Adler that metaphysics is not

238

logically dependent on empirical science, still, because of human limitations, it is bound to be strongly influenced by such science. Adler concedes something of this influence but in my opinion grossly underestimates its extent. He also greatly underestimates the need, even apart from scientific development, for a long period of intellectual experimentation to go through the doctrinal possibilities and discover, by discussion and refutation of proposals (Popper), which of them are exaggerations or oversimplifications. Aristotle needed Democritus, Heraclitus, Parmenides, and Plato, at least, with Greek mathematics and natural science, to do even as well as he did. We, with not only the Scholastics, but also the enormous modern development in science, philosophy, and theology, plus awareness of Buddhism and Hinduism, should do much better than Aristotle, Thomas, or Maritain.[3]

Notes

1. Of Adler's numerous books, I have read: *The Conditions of Philosophy* (New York: Atheneum, 1965); *The Difference of Man and the Difference It Makes* (New York: Holt, Reinhart and Winston, 1967); *The Time of Our Lives: The Ethics of Common Sense* (Holt, Rinehart and Winston, 1970); *The Common Sense of Politics* (Holt, Rinehart and Winston, 1971); and *How to Think About God* (New York: Macmillan Co., 1980).

2. Since writing this essay I have become more impressed by the obstacles to world government and the dangers of tyranny and civil war in the idea. For a discussion of the issue see *The Nation*, 237 (Sept. 17, 1983), 196–197, 201–207.

3. See *The Ways of Things*, pp. 612–647. Montague's address was also published in *The International Journal of Ethics*, 45, no. 2 (1935), 138–169.

CHAPTER 21

Roy Wood Sellars and Wilfrid Sellars on Quality and Structure

The two Sellarses, father and son, or RWS (1880–1973) and WS (1912), have spent some decades chipping away at a philosophical statue of the human knower. In substantial agreement, as it seems to me, they reached a result that is neatly described in Wilfrid's essay, "The Double-Knowledge Approach to the Mind-Body Problem." [1] The position is realistic and in a sense materialistic, but with a subtle kind of dualism that a psychicalistic realist finds instructive. [2]

In the approach of the physiologist to the psychophysiological problem, structural properties only are dealt with; in "intuition or inspection of mental states," qualitative content as well as structure is present. Moreover, WS continues, merely structural knowledge is incomplete, it lacks qualitative content. And "being must have content." RWS's colleague DeWitt Parker may have influenced him in this. Parker used to argue that structural notions, shapes for instance, by themselves are abstract or indeterminate. Blue circle, red circle, are more determinate than mere circularity. The concepts of physics are determinables, not determinates. They could not be complete descriptions of anything. All three of these philosophers agree with Whitehead that there cannot be (qualitatively) "vacuous" actuality. Russell was of the same opinion. But whereas Parker and Whitehead are psychicalists, Russell, RWS, and WS are not. What then is the issue between these two groups?

All five writers agree that there cannot be a dualism of merely structured physical systems and those that have also properties "in the qualitative dimension." "We know (somehow)," writes WS, "that every being must have a qualitative content of *some* determinate nature." However, we need not "postulate that in every case the content has the *specific* character of *feeling.*" Our only definite knowledge of content is acquired when dealing with "beings sufficiently like ourselves for there to be some point to reasoning by analogy." In other cases the content is unknowable.

The nonpsychicalist assumes that the structure-quality contrast, when fully generalized, permits "quality" to have a universal meaning and that what Peirce called "feeling-quality" is a special case of a more general meaning; whereas psychicalists, and this includes Peirce, hold that the distinction between feeling-quality and quality not that of feeling is merely verbal. Quality as contrasted to structure is knowable only by feeling, and when thus known, the species of quality and the species of feeling are one. The nonpsychicalist is making a distinction without a difference. Or, he has failed to generalize 'feeling' to its limit while claiming to generalize quality still more widely.

The psychicalist can agree with his opponent that systems to which we can reasonably attribute feeling must have some analogy to ourselves. And he can agree that not all physical systems exhibit such analogy. But each of these points of agreement is associated with an element of disagreement. Not all knowledge of feeling-not-our-own needs to be arrived at by reasoning from analogy. There can be direct intuition of feeling not simply one's own. Also, physical systems belong to two different logical types, first clearly distinguished by Leibniz, the type of dynamic singulars and the type of collectives of such singulars. Every dynamic singular may feel without every group of such singulars being a subject that feels.

Ordinary macro-objects other than animals are collectives. A psychicalist need not regard rocks, clouds, planets, or even trees, as sentient individuals; for he can deny that these are dynamic agents, each acting as one. All feeling expresses itself in action, and the actions as well as the feelings in vegetable or mineral collectives can be attributed to their cells, molecules, atoms, or wave-particles. Moreover, in the human mind-body relation the cells are integrated active agents and our sensations are interpretable as our feelings of their feelings. We do not need to reason by analogy to intuit cellular feeling. I regard this as a phenomenological analysis. True, cells are not distinctly exhibited in our intuitions; but then all intuition other than divine is only relatively distinct, as Leibniz saw long ago. However, something in the body not merely our own feelings is intuited as aching or suffering when we experience physical pains. Durant Drake, referred to in the essay by WS, had some such view.

241

The psychicalist identifies the mystery of quality with the mystery of feeling, whereas the nonpsychicalist has an additional mystery, that of qualities not those of feeling, human or nonhuman. I for one find the second mystery unintelligible. The only feeling qualities we can definitely know are those that we can feel ourselves by directly intuiting them or those we can know by close analogy, as in the experiences of other human beings. All dynamic singulars have, as such, a genuine, though in the most numerous cases remote, analogy to ourselves. The more their degree or kind of complexity or simplicity differs from ours; however, the less definite our notion of their kind of feeling must be, except when we directly intuit them as members of our own bodies.

It is notable that RWS uses the word 'participate' to describe our relation to the qualities of the one physical system accessible to us in its qualitative dimension. Concretely, this system consists of cells; if there is human intuitive participation in the qualities of cells, which are integrated individuals, why is this not Whitehead's feeling of feeling? Do the cells participate in the cells; does the system participate in its cell members; what are the terms of this relation? Reference is made to G. E. Moore's analysis of awareness of blue as a relation between two terms. A process philosopher agrees, so far, with Moore, but unlike Moore rejects the absurd idea of awareness as "transparent," qualityless. Rather, as WS seems to hold and C. J. Ducasse also held, the awareness itself takes on the quality of what it is aware of. We have a suffering awareness of suffering cells, for example. The case of color is more subtle and less easily analyzed.

Psychicalism has advantages that few of its rejectors have seemed to be conscious of. It can find, in the concept of prehension as feeling-of-feeling, clues to causality, spatial and temporal relations, God's relations to creatures, creatures' relations to God, that is, all the central problems of ontology. Of course it is not easy to think of the feelings of an atom. Is it easier to think of the unfeeling content or quality of the atom? Are these really two mysteries, or is it only one? How other creatures feel is mystery enough for some of us.

Among the nonpsychicalists are included Paul Weiss, John Findlay, and Brand Blanshard. I do not see that this rejection of psychicalism adds to the intelligibility of their systems.

If materialism means the doctrine that the whole truth about reality can be stated using only the structural concepts of physical science, then, as WS has said in his essay and elsewhere, materialism is false. But even if quality is admitted as a necessary and universally applicable concept, materialism explains nothing that psychicalism can-

Roy and Wilfrid Sellars

not explain at least as well. The explanatory value of the concept of mere insentient matter is exactly zero. There are insentient wholes in nature—rocks and trees, for examples—but the assertion that these wholes are insentient also in their parts explains nothing whatever. It is not even needed to explain why many philosophers make the assertion. For that fact quite other reasons or causes are at hand.

In this case of the father-son philosophical relation, it is the son through whom the primary influence seems to come. It remains to be seen how strong this influence will ultimately be.[3]

Notes

1. *The New Scholasticism* 45.2 (Spring 1972): 269–289.

2. Roy Wood Sellars wrote *The Philosophy of Critical Realism* (New York: Russell & Russell, 1966). For Wilfrid Sellars's views see *Philosophical Perspectives* (Springfield, Il.: Thomas, 1959, 1967).

3. Sellars Senior was a strict determinist, Sellars Junior has argued forcefully for the compatibility of determinism with human freedom. Mark Pastin (*The Monist* 65.3, July 1982, pp. 365–384) defends C. I. Lewis's phenomenalistic argument for freedom and distinguishes between ordinary, commonsense freedom (acting as one wishes to act) and "straight" or metaphysical freedom (given the antecedent state of the universe, it is psychophysiologically possible that we will, or do, otherwise than we actually will or do). Pastin also remarks that W. S. regards philosophical issues as interconnected, so that to decide one is to decide many others. Pastin holds that the free-will controversy takes us to the center of metaphysics. I could not agree more. Compatibilism is bad metaphysics resulting from excessive reliance on the piecemeal method.

In the same issue of *The Monist* (p. 403) Sydney Pressman advocates a modified version of Sellars's *via media* between Cartesian mentalism and logical behaviorism. I agree that the truth is likely to fall between extremes. But I hold that Sellars has not found the genuine middle way in philosophy. If any view is extreme, unqualified determinism is so. The opposite extreme is the absurd proposition that there is no causal order at all, only sheer chaos. The absurdity of this proposition explains the popularity of determinism. For it is the simplest alternative to chaos. Between absolute order and absolute disorder an infinity of degrees of order in partial disorder seems conceivable. However, until the discovery of quanta, physics had no definite way of quantizing a possible degree of causal indeterminacy in nature. So it adopted the simple opposite of an impossible idea of mere chaos. It avoided a *via media* it knew not how to render precise.

As for the *via media* of mind and matter, here too Sellars has not, I think, found it. Mere dead, insentient matter is a negative absolute that no conceivable experience could disclose as such. What any experience discloses is at least qualities of feeling. If the social structure of all feeling is adequately recognized, thinking or cognition is seen as a complication of feeling about

243

feeling. The Cartesian *cogito*, if taken as generalized definition of what is more than mere matter, is a false intellectualism. Even God feels, does not merely know or intend, all creatures. Mere matter and mere thought are alike constructs. Reality is "an ocean of feelings" (Whitehead).

CHAPTER 22

Quine, Philosophical Logician

It is arguable that Willard Van Orman Quine (b. 1908), accomplished logician, ingenious philosopher, and lucid, readable, often witty, writer is the most influential of living American philosophers. After studying logic with Lewis and Whitehead at Harvard, he went as a student to Prague, where Rudolf Carnap was then teaching. This exposure to a European positivist and scientificist (who spent the latter part of his life in the United States) has had important consequences for professional philosophy in this country. That Quine and Carnap disagreed sharply about some issues leaves intact much basic common ground between them. Both are strongly reductionist physicalists, agnostic or atheistic in religious metaphysics; both are Humean in their conception of causality, denying internal or intrinsic relationships of events to their predecessors. Both incline toward determinism and deviate from it only so far as they feel forced to by physics. Both identify freedom with voluntariness, rather than with creativity in the ultimate sense of adding to the definiteness of reality. Neither is a complete nominalist, Quine departing from this extreme only so far as he judges necessary to meet the needs of mathematics, Carnap departing somewhat further in his modal logic. Was it this that caused Quine to indulge in his reported phrase concerning his admired former teacher, "that Gothic metaphysician" ? (He has forgotten making this remark but finds it not inappropriate.)

Neither of these two writers sees what Aristotle saw so long ago: the modal structure of time and eternity. It is the openness of the future of the creative process, the very principle of reality, that gives modal ideas their ontological relevance.

However different from and incompatible with process metaphysics Quine's philosophy may be, there are some views in common. As compared to Lewis's phenomenalism, Quine's realism, like Popper's,

245

is congenial to a process philosopher. And his "qualified nominalism" is more congenial to my partly Peircean view of this issue than Whitehead's eternal-objects theory. Also, the rejection of an absolute mind-matter dualism is common ground with process philosophers generally. The question is if there is not a covert but incurable dualism in admitting the idea of simply dead and insentient agents in nature. As Lewis (and the Sellarses) imply, the physical account of reality is "merely relational," that is, structural rather than qualitative. Qualities are found as sensory or emotional; they are known by intuition and cannot be conceptually constructed as mathematical ideas can be.

Russell and Whitehead saw the issue in these terms, and Russell reached the conclusion that although structure is conceivable only as clothed with qualities, the only qualities we can know are those in our direct experiences or in our nerve cells. The qualitative side of the rest of nature remains a mystery. Whitehead concluded that the only way we can throw any light on this mystery is to generalize the idea of experiencing far beyond the merely human form, far enough to make the idea of merely insentient, unexperiencing, yet concrete, singulars in nature unnecessary. Either Russell's agnosticism about the qualitative aspect of nature apart from human beings (or, perhaps, from vertebrate animals) or Whitehead's generalized psychicalism are the two rational options, divided between these two collaborators of genius.

Carnap and Quine seem not to see the problem. (I say this although I have heard Carnap claim to have solved it.) To physics it scarcely matters how the structure-quality issue is dealt with. But psychology, considering the mind-body problem, cannot be indifferent to the question. And for art, religion, and ethics, as C. I. Lewis recognizes, quality is what matters and mere structure by itself is nothing.

Quine's rejection of the analytic-synthetic distinction is perhaps not so important as some have thought. What is analytic depends partly on how we arrange our language. But the conditioning of the present by the past and the partial openness of the future (and hence contingency of all happenings, since each event was once only an incompletely defined aspect of the future) is not brought about by language. Also, that which can never have been merely future but is coherently conceivable as, and only as, primordial and indestructible because inherent in the creative process as such is necessarily real and eternal, whatever we say about it. To reject ontological modality is to radically restrict one's access to metaphysical truth. On this point Aristotle, Peirce, James, Dewey, and Whitehead could agree.

In several senses, Quine is a reductionist. By rejecting the idea of the strictly a priori in "Two Dogmas of Empiricism" he seemed to adopt monolithic or unqualified empiricism. Of course he has not really stuck very consistently to this "holistic" view. How could he? Nor does one get rid of the duality, a priori-empirical, by making everything a priori, as some holisms or organicisms seem to do. I believe Carnap was more nearly right here than Quine—and Popper than either of the two.

Like Carnap, Quine wants in some sense to reduce the psychical to the physical. If that merely means that all concrete entities have a spatial character, then I incline to agree; but Quine means more than that. The duality of structure-quality already discussed in chapter 21 is one of the difficulties. Similarly, Quine tried to reduce universal aspects of reality to mere particularity but in his set theory abandons that project.

It is interesting that recent trends in logic in this country, influenced by Saul A. Kripke, are returning to something like the classical duality of actual-possible. Indeed, some have come too close to the classical view in my opinion, as though a possible world were as particular as an actual one. On this issue it is not Leibniz but Aristotle that we need to return to, Aristotle and that great Aristotelian Peirce.

Notes

1. Quine's philosophy is found in his *From a Logical Point of View* (Cambridge, Mass.: Harvard University Press, 1953, 1961) and *Word and Object* (New York and London: John Wiley & Sons, 1960).

My chief disagreement with the second of these books is with the assumption, expressed in the chapter on time, of timeless truth as including contingent facts in their particularity. This medieval idea, lacking in the ancient world and rejected by three great logicians, Aristotle, Peirce, and Whitehead, also by James, Bergson, and many others, seems to me an invalid inference from formal logic, not one of its demonstrable principles. If time is the order of creation, of emergent becoming, and if what *is* determines what is true, then there must be emergent truths. Such truths, once emerged, are everlasting, and this everlastingness will yield all that we need, apart from the really timeless truths about abstract entities that are themselves strictly eternal, like the primordial nature of God and the general idea of a world of nondivine actualities.

CHAPTER 23

Tillich's Philosophical Theology

If Whitehead, the Anglo-American, has made a decisive contribution to our American thought about religion, another writer of foreign training, Paul Tillich (1886–1965), has also been important. Learned in the German fashion in the history of theology, also of philosophy, and, like Whitehead, an imaginative and original mind, Tillich has been one of the two most influential American theologians of our time, the other being Reinhold Niebuhr. Although I consider myself a philosopher, many of my readers are primarily interested in the theological bearings of my work. There are significant differences and some disagreements among Whitehead, Tillich, Niebuhr, and Hartshorne, yet, in their contrast to classical theism, all four have important elements in common. Not one affirms of deity an unqualified immutability or sheer independence of the world. In Tillich's case this is made clear by the statement in the third volume of his *Systematic Theology* that the creatures contribute to the divine life.[1] This aligns him with Berdyaev and Whitehead. One is reminded of Karl Barth's statement that "there is a kind of holy change in God." On this fundamental metaphysical issue the twentieth century differs strikingly from its predecessors. One is reminded also of a remark of Heidegger's associating the idea of deity with that of "infinite temporality." Dual transcendence, whether or not so-named, has at last become a respectable doctrine, no longer to be casually dismissed as the Socinian theology was dismissed by Leibniz, Spinoza, and the Seventeenth and Eighteenth Centuries generally. This is an important cultural change. Similarly, whereas in the times of Leibniz, Hume, and Kant, belief in classical causal determinism was widely demanded or simply assumed in science and philosophy, today many physicists and philosophers reject it. Those who expend their energies in affirming the compatibility of freedom and classical determinism are neglecting the prior question, "Why determinism?"

Tillich's doctrine that talk about God must be largely symbolic rather than literal has led one partisan of linguistic analysis to argue that Tillich is a theologian who does not violate good rules of linguistic usage.[2] It is remarkable also that one of the most dedicated disciples of Wittgenstein (O. K. Bouwsma) was a devout member of the Presbyterian Church. Tillich says that theological talk implies one statement about deity that is to be taken literally: God is being itself. Because of the ambiguity in 'being' (according to whether its contrasting term is taken to be nonbeing, unreality, on the one hand, or becoming, process, on the other) I have some objection to this wording. Yet I can give it a good meaning. The idea of all-knowingness implies that to be is to be for God, that is, known to God, so that reality and the content of divine knowledge are the same. But it is as true that to become is to become for God, to change is to change for God, to be possible is to be possible for God, and thus dual transcendence is entirely compatible with Tillich's theism, nay, is implied by it. Tillich came to realize this, but somewhat late and never achieved full clarity about it.

Where Tillich says "symbolic," I incline to the medieval term 'analogical.' Although I have not convinced the theologian Schubert Ogden, who in metaphysics tends to agree with me, on the validity of my distinction between symbolic and analogical, he would agree that there is a considerable difference between saying that God is our good shepherd and saying that God is love, on the ground that the idea of shepherd is much narrower than that of love as generalized to mean, as a minimum, some degree and kind of feeling-of-feeling. Deity is the not-by-others surpassable form of such feeling, and the lower animals are forms, in certain respects vastly more limited or primitive, of the same abstract idea. Ogden and I agree that terms like relative, dependent, or capable of increase, like their contrasting poles, absolute, independent, or an unsurpassable maximum, apply literally to deity, though (and hence without contradiction) not in the same respects, the one pole true of an abstract aspect of God and the other of the full divine concreteness—the concrete, as Aristotle and Whitehead held, including the abstract.

If one holds, as Peirce did, that all significant human thought is in some sense "anthropomorphic," this being tautological, one should consider with care the proposition that we are able to understand nonhuman creatures only by something like analogy with what we know ourselves to be. We are movable entities with sizes, shapes, and characteristic ways of changing. Physics generalizes size, shape, and ways of changing far beyond their limitations in common sense. What physics deliberately does not do is to generalize attributes like feeling and thinking in describing nonhuman bodies. This does not mean that it denies sentience to parts of nature. Simply, it does not raise the question but leaves that to psychology. And psychology is less inclined today perhaps then some decades ago to worry about the feelings of other animals. It prefers to describe their behavior, as the measurable unambiguously quantifiable aspect. The problem of the place of mind in nature is not thereby solved or shown to be unreal. Instead, it is set aside. If philosophy also sets it aside, then one wonders if we very much need philosophy. To observe behavior, philosophers are not particularly needed; the scientists can do this quite well. What perhaps they cannot do is to illuminate intellectually what it is that is being missed if behavior is all that inquiry is to consider.

In many recent writers—some not American but well known in this country—one finds a strong disinclination to discuss theological topics, unless purely negatively, as well as a disinclination to take seriously the question, "Do the other mammals and still simpler creatures differ from us by having neither anything like thought as it is in us nor anything like feeling, *or* do they all have at least some form of sentience, however little they may be capable of thinking?" In short, what is behind or within these nonhuman behavings? In us we know what is within. Sir Karl Popper (or is it only his co-author, Sir John Eccles?) has doubts as to whether the lower animals have feelings. (He also says that theology is a lack of faith, in just what we are left to guess.) True, Sir Karl does say that where there is life there are values, and so I presume he holds that values (intrinsic ones?) do not require sentience.

It has been argued that Tillich's thought cannot be termed philosophical, because he says that the role of philosophy is to formulate questions to which only theology has the answers. There is a partial analogy here between Tillich and Augustine, Anselm, or Aquinas. The difference does not wholly favor Tillich. For the medieval thinkers mentioned held that some of the theological questions, including the one about the divine existence, are answerable by philosophical reasoning. Religious beliefs older than what is usually meant by philosophy gave rise to some central philosophical issues and many great minds have held that rational argument, independent of revelation, can give good grounds for a resolution of these issues. In any case there are competing forms of revelation. It seems that revelation as humanly expressed and received cannot be infallible, and that human reasoning, outside the truisms of arithmetic and elementary logic, is wonderfully subject to innocent and also not so innocent varieties of error. I agree with Reinhold Niebuhr on this matter; theologians and philosophers are both open to suspicion as at best thinking animals, not deities. And Tillich's view is really much the same in practice. He almost trusts Schelling and almost trusts Augustine, almost trusts his own reasoning and almost trusts the Gospels. There is no absolute refuge in our traditions. One does what one can.

Notes

1. The three volumes of Tillich's *Systematic Theology* were published by the University of Chicago Press in 1951.

2. Edward Cell, *Language, Existence, and God* (Nashville and New York: Abingdon Press, 1971). In America as in England, admirers of Wittgenstein differ startlingly in their evaluation of theism. Cell's awareness of the kind of metaphysics of which I am a representative is extremely minimal, to judge from this book. The discussions of the views of G. E. Moore, Bertrand Russell, A. J. Ayer, Ludwig Wittgenstein, John Wisdom, and Paul Tillich are helpful.

Cell discusses my use of the soul-body analogy in forming the idea of God (p. 211) but does not take into account the way in which I use the analogy (partly following Plato's *Timaeus*), not instead of, but in addition to, the person-to-person analogy—in both cases not forgetting the, in certain respects, infinite difference between the divine body or soul and ordinary bodies or souls. Dual transcendence is in both aspects genuine transcendence. Cell does not notice how the principle of contrast is respected in neoclassical metaphysics. The word 'contrast' is in the index of Cell's book only under Wittgenstein.

CHAPTER 24

Rorty's Pragmatism
and Farewell to the Age
of Faith and Enlightenment

"The pragmatist . . . can only say, with Hegel, that truth and justice lie in the direction marked by the successive stages of European thought. This is not because he knows some 'necessary truths'. . . . It is simply that the pragmatist knows no better way to explain his conviction than to remind his interlocutor of the position they both are in, the contingent starting points they both share, the floating, ungrounded, conversations of which they are both members." [1]

Richard Rorty (b. 1931) admits that judgments may differ concerning the "direction" European thought has taken. He knows only circular arguments for or against the view of Plato that philosophy should seek to "escape from time and history," in other words, to find eternal, necessary truths; or (with Hegel, as Rorty interprets Hegel) should regard this search as "doomed and perverse." All we can do is to "read the history of philosophy and draw the moral." (op. cit., pp. 736, 737)

My first comment is that Rorty has here constructed a somewhat mythical court of final appeal. There is no single, accessible, unitary thing called European thought or history of philosophy and no single set of starting points, the same for all of us. Moreover, I suspect that we are here confronted, after all, with the correspondence view (which in general Rorty seems to reject) of *historical* truth at least. Or was there no actual Plato or Hegel with whom our attributions to these writers are intended to agree? I hold that there was (and in a genuine sense is) an actual Plato and an actual Hegel and that each of us has real though limited access to their ideas; also that

252

we are not all equally well equipped to find out what they thought. I hold also that some very important aspects of the actual thoughts of past philosophers are omitted from most standard reference works, and in some cases the very names of some of those whose thoughts they were are scarcely to be found in those works. I do agree with Rorty (and Hegel) that a basic test of our philosophies is the light they throw on intellectual history.

Another comment is that I think, as Hegel already did, that we need to be less provincial than the limitation to *European* suggests. I think it is time that at least the Buddhist tradition should be taken seriously into account. I have argued for years that there are indeed non-European ideas that can serve "our European purposes better." But then it is notable that one (somewhat Americanized) European philosopher, Whitehead, has arrived, probably independently, at some central Buddhist insights, and that two Americans, James and Peirce, partly anticipated him in this.

Rorty's dismissal of metaphysics, defined as search for necessary truths, is not justified by a careful consideration of the historical facts about what has happened in metaphysics from the pre-Socratics to Peirce, Whitehead, and the present writer. Finding necessary truths is not the same as "escaping from time and history." Eternity, absolute necessity, according to the dominant metaphysics of recent times, can only be the most abstract aspect of becoming and cosmic history. A truth is necessary and eternal if it characterizes becoming as such, otherwise not. This is the point of the "ultimacy" which Whitehead assigns to "creativity." Furthermore, our human knowledge of the ultimate is not itself ultimate in the same sense. If we manage to arrive at a correct view of the necessary, this is a contingent achievement; and it is conditioned by historical factors. Mistakes can be made even in arithmetic, much more in metaphysics (including theories of the eternal and necessary aspects of deity). Knowledge of necessary truths is not infallible knowledge of them except in the divine knowing, which is infallible whether it is about necessary or contingent truths. Human knowledge is fallible in both aspects. And one needs to make use of intellectual history in seeking necessary truths and in evaluating claims to have found them.

Whether or not we can know necessary truths, the question seems logically in order. Do not the following three propositions exhaust the possibilities? (1) There are no necessary truths; (2) There are necessary truths, but we cannot in any reasonable sense know them, or sensibly seek to know them; (3) There are necessary truths, and we can (to some extent, or with whatever qualifications as to precision or certainty) sensibly seek to find them.

If one accepts (1), then the principle of contrast can be invoked to justify the criticism that "contingent" loses its meaning if "necessary" has no application. Moreover, the necessary is easily explicated as what all possibilities have in common (or what will obtain no matter which possibilities are actualized). It seems extravagant to suggest that they have nothing whatever in common.

If one accepts (2), one is by implication admitting that when we speak of contingent (in contrast to necessary) truths we do not know what we are talking about. Similarly, with the idea of eternity, if we have no understanding of that, then "temporal" is not adequately understood either. What all possible times have in common must either be sheer nothing or whatever it is that is eternal.

Of the three options the third seems to me the most credible. One reason this is difficult for some to see is that the role of the necessary or eternal has been badly misconceived by many philosophers and theologians. The purely eternal has been taken to be the "most real," whereas it is an extreme abstraction, by implication of its very logic as set forth first by Leibniz (with some mistakes about the meaning of 'possible'). In ethics the attempt has often been to make the most abstract principles of good or right (which alone can be necessary) do all the work of ethics or, at any rate, to expect more from them than they could logically deliver. Another confusion is the one already dealt with between the necessity of the proposition and the certainty of our knowledge of it. Connected with this error is the failure to take adequately into account the semantic problem of expressing necessary truths in language, which primarily evolved and is primarily used for discussing contingent truths, that is to say, all truths other than the most abstract or universal, applicable to all possible existents, or, in ethics or logic, to all rational beings.

That the method of reason is the method of "conversation" or discussion, mutual criticism, is an acceptable view common to Rorty and Popper. Discussion about necessary truths is one form of the general discussion. Success in this special form is of course no guarantee of success in other forms. That is not its value. It is a logical truism that contingent truths are not deducible from necessary ones alone. Metaphysics is not "foundational" in that sense. Neither is mathematics. Yet both may have their uses. What all possibilities have in common may yet distinguish them all from various seeming possibilities that are really verbal confusions. And certain ideas often supposed impossible may in truth be among the common aspects of all genuine possibilities. Thus freedom as at least minimal transcendence of causal necessities may be a requirement of all possible occurrences. If Einstein had accepted (as Bergson and Peirce did) the metaphysical truth of the essentially creative aspect of becoming as such, his last decades might have taken a more constructive turn, more congenial to his scientific colleagues in quantum physics.

Metaphysical truth cannot dictate any more specific truth, but it might (for those who claim to know it) forbid certain negative extremes such as the absolute absence of emergence in becoming or of mind as such in the lower levels of nature. Such negative absolutes are unobservable and a veto upon them need not hamper observational science.

Since (unconditionally) necessary truths are strictly universal, what makes them true must be in everything. They must be implicit in all ideas. How far it is important for a given purpose that the implicit metaphysical content of beliefs, any beliefs, be made explicit depends on the purpose and the situation. Scientists have long ago absorbed at least part of the metaphysics they need and may do well much of the time to let others worry about formulating that part. They embody it in their practice. On the other hand, extreme crises, such as those that have been produced by the difficulties of combining relativity physics with quantum and particle physics, may make it worth while to pay attention to metaphysical issues—about the asymmetry of time and the independence of earlier from later events, or about the place of mind as such in the cosmos, or the relations between continuity and discreteness, or the finitude or infinity of the spatial aspect of reality, or the mutual independence (or?) of contemporaries.

Theologians have tried periodically to do without metaphysics and have repeatedly found that they cannot do so. The Barthians tried it in one way and some positivistic theologians, Van Buren, for example, have tried it in another way. The success of either approach is problematic. So is that of the Marxist version of, or substitute for, religion.

Whether the renunciation of metaphysics is a viable human option for an entire culture, Rorty admits he does not know. I salute his candor on this point. But even if it is culturally viable I fail to see that it represents our best or most intelligent option. Why should we give up all efforts to satisfy such natural curiosity as that about the eternal or necessary aspects of reality, in contrast and relation to which the contingent and emergent aspects alone have their full sense and definition? To what extent we shall ever reach a consensus on these topics is not itself a metaphysical question. An absolute consensus is hardly possible in any science or human inquiry; but we can sensibly strive to minimize misunderstandings and do our best to persuade one another of what truths we think we discern.

Always there have been both more and less speculative minds in philosophy. Some periods give the critics of speculation more prominence and attention than others. Ours is a somewhat antimetaphysical culture, except that the skepticism of academics and intellectuals is balanced by waves of popular religiosity and superstition suggesting that the human species is not about to accept a merely positivistic or merely anthropocentric view of things.

It is amusing to think of Peirce or James reading Rorty. It is perhaps hard to say which of them would have liked his views least. Probably it is Peirce, for whose pragmaticism the conceivable practical import defined meaning but not truth. Moreover, in developing his categories Peirce was looking for necessary truths. As Rorty well knows, James was seeking a way to justify some ethical and religious beliefs, especially in freedom transcending causal determinism and in some form of theism—however qualified in the attributes assigned to deity. One might say that in Rorty, James's "will (or right) to believe" becomes a will or right to disbelieve. There is at least a very sharp difference of emphasis.

In Rorty's thinking there is much subtlety and a wide acquaintance with contrasting philosophies. However, in dealing with some topics of interest to me, also to Peirce and James, he becomes crude or dogmatic. Determinism, rejected for carefully analyzed reasons by both the founding pragmatists, is apparently acceptable to Rorty, as is materialism, of which Peirce said that it "leaves the world as unintelligible as it finds it." Rorty holds that only science can inform us about nature. Science is now telling us that chance is a real factor in all process, that the valid laws are statistical, not absolute. And Rorty tells us next to nothing about the recent history of this problem, whether in metaphysics or in physics.

In the preface to his *Philosophy and the Mirror of Nature*, Rorty admirably explains how six teachers, of whom I was one, brought him to the conviction "that a 'philosophical problem' was a product of the unconscious adoption of assumptions built into the vocabulary in which the problem was stated—assumptions which were to be questioned before the problem itself was to be taken seriously." Dewey has said that philosophy should not be a method of solving problems invented by philosophers, but a method, cultivated by philosophers, of solving problems of human beings generally. Of course, either way one is using a vocabulary. I have long accepted the view that metaphysical mistakes do consist in part of misusing terms but have argued against the view that such misuse is the very definition of "metaphysics." The ultimate source of metaphysical concern is not merely terminological. Human mortality presents us with the question, "How do we adjust ourselves to the certainty of our own eventual death and, for all we can know, even the eventual extinction of our species?" Conflicts of purpose with other human beings, or even more generally with nonhuman animals, present us with the question, "How do we relate concern for our own welfare or advantage to concern for that of others?" Are Buddhists right or wrong in their criticism of the idea of personal identity, taken as final in ethics and religion? Conflicting religious and antireligious beliefs and attitudes present us with questions about immortality, or at least about the permanence or lack of it of our achievements, and about God, or other allegedly superhuman beings. The progress of scientific explanations of events through their causes presents us with the question, "Are our choices or decisions mere links in a causal chain in which what happens is in each case the only thing that then and there could have happened, *or* is causality less determining, so that at each moment there is at least a small range of possibilities, an indeterminate but determinable potentiality that only our deciding makes determinate?" In more technical terms, are there antecedently *sufficient* as well as necessary conditions for decisions, or only necessary conditions? The vocabulary in which this is stated does not produce the problem that is presented by the scientific tradition and successes. It arises from the mathematics of classical physics and astronomy. Quantum physics has a new mathematics that changes the problem somewhat. But even before quantum physics a few philosophers and scientists were advocating, stimulated by the laws of gases, a nonclassical view of natural laws.

I find in Rorty a dearth of interest in the kinds of problems hinted at above. He focuses rather on "epistemological" problems. With Gustav Bergmann, I hold that epistemology is merely the metaphysics (he says ontology) of knowing, rather than a propaedeutic of metaphysics. Rorty also talks much about "foundationalism," a jargon term for which I see no great need. I do doubt that I am a foundationalist or that Whitehead was. On the whole, I think Rorty is overconcerned about problems invented by philosophers and too little concerned about problems of human beings, aware, unlike other animals, of their mortality, aware also that their choices are largely

257

predetermined by the past, yet with the sense of these choices as really determining what was previously somewhat undetermined.

In the indexes of Rorty's two books the words 'determinism,' 'freedom,' 'choice,' 'decision' do not occur. Nor do the words 'time,' 'past,' 'future'; 'contingency,' 'modality,' 'possibility'; 'potentiality,' 'actuality'; 'abstract,' 'concrete'; 'relation'; 'universal,' 'particular'; 'infinite,' 'finite'; 'absolute,' 'relative', 'becoming,' 'creativity', and other similarly abstract terms. Nor, finally, does the word 'metaphysics' appear in the index, although it occurs in the text. 'Mind,' with many entries, is indexed in *The Mirror*, but not 'matter' or 'physical.' And not 'God.' 'Necessary' occurs but is explicated (mistakenly) as the highest degree of noncontroversiality, not in terms of its relation to possibility and contingency, or to becoming and the openness of the future. The Aristotelian and Peircean ideas of the future as modally different from the past and of the unconditionally necessary as what is, without first coming to be, are ignored. The really enduring philosophical problems are not discussed.

Rorty mentions my and Whitehead's panpsychism (which I usually term psychicalism). He astonishes me by the statement that panpsychists reject the statement, "Neural processes are physical events." Rorty also says that materialists deny that "mental" and "physical" are incompatible predicates. I also deny it. If physical means, as in Descartes, extended, and if what is localized but not punctiform is extended, then I hold that physical things are all either aggregates or, if singular, for example, nerve cells or some of their constituents, then they at least feel. Whitehead says they also have at least minimal forms of what he technically terms mentality, that is, some sense, however limited, of the contrast between actual and possible, or past and future.

Rorty also says that my or Thomas Nagel's "panpsychism tends to merge with neutralism," defined as the doctrine that "the mental and physical are two 'aspects' of some underlying reality which need not be described further." This recalls Spinoza more than it does anything I have ever said or meant. I hold that the physical is simply the psychical considered only in its aspects of causal and spatiotemporal relations or structures, abstracting from nonstructural, qualitative aspects (see above, chapter 21).

In his essay "Mind As Ineffable" in *Mind in Nature*, Rorty clarifies further his conception of the psychical. He tries to show that 'mind' has no distinctive meaning, no special character as contrasted to physical realities. If this means that a psycho-physical dualism is unfounded, then I grant it. Psychicalism is precisely the view that the psychical as such is not a special kind of reality but is reality itself or as such. Concrete and singular realities at least feel or sense, however little they may think; abstract realities are abstract aspects of the psychical, aggregate realities are groups of sentient singulars; subhuman realities if singular are subhuman psyches; superhuman realities are superhuman psyches. The difference between reality or actuality and the psychical or mind in the most generalized sense is that the second set of words gives positive content to the terms by expressing them in relation to our experience or knowledge. What we experience is itself experience in some form, what we feel is itself feeling in some form. *Mere* stuff or *mere* matter is not positively experienced or felt but only seems to be because of the low levels, or radically nonhuman forms, of its feeling quality.

The reason for psychicalism is not to escape a skepticism generated "by the naive metaphysics of common sense." The basic reason is that the notion of mere physical stuff or process is not self-explanatory, let alone explanatory of mind. Mind, as Peirce said, is self-intelligible and the explanation of all things, so far as they are open to explanation. It is mind that knows (other) mind, experience that discloses (other) experience. Mere matter is an empty negation that explains nothing. Matter or the physical in ordinary language is simply sentience on low levels that we can experience only indistinctly. It is mind, the psychical, that we must deal with; what we need matter for is adequately furnished by appropriately nonhuman forms of mind. Otherwise, it is an idle, superfluous term. In Rorty I find no evidence for a need to abandon this position.

An oddity of Rorty's *Philosophy and the Mirror of Nature* is that, although he says that we may expect a philosophy to throw some light on belief in God, what he says on the subject suggests that he knows next to nothing about the form this belief has more and more been taking for several centuries in theology and philosophy. Rightly, he holds that if deity is equated with infinity, it is an empty idea, devoid of religious value. This objection is as old as Carneades; the reply to it is as old as Socinianism and is entirely in harmony with some of the most influential forms of philosophical theology today. That 'divine' and 'infinite' say the same thing does not harmonize with Karl Barth's or A. N. Whitehead's beliefs, to mention two of many recent writers of prominence. Berdyaev is another. From Hegel to the writer of this book those really conscious of the history of theism and the metaphysics of religion are not likely to take for granted that worshiping God is the same as adoring the idea of infinity—or mere unlimitedness, or mere eternity, or mere absoluteness, or any other single one-sided abstraction of this kind. In some sense, the Hegelian saying, "truth [at least, metaphysical truth] is the unity of contraries" is widely accepted in theology.

Vaguely generalized metaphysical agnosticism like Rorty's may be fashionable. But I do not see what other reason those of us interested in metaphysics have for allowing this fashion to deter us from trying to arrive at reasonable metaphysical beliefs. We will not convince everyone to share our beliefs. Neither will Rorty do that with his unbeliefs.

A very neat expression of his attitude is Rorty's remark that we deal with things not by knowing what they are but by "coping, merely coping" with them. One reply might be that the insects cope quite well; we, however, are creatures that find meaning in life partly by thinking we can come to know at least approximately, or with whatever qualifications, what things are. We want to participate in what Wordsworth deliberately called "the life of things." Scientists want to participate in the beautiful causal structures of the world, patterns embodied in one way in scientists' thoughts and in another way in nature generally. What natural science does not try to do, at least at present, is participate in the qualities of feeling in nonhuman animals and perhaps in plants and in all nature. The correspondence sought in science is purely intellectual, not emotional or sentient. Yet Darwin and doubtless most biologists have attributed feelings (of perhaps not humanly knowable kinds) to all animals. Darwin seriously wondered if plants were to be excluded in this connection.

Rorty perceptively realizes that religious people and scientists have in common a greater faith in the objective validity of our thinking, its correspondence with reality, than he has. To be religious, he suggests, is to find, or hope to find, a "connaturality" of ourselves with the rest of reality. I agree, and I think that scientists are at heart religious in this sense. Some of the greatest among them have been conscious of this. I also hold with Peirce and others that to understand is in principle to succeed in the endeavor to find analogies between ourselves and other realities.

A teapot (an example of Wittgenstein's) is scarcely analogous at all to a human being. But the molecules and atoms into which physics analyzes teapots are not nearly so different in certain essential respects from ourselves. They, and not the teapot, share with us self-activity; they, and not the teapot, are partly unpredictable in their actions, as (*pace* some psychologists) are we. Also, the inclusive physical cosmos is more like us than like a teapot. The teapot has no unique principle of order; its chemical atoms behave according to the laws of their kind in the teapot's environment. But the inclusive cosmos, in comparison with other conceivable universes, has its unique laws pervading all its parts; and each of us, unless an identical twin or quintuplet, has a unique gene structure which gives us a specialization of chemical capacities not shared with any other. Even an identical twin has a uniquely developed nervous system influencing and orchestrating all its activities. Thus you and I, or a cell of one of our bodies, or, more problematically perhaps, a molecule or atom, or at the opposite extreme, the universe are all dynamic singulars in a sense in which teapots are not. Before Leibniz no one was nearly so clear as he came to be about this distinction between dynamic singulars and aggregates. Perhaps he actually made too much of it in some ways. Whitehead was, on the main point, a neo-Leibnizian, as am I.

Is human thinking a mirror of nature? If what is meant by mirror is a medium reflecting with absolute distinctness and precision, then of course the human mind is no mirror. (Nor is an ordinary mirror that.) But if the criteria for mirroring are suitably relaxed, why is one's mind not analogically a mirror? I find no very impressive argument in Rorty on this point. Consider a geographical map. It is not correspondent to its region with infinite precision or without qualification. But it is roughly, and for some purposes sufficiently, thus correspondent. Things more or less like maps are important elements in human thinking. They are merely the most obvious examples of the validity of the (suitably qualified) correspondence theory of truth. I am somewhat mystified by those who seem unwilling to grant this.

Rorty says that the success of our predictions does not prove the (strict?) correspondence truth of the theories from which the predictions are derived. Popper says this, too, and with emphasis. But Popper also says (with some wavering and apparent inconsistency) that we can reasonably hope on the whole to achieve some partial or approximate correspondence with things as they are and to keep increasing this correspondence. We cannot simply capture the "essences" of things; but still we eliminate erroneous views of them and thus make our pictures of the world more nearly correspondent with the realities. The two extremes: We know exactly what things are, We know nothing of what they are, are both unjustified. If Rorty's view is not the second extreme, it is not easy to see the distinction.

Some people set great store by the goal of not believing too much, others on not believing too little. Here, as everywhere, I am chronically a moderate and distrust extremes. My admiration for Popper arises partly from his avoidance of at least many extremes. In distrust of metaphysics he is less extreme than the positivists but still too extreme for my taste.

The metaphor of the mirror is not ultimately necessary. What is necessary is prehension as feeling of (others') feeling, by which not only the relation of experience to what is experienced is explained but also the relations of effects to causes, or earlier conditions to subsequent results. Among the essential results of modern, also of much older Asiatic, metaphysical thinking, neglected or dismissed by Rorty, are the criticisms of substance or genetic identity by Hume and the Buddhists and the alternative analysis of (partial) identity in change by Buddhists and, most clearly, by Whitehead. As a result, Rorty's analysis of internal and external relations in the *Encyclopedia of Philosophy* misses the basic point partially explicated by Peirce in his concept of Secondness, more precisely implied by Whitehead in his definition of prehension, and emphasized by me in many writings, that is, the point that the basic relations are internal for one term and external for the other. These relations hold not between substances or individuals taken as identical but between momentary actualities whose sequences constitute in many cases the careers or the concrete actualities of enduring individuals. Physics has come in this century to conceive the world in terms of "events, not things." Peirce wavered and never achieved full clarity on the question, hampered by his overextended doctrine of continuity-ism or synechism. Whether becoming is continuous or quantized is another of the essential and not artificial problems of metaphysics that are ignored by Rorty. The issue is not wholly new with quantum physics or Whitehead but was suggested by some Islamic as well as all Buddhist thinkers long ago, and by Hume more recently.

On one point neoclassical metaphysics can agree with Rorty. According to him the only metaphysical synthesis that could conceivably fulfill the traditional philosophical ambition of significantly supplementing and completing the account of reality given by science is idealism. But idealism, Rorty insists, has collapsed and is not likely to win acceptance again. However, what has collapsed is what was called idealism at the turn of the century, and this, as I have repeatedly argued, is a mixture of genuinely idealistic motifs (meaning ways of using the idea of mind or experience to explain reality as such, including physical reality or matter) with motifs which not only do not follow from the idealistic one but are implicitly incongruous with it. Examples are: the denial of the reality of becoming, the classical deterministic view of causality, and the notion of physical objects as insentient not only as wholes but in all their constituents. In addition, historical idealists tended to blur or deny the distinction between eternal, necessary, metaphysical truths and contingent, empirical ones. Rorty knows, I presume, that the idealism of Peirce and Whitehead, and still more explicitly my own, contrasts rather sharply with the views taken as definitive of historical "idealism." He goes so far as to say that this historical world-view is believed nowadays by "no one." Perhaps so, but nothing, or not a great deal, follows from this concerning the future prospects of an idealism purified from the far from small mistakes or contaminations referred to.

Perhaps the most useful thing Rorty has done (in *The Consequences of Pragmatism*) is to survey the variety of activities going under the name of philosophy today. He finds fantastically diverse things. One possible conclusion that I am tempted, but not ready, to draw is that what some of us are still doing, that is, trying to reflect rationally on metaphysical questions concerning necessary truths (those with which any conceivable experience is at least compatible) may in the near future be carried on as much or more by liberal theologians as by those calling themselves philosophers. After all, in considering the history of philosophy many of us study Philo, Augustine, Anselm, Aquinas, all very definitely theologians, but theologians who saw an important role for philosophy as well as for science. Antiscientific, unphilosophical theology, fundamentalism, is a different matter. However, in an age facing threats of nuclear, biological, and chemical warfare, who dares to make predictions about our human future?

My ethics, which has a metaphysical aspect, tells me that, despite these awful dangers, we are obligated to do the best we can with a situation one would not have chosen to be in, but which has been brought about by freedom, the source of both good and evil. There seems no way in which giving up the metaphysical quest would lessen the dangers and some possibility that pursuing the quest would increase our powers to avoid them. It is heartening that the Catholic Bishops of this country (with at least many of whom I would have grave disagreements about some matters) are moving to counteract our present administration's enthusiasm for increasing our stores of nuclear weapons at the cost of doing less and less for social justice to millions of unfortunates, huge budgetary deficits, and yet with no clear relation to the professed goal of saving us all from utter nuclear catastrophe, or with the implausible claim that damage done by nuclear war could be kept within reasonable bounds. (The genuine experts seem far from encouraging on this subject.) Perhaps theologians and scientists may prove akin in these matters also.

Notes

1. From Richard Rorty's *Consequences of Pragmatism* (Minneapolis, Mn.: University of Minnesota Press, 1982), pp. 173–174.
2. *Philosophy and the Mirror of Nature* (Princeton, N.J.: Princeton University Press, 1979).

CHAPTER 25

Neville on Creation
and Buchler on Natural Complexes

On this chapter I consider two thinkers who deal elaborately with metaphysical problems, Robert C. Neville (b. 1939) and Justus Buchler (b. 1914). Both are well aware of the philosophy of Whitehead, and at least one, Buchler, of that of Peirce. Neville has paid me the compliment of searching criticism showing familiarity with my writings. He presents a new, but partly very old, form of philosophical theism. Buchler proposes a metaphysics of natural complexes.

A metaphysical system should be clear and definite (the vague truths have probably all been said); it should illuminate religious problems, scientific problems, and ethical and aesthetic problems, so far as these concern eternal and necessary principles. A metaphysician should see some truth in what the great speculative philosophers have said; for if they were merely foolish, why should we be supposed wise? On the other hand, if something has already been well said, merely repeating it is not a major contribution. In Peirce and Whitehead there is much that was not said with any clarity before; but both can claim to be in a great tradition or several great traditions. Peirce rejoins and clarifies Aristotle in his theory of ontological modality. He does the same for Leibniz in his overcoming of the mind-matter dualism of Descartes. Whitehead independently confirms Peirce in both of these respects, but he also radically clarifies the concept of individual, which was definitely misconceived by Leibniz and was left somewhat vague by Aristotle and even by Peirce. Both men from the outset take Kant's criticisms of metaphysics into account. In addition both show a deep awareness of inadequacies in the medieval and early modern theologies of the West, and an awareness of the Buddhist alternative. Whitehead makes a clear advance toward a third religious conception that is vaguely or ambiguously anticipated by a considerable number of philosophers and theologians (most of them probably unknown to Whitehead) of the last three or four centuries. This third conception to some extent bridges the gap between Occident and Orient of which Peirce showed his awareness—and sense of the need to remedy—by his formula "Buddhisto-Christian." Whitehead also had Chinese modes of thought in mind.

It is to be expected that there would be disciples, some faithful, some more or less deviationist (as is said of Marxists), and some searching critics of these two men. Robert Neville is a deviationist Whiteheadian, with a different idea of the relation of God to the world.[1] Justus Buchler, exposed intensively to the writings of Peirce, reacting also to the Whiteheadian literature, has his own new system.[2]

Neville is one of the most vigorous and resourceful critics of process and neoclassical conceptions of God as supreme creative power. He understands and largely accepts Whitehead's cosmology and finds seven points of my system that he regards as persuasive. Yet his view of God is quite different, as he realizes, from mine or Whitehead's. According to Neville, God creates *ex nihilo* the entire detail of the world. Creatures are partly self-determined so far as other creatures are concerned (the doctrine is not deterministic in the cosmological sense). However, our decisions are fully determined by God. Our self-determination is simply a portion, as it were, of the divine self-determination. This reminds me of Royce. Apart from the world, God is indeterminate, and any goodness we attribute to God is known only through the degrees and kinds of goodness found in the world. God makes the bad as well as the good. This, too, is in Royce, and can reasonably be read into Aquinas. Plato, with whom Neville is in some respects sympathetic, would not have liked it at all!

This is not the place to deal with the many subtle and complicated details and nuances of Neville's criticism of my theism. At some points there is perhaps some misunderstanding of my intended meanings, but primarily the difference between us is in basic intuitions. We both make some appeal to intuitions, or to lessons of experience in some sense. I think the idea of God must be, in some aspects, analogical. Neville overstates somewhat my assertion that we can think literally about God, and I find no analogy to give meaning to the idea of divine-creaturely relations in which the first party simply makes the decisions of the second party. Also, I find repulsive the idea of a God that inflicts definite evils upon creatures, supposing that it makes sense at all.

A basic technical contention of Neville's is that any definite multiplicity is contingent and derivative. The ultimate prius then is a pure One, or the indeterminate. So we seem to have Plotinus, or Advaita Vedantism. My proposition is that nothing is contingent unless it excludes something positive and possible, *this* instead of *that*, where that was not absurd, impossible, or a mere negation. Also, nothing is contingent unless it comes to be or has a beginning. (Possibility is futurity, actualization is creation out of previous definite actuality.) The eternal metaphysical structure that I attribute to the divine-creaturely creativity as such excludes only something negative, the merely indeterminate, or merely unitary, hence it requires no causal explanation or creator back of it. I grant to Neville that God would be indeterminate if wholly without a world; but this shows me that God's having a world is an eternal necessity. I conceive the eternal as having no positive alternative and as requiring no decision to bring it into being. Each particular world or cosmic epoch requires divine decision, but between having some world or having none can never have been an option for God. Nor does the eternal consist of single, definite items (eternal objects) of quality, such as an exact shade and hue of green, or a quality of emotion. The eternal possibilities of quality form continua, and continua have no least parts.

In addition to Plotinus, Neville's theism reminds me of the conclusion of Hume's *Dialogues*, where Philo holds that the power ordering the world must be absolute, since the order is absolute; but because of the evils in the world the power cannot be good as we understand good. Thus Neville has the worst of Philo's God without his excuse of cosmological determinism. I am also reminded of Kierkegaard's saying, "The idea of God's creating creatures free over against himself is a cross that philosophy has been unable to bear." The Danish thinker was not the first to advocate bearing that cross, and there have been many since.

Neville tries to recommend his radical step back toward an old tradition by various arguments. One is that Whitehead does not offer any appreciable freedom from control by God, who gives the creature its "initial subjective aim" and can use divine persuasion to influence the final concrescence. Here I really think Neville is making the worse appear the better reason. As he himself expounds it, the Whiteheadian idea of power or influence simply does not allow absolute determining of one power by another. Even God is for the creatures' experience a datum, the supreme datum to be sure, the synthesis of which with other data must be done by the actuality being influenced. No datum can dictate its own mode of reception.

267

In the case of low levels of creaturehood (and of creativity), such as in atoms, divine control can come close to absolute, hence the laws of physics. But to suppose this of creatures actively engaged in thinking, using universals indeterminate with respect to their particular instantiations, is not plausible. We understand in principle divine power of self-determination because we have an inferior—but not zero—form of this power. Creativity as such is a transcendental, applicable to God and also to every creature. Apart from the word transcendental this was Whitehead's almost unprecedented invention, though Peirce, Bergson, and Berdyaev were close to it. Creativity is not merely divine or merely creaturely, but both. Neville's combination of Whiteheadian cosmology and an old-fashioned idea of creation is original, but I am not the one to appreciate its value.

Neville likes to appeal to the Book of Job to support his view that God, though with absolute power, may be only relatively good. He reads Job differently from some of us. The voice from the whirlwind tells Job that he does not know what it means to create a world. Divine power is the more problematic concept, not divine goodness.

Whether in Whitehead's or my version process theology has been appropriated by a number of theologians, including my one-time students John Cobb and Schubert Ogden; also by the Catholic priest Jan Van der Veken of Leuven, Rabbi Jack Bemporad (formerly in Dallas, now in Los Angeles), the Episcopalian Norman Pittenger, and others. All of these are knowledgeable scholars.

Buchler's system has been praised for its "openness" because of its doctrine of "ontological parity," in contrast to Whitehead's notion that only certain things are "really real," res verae. I see this as a largely verbal point. Whitehead grants reality to universals as well as to his actual entities. Although the former are in actual entities, they are really in them—at least in God as actual. A quality that is in no actual experience (divine, human, or neither) is nothing for Whitehead; but that restriction does not exclude anything known to science or common sense. Numbers are real if there are multiple experiences or experiences of multiplicity; atoms are real, but so are their experiences or feelings. Whitehead denies nothing positive here. Physicists deal with atoms but do not as physicists discuss either their feelings or their lack of feelings. Nor do psychologists. Who can show us that we can experience or imagine any positive meaning under the caption, "Neither a sentient actuality nor an aspect or collection of such actualities?" Feelings, experiences, thoughts, we know; something absolutely other than feeling or thought—What do we know of that? What help does the assumption give to any science?

268

From Leibniz to Peirce and Whitehead great scientific-logical-philosophical minds have pondered this question.

Buchler is correct that anything you please, unless Neville's God apart from creating, is in some sense complex. Leibniz's monad was that, so is a Whiteheadian actual entity, or an eternal object. But that it is complex is close to the least informative thing we can say about a definite something.

The metaphysical aim at generality is not merely the search for a concept that bridges the distinction between logical types or levels. Whitehead has such a concept in defining "being" as availability as datum for (future) prehensions. But this definition implies the idea of actuality. Only actual experient occasions directly prehend or discriminate. Since Buchler does accept the contrast possible-actual, relations between which could not be wholly symmetrical, he should be more respectful of the contrast abstract-concrete. Which makes better sense, that universals are useful to particular subjects or experiences, or that the subjects are useful, valuable, to universals? If we knew everything that actualities could enjoy or achieve by discriminating or instantiating universals, what would be left to know about universals? But universals do not enjoy or achieve at all. Why this rage for symmetry? Apart from value in some sense, who cares about reality or complexity?

To adapt Wittgenstein's phrase, what Buchler has done is to invent a new philosophical language game. The game is played with truly remarkable skill. Among its basic rules seem to be: distrust terms like being, existence, abstract, concrete, entity, reality, appearance, in traditional philosophical usages; take instead, as universal concepts to be investigated by metaphysics, the idea of a complex (whose constituents or traits are also complexes), and the idea of acts of discriminating. A complex is anything that is discriminable. (No pure simples can be discriminated. With this I agree, and it is an important truism.) Another rule, not stated as such even indirectly, but obeyed in practice is, look for symmetry where others have thought to find asymmetry. If some say that concrete or particular entities are more real than abstract or universal entities, try to show that one can at least as plausibly reverse the alleged asymmetry and thereby establish (though this does not necessarily follow) "ontological parity."[3] Parity is symmetrical. I myself look for asymmetry where others allege symmetry. After all, we define equality in terms of greater or less than and its negation; interaction of A and B as A's action on B and B's action on A. If A and B know each other, A's knowledge of B is not B's knowledge of A read backward. So I am suspicious of a doctrine making a symmetrical idea so central as Buchler makes parity.

In speaking of a game played with skill I mean to praise as well as to suggest a slight lack of the deepest seriousness. I am troubled by the almost complete lack of value terms (other that those expressive of intellectual distaste) in this book. And I note as a weakness the way other speculative possibilities are criticized in less than their strongest forms. As in reading some of the Greek Sophists and Skeptics, one wonders if any possible system of philosophical ideas, including Buchler's, would make much of a showing against such resourceful and determined attacks.

To show that causes are not "more real" than effects, Buchler deduces absurd results from the assumption. But he does not consider that effects, even if not more real than their causes, might at least have more reality (or, if you prefer, more value) in them than the causes; thus the present richly variegated universe, with its probability of many inhabited planets, has more reality than the Big Bang. I do not myself feel a need to use "real" in a laudatory sense. Anything about which there is truth is real for me, as anything that is dis-criminable is so for Buchler. But I also believe that in all becoming additional value is created and none is lost for the cosmos (or at least for God). Here, and in many cases, as Buchler seems to concede, there may be an asymmetry in terms of value, if not of reality. The issue is partly verbal, but not wholly so. I see danger of an overstress on symmetry obscuring more important asymmetries.

Consider discrimination. If A discriminates B, does it follow that B discriminates A? I should think not. Moreover, I think there is reason to suspect that something like the verb discriminate is as "pervasive" as the complexity it is used to define. Thought discrim-inates, so does feeling or sensing. I believe certain nonsymmetrical verbs are at least as fundamental as complexity is. Buchler apparently thinks that the entire idealistic tradition (including Peirce and White-head) can be brushed aside. It includes Buddhism, a fair number of scientists dead or living, and many others in East and West. The point is not that "matter is unreal" but that, for all anyone can prove, mind in a form remote from our human form is what matter is for one whose imagination fully generalizes the idea of mind or the psychical.

The emphasis (to which Buchler objects) by some idealists on feeling rather than thought or cognition is supported, among other considerations, by the fact that infants show slight signs of thinking but plenty of signs of feeling, and the same goes for animals generally, apart from the very highest forms. My psychicalism generalizes this for cells, atoms, wave-particles. For Buchler, this view humanizes the world or is anthropomorphic. But the idealistic argument is that only an anthropomorphic narrowness in the idea of mind can appear to justify the contention that the descriptions of the physical world given by physicists could not apply to a form of mind sufficiently different from the human and lacking in thought or cognition unless in some extremely minimal kind or degree.

Buchler says some true things about actuality and possibility; for example, that where one is so is the other. (I could not agree more. This symmetry does obtain. I apply it to God, for there are divine potentialities.) But as always there is a subtle and immensely important asymmetry. The possibility for tomorrow consists in (or is entirely determined by) the actuality of today. But the actuality of tomorrow will add values, determinations, not in today's values or determinations. Potentialities, real possibilities, are the properties of events that they necessarily will be followed by later events with new determinations, conditioned, not fully determined, by their predecessors. Possibility is inseparable from futurity. If actualization does not add value, why do we bother to live?

Buchler speaks of the "integrity" of a complex. Consider a wave or ripple in a body of water; it is complex and has integrity or unity, or it would not be *a* complex for anyone. Clearly this is a trivial integrity indeed compared to that of a person through change, or to the unity of a momentary experience of a person, say in no more than a tenth of a second. It is even trivial compared to the unity of an atom.

Much practice would be needed to enable one to play the Buchlerian game well. But I see good reason for preferring a metaphysical game less far from the tradition than Buchler's. I do agree with his rejection of Husserl's form of idealism and his rejection of Quine's rejection of ontological possibility (here, I presume, he has learned from Peirce, as Weiss and I have). I accept his implied rejection of God as absolutely "prevailing" or all-determining. I do not defend the Whiteheadian elevation of universals like "blue," or some other quality of feeling, to the status of an eternal object. In some ways Buchler has learned from recent metaphysics.

There is much in *The Metaphysics of Natural Complexes* about relations as traits of complexes. It is apparently admitted that some relations are intrinsic or constitutive, others are not. At least, there is talk of dependence and independence, which for me is the same distinction more clearly stated. But then we are given a demonstration that the independent is not as such superior to the dependent. Here, as often, Buchler refutes a weak rival to his view, not a strong one. The truth is that the dependent is in principle *more* than the independent. Dependence is a positive thing, not a privation. The proof is simple: knowledge that something exists is impossible if the something does not exist. Knowing is a form of depending. But that something exists is not dependent on whether or not a given case of knowing embraces the something. Knowing is a form of asymmetrical dependence, yet a case of knowing is a positive reality—if you will, a positive complex. It is non-symmetrical. That I know about Shakespeare does things to me; but no one can show us that it does anything to Shakespeare as a certain human life and career. My knowing about Shakespeare enriches the world. It enriches God. If God is wholly independent, then God is an empty abstraction, as Aristotle practically confessed with his mere "thinking of thinking." Medieval theology tried to have it both ways at this point.

In spite of the clever arguments of Buchler, I do believe, with Leibniz and Whitehead, that although there are no absolute simples there are singular actualities. True, I accept the Whiteheadian proposition that each actuality prehends its predecessors, however faintly and indistinctly. But the prehended actualities are in the prehending actuality by the subjective forms of feeling of the former furnishing objective forms of the latter's feeling. Whitehead does have resources to defend the singularity, though not the sheer simplicity, of a single actuality.

Surely it is true that if there are groups of persons then there are single persons, if there is a definite succession of actualities there are single actualities. If there is discrimination, there are discriminators that can be considered one by one. The final discriminator is I-now or you-now, not I or you as the same from birth to death. Whitehead is trying to find the discriminators that do not consist of subdiscriminators of the same kind. Other animals discriminate; it can be argued that so do cells, atoms, and particles. But not (as single discriminators) clouds, rivers, or even trees. The problem of plurality and singularity is not really solved by Buchler, in spite of all the dialectical fireworks.

I do not find in Buchler any cogent arguments against the view, fundamental for the two greatest modern metaphysicians (if Leibniz is considered modern), that if there are definite multiplicities, real independently of our so conceiving them, then there are equally definite singulars. If a definite multiplicity is as such concrete, say a society, then its singulars are concrete. That all concrete singulars are dynamic is a truth missed or seen at best darkly by Plato and Aristotle but seen sharply by Leibniz and more accurately by Whitehead.

Buchler's challenge to process metaphysics is ingenious. We should be able to learn from it. As Whitehead said, limitations of language make it impossible to construct a perfect metaphysical system. As my first teacher in the subject (Rufus Jones of Haverford College) put it, "Every system has an impasse in it somewhere." There are, however, degrees of such deficiencies. Once when Herbert Feigl of the Vienna Circle, talking to some admirers, had just said, "A philosophical system is like a blanket that is too short; you pull it up to keep your shoulders warm and expose your feet to the cold," the late lamented logician C. H. Langford whispered to me, "He must be a centipede."

An indispensable element in philosophizing is one's intuitive sense of existence. I intuit it as an affair of successive experiences, not as a collection of complexes, I find these experiences to be inclusive of abstract entities in nonsymmetrical fashion. I find actual experiences to realize possibilities constituted by past actual experiences, mine and others', human and nonhuman. Each experience is a potentiality for future experiences to have as their datum, however indistinctly or little consciously discerned, however vividly or faintly prehended. Complexity apart from all experience whatever is for me, as for Whitehead (also Peirce), "Nothing, nothing, bare nothing." True, experience without complexity is also nothing, but complexity refers to structure, and experience (chapter 21) is quality as well as structure. Experience is more than complexity; it is the enjoyment of complexity. If complexity could not be enjoyed or suffered it would be nothing for us. As Plato said, the good is being and more than being. It is, we may say, more than complexity. Valuation is ultimate; sense qualities, as I argued in my first book, are value qualities. There is complexity because experience is social, as is shown not only in language but in all basic aspects of experience. Feeling is feeling of others' feelings enriched by the contrast and diversity of the others. Thus the good is love, as Plato almost knew in spite of himself. Ikhnaton of Egypt virtually said so three thousand years ago. Or, as another put it, "God is love."

To the charge that the foregoing is anthropomorphic (a term used somewhat scornfully, I feel, by Buchler) I reply with Peirce and Whitehead (also Heidegger, perhaps) that we achieve positive meaning for our concepts only by accepting analogies, close or remote but genuine, between our natures and whatever we wish to understand. There is good and bad anthropomorphic thinking, otherwise only an absence of meaning for our words.

Not all analogical thinking is a case of arguing by analogy. In sensation we directly experience feelings as in our bodily constituents as the feelers, not as merely our feelings. This is a phenomenological judgment, not a mere argument. We feel the otherness of the feelings. A pain is not merely in our minds, there only because some cells (or at least something not simply our minds) are (is) hurting. An agonized voice enabling us to sense the suffering of another person is a less direct intuition of another's feeling. The agony we immediately intuit is in our auditory system, not in our neighbor's mind or body. When automobiles scream as though in pain we are deceived if we think our immediate (relatively distinct) datum is the automobile or any part of it. But in us, mind and body, there is a two-story form of enjoying or suffering, a higher level of feeling actually enjoying or suffering a lower level (not merely mirroring it, as in Leibniz). This is a rather new doctrine, scarcely to be found before this century. It takes the cellular constitution of our bodies seriously. Leibniz anticipated that in essence, but his exaggerated idea of personal identity through time, on which his denial of interaction between individuals is based, also his medieval idea of God, limited what he could do with this flash of genius.

Buchler objects to Whitehead's contention that groups of actualities are real only in their members. Each member has a perspective on its predecessors and is complicated by relations to them. Still it is itself a single actuality. Buchler wants the idea of concrete singular to lose all distinctive meaning in the utterly abstract idea of a complex. I think almost the entire history of philosophy is against such an idea. A mere group of related actualities is merely those actualities, those singulars, not itself a kind of supersingular. It may be associated with such a supersingular. My bodily cells are associated, at a given moment, with me as conscious, as super-cellular singular; and (by the Platonic analogy) all lesser actualities are associated with the supreme singular, or society of singulars, God. (If society, then each member prehends its predecessors.) Togetherness of actualities must be in actualities. Logicians, even Peirce, sometimes attribute relations to "pairs of entities." But the unity of a relation must have its reality in some term as one. Otherwise, there is a truly vicious regress. This was a valid aspect of Bradley's argument against (merely) external relations.

Buchler's dialectic is too partial to his own cause, his own invented scheme, to inspire full confidence. That one mind can be so ingenious is surprising and to be admired, but hardly proof of comparably unusual profundity. Nevertheless, it has at least the value of showing something that Whitehead often insisted upon, the "limitations of language." Whitehead's "Apart from actual entities, there is nothing" can indeed be countered by "Apart from eternal objects there can (according to Whitehead) also be nothing." However, suppose Whitehead had said, "In addition to actual entities (including God as somehow actual) and what they have as their traits, aspects, or constituents, there is nothing." To reject this would be to assert that there are realities that are neither actualities nor traits, aspects, or constituents of them. And this would be harder to justify than Buchler's counter-proposition.

Buchler's challenge to twentieth-century metaphysics may deserve to be taken seriously as a language game the playing of which by some scholars might prove illuminating. But it seems doubtful indeed that there can be, for science, religion, practical life, or philosophy, a serious rival to individual things, persons, events, or experiences, as the basic units of reality. For twenty-five centuries these (apart from mystic monism) have been the principal options. Only considerable courage could have made it seem worth while to challenge this tradition.

Influenced by Buchler, Stephen D. Ross (b. 1935) has a somewhat different perspective.[4] Instead of the abstraction *complex* he prefers *order* as the basic term. He concedes that no metaphysical theory is without qualification more valid than others and thinks that metaphysics is nonprogressive. His thinking reminds me of McKeon's in seeming to be metametaphysical—about thought-systems more than about extra-linguistic reality. As such it is interesting. I see in it insufficient attention to basic asymmetries: concrete-abstract, actual-possible, subject-object, effect-cause. And I think that the nonprogressiveness of metaphysics is overstated.

Notes

1. My discussion of Neville is based on *Creativity and God: A Challenge to Process Theology* (New York: Seabury Press, 1980). I find much to admire in this brilliant book. Neville has also published a number of other works, including *God the Creator* (Chicago: University of Chicago Press, 1968), *The Cosmology of Freedom* (New Haven: Yale University Press, 1974), *Reconstruction of Thinking* (Albany: State University of New York Press, 1981), and *The Tao and the Daimon* (Albany: State University of New York Press, 1982).

Another deviationist Whiteheadian, like Neville differing especially from Whitehead in his form of theism, is the logician R. M. Martin. Agreeing with many logicians (and theologians) that all truth is timeless, he argues that Whitehead's Primordial Nature of God is the inclusive aspect of deity, making the Consequent Nature superfluous. Martin is also an expert on Peirce. He is perhaps the most metaphysically concerned of living logicians. That all truths are timeless is a view that Plato, Aristotle, Peirce, and Whitehead, as I interpret them, reject. It is arguable that these are, with the sole exception of Leibniz, the greatest of all the philosophers who were also outstanding as logicians. Until I can be shown otherwise, I cannot take altogether seriously any philosophy that eternalizes truths about specific or particular, contingent or concrete actualities. Truths about entities themselves eternal (and abstract) are of course eternal. The others are everlasting, once they come to be at all. Creation is cumulative; its products are not eternally there to be known. As noted above in Chapter 14, Martin's view of God's knowledge was influenced by Wilmon Sheldon's eloquent lecturing on this subject. Whether or not unqualified consensus in metaphysics is an ideal, it is certainly not in sight as a fact. Partial or qualified consensus is another matter. Martin and I are more nearly in agreement than Sheldon and I used to be. All three of us agree on some important issues.

2. Buchler expounds his new metaphysical system in *The Metaphysics of Natural Complexes* (New York: Columbia University Press, 1966). Two others of his books by the same publisher are: *Nature and Judgment*, 1955, 1965; *The Concept of Method*, 1961. In addition: *The Main of Light: On the Concept of Poetry* (New York: Oxford University Press, 1974) and *Toward a General Theory of Human Judgment* (New York: Dover, 1980). Buchler has also written a book on Peirce's empiricism and has edited a useful book of selections from Peirce.

3. See my article in *The Journal of Philosophy* 67, no. 23 (1970): 979–986.

4. *Transition to an Ordinal Metaphysics* (Albany: State University of New York Press, 1980).

CHAPTER 26

Nozick's Indecisive Dialectic
and the Meaning of Life

The ideal with which Descartes inaugurated modern philosophy, that of discovering formulations of truth so clear and distinct that their correctness would be indubitable, has in this century been largely abandoned in philosophy, apart from Husserl, who consciously endorses the Cartesian optimism in this respect. In a very large book, Robert Nozick sets forth and elaborately illustrates a program of exploring possible explanations of basic aspects of existence for the truth of which he thinks there cannot be absolute proof.[1] He does not go so far as Rorty in depreciating the idea of truth and substituting for it the "pragmatic" idea of usefulness in a highly relativistic sense, according to which all we know is whether, or how effectively, a position can be defended and used in our cultural situation. Nozick seems more tempted and intrigued than Rorty by traditional metaphysical speculations but makes little pretense to demonstrate where the truth lies.

I have elsewhere discussed Nozick's book at length and have sought to show that, with all his sensitivity to various points of view and knowledge of the history of ideas, he underestimates and understates the force of the arguments available for certain metaphysical positions, including some positions that he appears to accept, such as the reality of freedom as more than mere voluntariness taken as "compatible" with strict determinism.[2] To be free in the sense he inclines to favor is to originate definiteness where the antecedent causal conditions do not entirely determine the outcome.

In the article referred to I discuss Nozick's evaluation of the widely held belief that the meaning of human life is to be found in the relation or relations in which we stand to God. I maintain that Nozick greatly understates the defense that can be given of the belief in question provided one gives the ideas of God and our creaturely relation to God as supreme creator their best formulations. Only very vaguely does Nozick refer to such formulations. Much of what he says about God is scarcely relevant to what some of us mean by the word.

Why do we look beyond our species for the meaning of our lives? Nozick discusses one alleged reason, our mortality, the impermanence of our individual existences. Against this Nozick sets, among other considerations, the following. If value requires permanence, then the most permanent things ought to be the most valuable, for instance numbers, which are timeless and indestructible. What Nozick misses here is that death justifies looking beyond ourselves for meaning, not because we are less permanent than numbers but because, though unlike numbers we are concrete, we seem destined (in this also, unlike numbers) to drop out of concrete reality forever. Only concrete realities actualize (enjoy) whatever values abstractions are capable of contributing; but if each concrete reality ceases to be after a time and if, further, the higher types of concrete reality may no longer have instances (as the human species and perhaps the other earthly animals cease to exist), then it seems deeply problematic what importance our actions can have, considering the eventual future as we are able to foresee it.

If there are conscious or at least sentient beings, then abstractions can contribute to the values they enjoy. Otherwise it is hard to see meaning or value in anything, including numbers. What death conflicts with is not "permanence" in the sense in which numbers are permanent but, as Whitehead expresses it, "everlastingness." Our having lived as we have ought to continue to make a difference. While we live, memory gives our past satisfactions some significance; for we still in some measure re-enjoy them. And our friends participate somewhat in this retrospective enjoyment, especially if we are eloquent in communicating our experiences, perhaps in writing or works of art. Also, our physical labors have significance for us if we see them as helping to make good experiences, for us or those we care about, possible in the future. Each moment of experience more or less consciously intends to contribute to future moments; and to be human is to be much more conscious of this contributiveness than the other animals probably can be. But our situation in the cosmos makes the ultimate reception of our contributions entirely problematic. Perhaps there will sooner or later be no recipients.

Besides, can we really convince ourselves that what gives our lives value in the long run is merely what our human posterity will derive from it? A God who is strictly immortal and who cherishes all creatures and loves them more adequately than they can love themselves or one another is a definite solution to the problem as just formulated. For by living richly and beautifully and helping our friends, children, and others to do so, we optimize our contribution to future experience, at the least, future divine experience. In Nozick's discussion of God the word 'love' is missing, and so are any clear synonyms for it.

In the previous paragraph I assume, with Berdyaev and a number of others, that there is a future even for God. God changes, but not by decaying or possibly dying and not by forgetting values once possessed, but by addition only. Nozick vaguely considers that God can be conceived as in process, but much of his discussion of religious ideas is too far from clarity or vividness to do any justice to the problems he discusses.

I agree with Nozick that the mere idea of God as indestructible does not give the divine existence meaning since "we can step outside (in thought) of any whole" and ask about its meaning. However, if God changes (though only by increase), then each moment there is a new divine whole. So the meaning of God lies beyond God-now. But it is not something beyond God. For what is beyond God-now is simply God in a later phase. God is no mere whole, complete once for all. Each of us is a new whole each moment, much more is God, whose increase is uniquely eminent since it is inclusive of all the increase there is.

Were God a mere abstraction, then belief in God would not provide the everlastingness that is needed. And the main line of modern metaphysics, beginning with Hegel and Schelling, has rejected the idea that a mere timeless or immutable deity can be more than an empty abstraction. Nozick does mention the possibility that the supreme reality may be thought of as having an aspect of becoming or change. But he does little with the idea and fails to see its full significance for the problem of meaning. Similarly, he does too little with his own idea of freedom as originativeness in considering cosmic and theological problems. The full value of a philosophy of freedom as creativity of new definiteness is to be seen only if it is taken as a universal principle, in the medieval sense a "transcendental," applicable to every creature and, in eminent analogy, to God. Peirce was groping toward such an idea, as was Bergson; W. P. Montague developed it, inspired by Peirce; Whitehead, influenced by Bergson, made it the crown of his system. Still others could be mentioned as contributors to this modern tradition, the history of which is not to be found in the literature apart from the writings of the author of this sentence.

It is refreshing to find a contemporary philosopher (who is rapidly becoming widely known) so interested in the great problems. If his treatment of them has considerable limitations, still, in view of his comparative youth, there may be possibilities of substantial deepening of his thinking.[3]

Notes

1. Robert Nozick, *Philosophical Explanations* (Cambridge, Mass.: Belknap Press of the Harvard University Press, 1981).

2. My essay, "God and the Meaning of Life: Reflections on Nozick's *Philosophical Explanations*," is to appear in Boston University Studies in Philosophy and Religion, ed. L. S. Rouner (Notre Dame and London: University of Notre Dame Press, 1983) Vol. 4.

3. Nozick has also written *Anarchy, State, and Utopia* (New York: Basic Books, 1974).

CHAPTER 27

Conclusion

American philosophy, from Edwards to Peirce and Whitehead, constitutes a success story from the standpoint of neoclassical metaphysics. The problem of causality and freedom has been redefined in terms of self-determining experience that furnishes content for its later instances. The "furnishing content" aspect is the causal conditioning. Peirce was nearly clear about this, Whitehead was essentially clear. The mind-matter problem is in principle solved by the same idea, taking into account the Leibnizian distinction between imperceptibly small active singulars and their aggregates and also that between low and high levels of experiencing.

The problem of God is, if not solved, at least greatly alleviated by the conception of Deity as the eminent form of finally self-determining experience, grasping as its content already actualized experiences. The principle of dual transcendence (toward which Channing, Royce, James, Peirce, Brightman, Hocking, and others seem to have been groping) then applies, since God as experiencing the world must be, insofar, relative and changeable rather than merely eternal, absolute, or independent. The abstract defining characteristics of deity are indeed independent or absolute, strictly necessary and eternal. These defining characteristics include an eminent or divine kind of relativity and changeability. In this matter Peirce is somewhat unclear, but he does hint strongly that God is not in an unqualified sense immutable. Whitehead definitely implies that God has an "infinite" and "absolute," but also a "finite" (and relative) aspect, the one primordial and changeless, the other in its specific content "consequent" and "in flux."

In the United States, as in a number of other countries, there has in recent times been a slow approach to the dipolar or dually transcendent conception. Brightman's defence of the finite-infinite,

281

temporal-eternal God was one twentieth-century instance of this, preceded by Channing's vaguer qualification of the divine infinity, and by various hints in Peirce's discussions of the idea of God. James knew that sheer infinity or absoluteness was not the answer to the question, "What is the divine nature?" However, his empiricism gave him no clue to the required qualification. Brightman called his view empirical but lacked a sharp criterion for the application of this term. He assumed that God must definitely have eternal and infinite aspects to be the God of the high religions—but then, some might object, perhaps the high religions ask more of reality than reality provides. To deal with this objection, more than empiricism is required.

Thinking of the American writers who, before Whitehead, tried to find a remedy for the notorious logical problems of classical theism, or the notorious logical problems of historical idealisms, I recall Santayana's *Winds of Doctrine*, and the conclusion of its first chapter:

These are but gusts of doctrine, yet they prove that the spirit is not dead in the lull between its seasons of steady blowing. Who knows which of them may not gather force presently and carry the mind of the age steadily before it?

Perhaps Santayana overestimated the capacity of our twentieth century culture to arrive at a consensus. It is true that Wittgenstein's thought seems to some to give a definitive direction to recent philosophizing, and Heidegger so appears to others. Rorty, who has learned from them and from McKeon's historicism, is impressive to some, Wilfrid Sellars to others. If we must settle for a nontheistic view, then I question if Dewey and Mead have been surpassed. In their vein is Charles W. Morris's *Paths of Life*. Like many Americans, including Montague, Morris was aware of the challenge of Buddhism. Somehow it is not for nothing that the waves of the Pacific beat upon one of our principal shores.

Many Unitarian clergymen are trying to foster life in their religious communities without benefit of a definite idea of God. Considering the complexities and subtleties of our cultural situation in its bearing on the theistic question, one cannot wonder that this should be so. As Montague nicely put it, a theist should not look upon the efforts of such humanist thinkers with hostility. Rather, one should admire their courage in a difficult situation. Without the inspiration of a definite belief in divine love, they are trying to achieve an adequate love for their human fellows and to derive as much inspiration as they can from science, the arts, and the history of human greatness and nobility. Belief is a gift, a blessing, or an achievement, not a duty one can simply demand that all should perform. What may be a duty is that one should not "bar the path of inquiry" (Peirce), including inquiry into the pros as well as the cons of the metaphysical belief that is theism and into the relative merits of various formulations, new as well as old, of this belief.

On the question of method, I have at least some slight quarrel with all the persons I have discussed. I agree with Parker, Emerson, and Royce in acknowledging a priori metaphysical elements in knowledge and valuation (the English poet Coleridge, with his *Aids to Reflection*—American edition in 1828—was influential here); but I miss in them an adequate grasp of the empirical elements. The total denial of contingency, implicit in Emerson and at best only ambiguously and consistently avoided by Edwards, also close to the surface in Royce, makes the inadequacy clear. The unconditionally necessary could not be known empirically, nor could the contingent be known a priori. What could be known a priori is that the category of contingency necessarily has some instances or other, so that it is an a priori truth that some truths must be known, if at all, empirically. This applies even to God's knowledge. God could not, in spite of Thomas Aquinas, know the contingent world by intuiting the eternal and necessary divine essence. Rather, God must directly perceive the contingent creatures by contingent acts of prehension.

In Peirce and Whitehead the empirical aspects of knowledge are fully recognized. It is perhaps less clear what for them is *not* empirical. They seem not to make explicit use of Popper's criterion, the most useful one of all, for empirical statements, that they are those to the *falsity* of which some but not all conceivable experiences could testify. Peirce virtually uses this criterion in explicating the rationale of induction but not in explicating the terms 'empirical' or 'a priori.' Whitehead puts no special stress on falsification. He seems sometimes to imply that metaphysics is merely the most general form of empirical inquiry. Like Peirce, he thinks of metaphysics as "descriptive" of the most general data of experience, those common to all conceivable experiences. But by Popper's valuable definition, knowledge of these data, since it is unfalsifiable by conceivable experience, is nonempirical. Its truth is that of pure reason, as Kant would have it.

Is such truth synthetic a priori? I agree partly with Quine but partly also with Carnap here. What is analytic or synthetic depends somewhat on how we arrange our language. What is, in one linguistic framework, synthetic a priori may also, by meaning postulates, be made analytic. Judgment as to what meaning postulates are legitimately used in this way is precisely the metaphysical question. I hold with Peirce that it is an ideal to arrange our language so that objectively necessary or merely possible relations appear respectively as formally analytic or formally synthetic, and I agree with him and with Aristotle that contingent possibility and futurity are essentially one and that truths about strictly eternal aspects of reality must be objectively necessary. They are the metaphysical truths. No empirical science could establish or disprove them.

A similar distinction is required in evaluating the pragmatic criterion of meaning. James badly blurred the distinction between criterion of meaning and criterion of truth. Royce called himself an "absolute pragmatist," and, although he didn't say so, this meant an a priori pragmatist. All truths whatever, he seems to imply, have the same objective status logically, since all are made true by the unique, eternal, Absolute Experience. There is, for Royce, no genuine temporality, hence no genuine contingency. One was still, in Royce, with Emerson's "There is no chance, no anarchy." Here James was the wiser man in proclaiming, with Peirce, the reality of chance. But James tried to make his pragmatism wholly empirical and yet a criterion of truth. How badly this worked we saw in chapter 5. What James missed was that the pragmatic criterion is valid for truth as well as meaning only in application to strictly necessary and eternal aspects of reality, because in that application value and truth, being alike necessary, are equally a priori matters. In empirical applications, value is contingent upon truth, upon how the world happens to be; so that reasoning from the value of the mere idea begs the questions of both truth and value.

Peirce was largely clear about his pragmatic criterion. He made no attempt to derive contingent truth from it, although he did hint that it could be used to support the truth about noncontingent questions, such as the existence of God.

Whitehead's pragmatism comes out at least vaguely in his definition of metaphysics (or "rationalism") as "the search for the coherence of the presuppositions of civilized living." He means here, presumably, the indispensable or necessary presuppositions and ideals (however poorly actualized) of any conceivable society of thinking animals. Peirce's "critical commonsensism" is another approach to the same issue. Since there is no absolutely perfect way to express metaphysical truth in language, it will probably always be possible to argue plausibly that any particular way of doing so is unsatisfactory and that some other way would overcome certain difficulties in the given way. But the claims for a greater "openness" of Justus Buchler's "ordinal metaphysics," characterized by a principle of "ontological parity," are stated in a manner that I find insufficiently impressive to tempt me to spend the effort required to master the system. To say, as Aristotle, Whitehead, and many others have done, that abstractions are real only in something concrete does not mean that, as in the concrete, they are not real. Numbers, for example, are real insofar as there are multiple concrete actualities, also insofar as there are thoughts with multiple aspects, entertained by human or superhuman actualities.

My difficulties with Weiss's philosophy are somewhat similar to those I have with Buchler's. Both of them seem to misplace concreteness, or confuse levels of abstractness, and to fail to find a coherent way of conceiving the inclusive reality for the sake of which alone the less inclusive realities have their significance.

Where there is no perfect method there may always be some point in trying other ways than those already tried. So Buchler's principle of ontological parity, or idea of natural complexes, (or Weiss's finalities) may be worth more consideration than I have given them.

On the question of political equality and sovereignty, I make more modest claims to progress in our American philosophical tradition. Our Founding Fathers were men of astonishing wisdom. But they left political problems that are still troublesome. As Mrs. John Adams pointed out, they omitted women from the scope of political equality. They also omitted Blacks. Theoretically, we have overcome the second anomaly and have made a start toward overcoming the first. However, in our practice, and in the fine points even in our theories, there is still much to be desired under both heads. It is perhaps worth noting that at least two of our philosophers explicitly conceded full rights to woman. They were Emerson and Whitehead.

The essential social problem, which is economic as much as political, and international and military as much as domestic, is today our problem of problems. It is not metaphysical, except somewhat indirectly; for it involves rather specific and contingent aspects of human life on this planet. Jefferson himself could not see how equalitarian democracy was possible in a largely urban and industrialized society; yet that is the society we now have.

That many of our philosophers (for example, Rawls and Nozick) are now focusing on ethical and political questions, especially problems of economic justice, seems in order. Ideally, there is need for a synthesis of the results of this inquiry with the metaphysics of freedom that James, Peirce, and Whitehead, have together made possible.

It is important that philosophers realize how technology has transformed value questions. It has done this by altering quantitative factors whose changes, as Marxists rightly say, bring qualitative changes with them. The simple fact, for example, that modern hygiene makes anything like a balance of birth and death rates possible today only if women bear perhaps a third as many babies as formerly alters substantially the appropriate life-styles for women in general. Many other technological changes, quantitative and in effect qualitative, go with this. The problems that Blacks as such face are also altered by these changes. And everyone's problems are affected by the discovery of nuclear fission. Neither Jefferson nor Marx foresaw these formidable issues.

Perhaps for the near future Dewey's focus on middle-sized ideas more than on metaphysical ultimates is appropriate. But it is also true that most people still show a need for such ultimates. In this way a diversity of concerns by philosophers, such as does actually exist, may be healthy.

If Leibniz could have been alive during the past ten decades, from whom could he have learned most, metaphysically? I think the answer is obvious: Charles Peirce and Alfred North Whitehead. They were the ones who understood his problems better than he was in a position to do, with a better mathematics, logic, and physics, more comprehensive knowledge of the history of philosophy and religion, and with comparable imaginative power, intellectual daring, and lifelong devotion to intellectual pursuits. They had one more advantage over Leibniz: they knew about him, while he did not know about them. If it is really true that there is no progress in philosophy, then philosophers must be fantastically stupid. They are indeed limited and fallible—but not *that* stupid.

I reiterate my conviction that in metaphysics no country is in a better position than this country and that all whose language is English have ready access to an unsurpassed metaphysical tradition. This encouraging thought needs to be balanced by the sobering one that only a small minority of our population has any knowledge of our philosophical tradition. Many of our citizens are functionally illiterate in philosophy and comparative religion. In their grasp of the philosophy of religion our Founding Fathers were worlds removed from countless writers of letters to newspaper editors today. How Jefferson would have shuddered to read some of these letters! Teachers of philosophy and religion or theology have a responsibility in this regard. It will not suffice to teach only agnostic or atheistic perspectives, for most people will insist on something positive. Jefferson and Lincoln had a positive view of life and the cosmos. Marxist leaders may be able to do without belief in a superhuman cosmic reality. It is not clear that ours can do so. In any case, people have a right to know what the positive options are in their best contemporary or recent formulations. If this book increases their chances in that respect it will have attained its end.

Index of Names

Index of Topics

96924

HARTSHORNE, CHARLES
CREATIVITY IN AMERICAN PHILOSOPHY.

DATE DUE

GAYLORD

PRINTED IN U.S.A.